T0367886

Causes,

Agents,

Explanations,

and Free Will

Causes,

Agents,

Explanations,

and Free Will

MARTIN GERWIN

ARCHWAY PUBLISHING

Archway Publishing books may be ordered through booksellers or by contacting:

Archway Publishing
1663 Liberty Drive
Bloomington, IN 47403
www.archwaypublishing.com
1 (888) 242-5904

Because of the dynamic nature of the Internet, any web addresses or links contained in this book may have changed since publication and may no longer be valid. The views expressed in this work are solely those of the author and do not necessarily reflect the views of the publisher, and the publisher hereby disclaims any responsibility for them.

Any people depicted in stock imagery provided by Thinkstock are models, and such images are being used for illustrative purposes only. Certain stock imagery © Thinkstock.

This book is a work of non-fiction. Unless otherwise noted, the author and the publisher make no explicit guarantees as to the accuracy of the information contained in this book and in some cases, names of people and places have been altered to protect their privacy.

ISBN: 978-1-4808-5681-3 (sc)
ISBN: 978-1-4808-5682-0 (hc)
ISBN: 978-1-4808-5683-7 (e)

Library of Congress Control Number: 2018900259

Print information available on the last page.

Archway Publishing rev. date: 02/09/2018

For
Judith

ACKNOWLEDGMENTS

It would be impossible to list all the people whose thoughts, inspirations and stimulating criticisms have shaped my own thoughts during the long process that has led to the writing of this book. I will therefore confine myself to mentioning the outstanding few.

Amongst the many faculty members, visiting scholars and fellow graduate students with whom I had valuable discussions while I was a degree candidate at Princeton University, I owe a particular debt of gratitude to my dissertation adviser, Calvin Normore. His searching, sympathetic and imaginative criticisms of the early drafts of this work were simply invaluable, and the time and support he devoted to furthering my project went far above and beyond the call of duty.

During my years as a faculty member at the University of Manitoba, I profited from discussions and conversations with colleagues and students from far and wide. I am immensely grateful to all of them; but special mention must be made of two Manitoba colleagues, Jack Bailey and Murdith McLean. The journey whose destination is to be found in the thoughts set down here included many hours of lively and fruitful conversation with them. I only hope that their memories of those talks are as pleasant and satisfying as my own.

I wish to express my thanks to the University of Manitoba for support during research-study leave time that was devoted to work on these topics.

I extend thanks to Cambridge University Press for giving permission to include reworked material from my article "Causality and Agency: A Refutation of Hume", which was originally published in *Dialogue*, vol. 26 (1987), and to Taylor & Francis Ltd. (http://www.tandfonline.com) for permission to reprint my Critical Notice of Bas C. van Fraassen, *The Scientific Image*, which appeared in the *Canadian Journal of Philosophy*, vol. 15 (1985).

Last of all, I would like to thank my family for bearing with me at the times when the work took my attention away from family life.

Toronto,
August 2016.

CONTENTS

FOREWORD

In setting these thoughts before the reader in their present form, I feel obliged to offer some explanation of what is, and is not, to be found in this book.

I have been reflecting on the philosophical problems connected with causality, explanation and free will ever since I was an undergraduate more than half a century ago, and the main outlines of the ideas presented here were worked out in the years prior to 2000. Although I am not aware of any points that would need to be retracted or modified in the light of recent discussions of these issues by philosophers, I have not undertaken to provide a response to the most recent contributions to the literature. How great an inadequacy this represents, I leave it to others to judge.

The book contains material of different kinds; and some readers, I expect, will find themselves interested in certain parts and not others. The main argument is a contribution to the centuries-long conversation concerning the nature of cause and effect, the practice of explanation, and the relationship between causality and human free will. As such I hope it will be of interest to a large number of philosophical scholars and students of philosophy in the broadest sense. But since it is claimed that certain patterns of modal inference underlie our common ways of reasoning about causes and effects and free choices, I have seen fit to include the elementary formal development of a system of modal logic that will represent those patterns of inference in a precise way. The system I present borrows heavily from other systems of modal logic discussed in the literature, but is not completely identical to any of them. The sections in which it is presented are designed for readers with an interest in formal logic, but may be skipped over without losing the overall thread of the argument.

In addition, the book contains extended criticisms of the work of others who have made significant contributions to the conversation, such as Hans Reichenbach, Wesley Salmon, J.L. Mackie and Bas van Fraassen. Some of these critiques are germane to the defence of my own views only to the extent that they provide grounds for ruling out certain alternative views. One could disregard them, also, without losing the overall thrust of the argument. I have included them, not only because the work of those authors was of immense value to me in the development of my own position, but because I believe that philosophical work of such towering merit deserves all the detailed and strenuous criticism that fellow practitioners of philosophy are able to offer, and I have not encountered these particular criticisms elsewhere in the literature.

In closing this foreword, I will mention – without apology – that the text contains a number of lengthy quotations from the writings of other philosophers. In this instance I would like to encourage the reader *not* to skip over them, as though they were mere asides, but to view them as part and parcel of my own argument, since they formed a significant part of the process that led me to the conclusions defended in these pages.

CHAPTER 1
Introduction

The main task undertaken in this book is an examination of causation: the cluster of concepts by which we speak of causes and causal connections, the processes and connections themselves that those concepts designate, and the means by which we come to know of their presence. But my thoughts on these matters originated in reflections on the problem of determinism and free will. I was attracted from the start to the position of libertarianism – the view that when human beings act or make decisions, as we say, of their own free will, they exercise a power of choice of such a kind that it is possible for them, at the time and in those very circumstances, to act or decide otherwise. I was suspicious of the arguments of the compatibilists, which purported to show that the existence of free will in the sense just mentioned is compatible with the truth of determinism – the view that for every event or condition, human actions and decisions included, there are causally sufficient conditions which make it impossible, given the laws of nature, for them to unfold in any way other than as they do. Compatibilists find it necessary to observe a strict separation between the sense in which it is possible for people who choose freely to choose otherwise – the human-agency sense of 'possible' – and the sense in which it is not possible for them to choose otherwise – the causal sense of 'possible'. I was always doubtful that such a separation could, in the last analysis, be maintained. Yet at the outset I found it difficult to say why. It is plain enough that the two senses of 'possible' are not the same; the burden of proof would seem to lie upon those who wish to conclude that the two are connected in a way that would rule out the truth of compatibilism.

To this problem, posed in the context of the issue of determinism and free will, it seemed to me that there might be a solution stemming from another line of argument that had always appealed to me. This was the argument that our concepts having to do with causation and causal connection are derived, not solely from our experience of the constant conjunction of similar sequences of phenomena, as Hume taught, but primarily from our experience of interacting with the world as agents rather than as passive observers. Hume had neither the first word nor the last word on this subject. What I will call the "agency" view of the origin of causal concepts predated Hume's "regularity" view, and has endured in a form that takes account of Hume's arguments. My intention in writing this book is to contribute to the development of the agency view, and to do so in a way that displays the relevance of this analysis of causal concepts to the issue of determinism and free will.

This will be a project in the spirit of traditional empiricism. The aim will be to show how our concepts related to causation, and our knowledge of causal connections, are grounded in experience. My procedure will be to take the complex, interrelated cluster of ideas by means of which we think and talk about causes, and identify some fundamental ones in terms of which the others may be defined or explicated. These fundamental ideas may be thought of as logical primitives for the purpose of a systematic explication of the family of causal concepts. Each one of them, it will be argued, can be seen to be based on or derived from experience in the sense that there is a common experiential situation which occurs early in the lifetime of every normal human being, and which unequivocally instantiates the concept in question. A person in that situation would be able to say to himself or herself, "What I am now experiencing is without any doubt a member of the extension of the target idea".

While I maintain that this procedure is in the spirit of traditional empiricism, I do not share many of the assumptions of traditional empiricists. I do not assume that the judgment of a human cognizer that he or she is experiencing a clear instance of a given concept is an infallible or incorrigible judgment. It is a judgment that one might conceivably be forced to revoke or revise in the light of subsequent experience. Nor do I assume that the *a priori* methods of philosophical analysis can lead us to conclusions about what goes on in the minds of pre-verbal children. For this the experimental investigations of developmental psychologists are called for – and their results are often quite surprising. One thinks, for example, of Jean Piaget's research into the development of young children's concepts and thought patterns.[1] Neither do I wish to commit myself to any particular theory about the nature of concept formation; I assume only that it is a creative process whose end product is a mental item with a logico-semantic function. I am quite certain, however, that Hume's copy theory of concept formation, according to which what is produced is invariably an idea that copies an impression of sensation or of reflection, is egregiously inadequate to the phenomena of common experience.[2]

I found it necessary to name three fundamental, logically primitive concepts relating to causation, and I doubt very much that it would be possible to reduce the set of primitive concepts to a smaller number. All three can be grounded by reference to experiences that are part and parcel of the experience of being an agent.

The first is the notion of causal efficacy: bringing about an event or condition; making something happen. A cause brings about its effect, makes it happen; and we understand what we mean by that because, as agents, we have the first-hand experience of making things happen. The prime example of the kind of event we can make happen is a movement of our own bodies or members. This is not a new thought: it goes all the way back to Locke. But I believe there are some novel things to be said in its defence, and that is the justification for producing yet another book on this well worn topic.

One consequence of taking a notion of causal efficacy of this sort as a foundational element in the analysis of causality is that one is led to a singularist view of causation. Efficacy is present in each single case of causal connection; it does not depend for its existence on being an instance of a law-like regularity. The law-like regularities, I suggest, are indispensable for our knowledge of causal connections. But they are not essential to the connections themselves.

The second of the primitive notions presented in this essay is a modal term related to the 'can' of human ability. Since a significant part of our conceptual apparatus for dealing with causes and effects consists of a family of modal terms – causal necessity, possibility, impossibility – it would seem to be indispensable to have a modal term included in the primitive basis of the whole structure. Otherwise one would be faced with the impossible task of defining modal terms by means of non-modal ones. The modal term presented as logically primitive is an artificial creation: 'It is possible to agent A at time t that p'. This term, it is safe to say, never figures in the conversation of ordinary human beings. Yet it can, I maintain, be seen as a central element in the thought and perception of an unsophisticated human who sees himself or herself as an agent possessed of a capacity to bring about certain effects. Thus it can be related in the needed way to human experience at a psychologically elementary level.

The third and last of the proposed primitive concepts is that of doing one thing *by* doing another. This provides the basis for defining the familiar asymmetrical relation between cause and effect, which in turn is the basis for explicating the direction of causation and the asymmetries of explanation. The proposed derivation from a young agent's psychologically uncomplicated experience of doing one thing by doing another provides an experiential grounding for a concept with the logical feature of asymmetrical relatedness. It does so, moreover, without mentioning the direction of time. Thus it is not portrayed as a matter of logical necessity that a cause should precede its effect in time. Causes that are strictly simultaneous with their effects, and even causes that work backward in time, are not ruled out as absurd or self-contradictory. It is my contention that this is in accord with our common conceptions. Weird though it would be to have a cause that occurred later than its effect, there are, I maintain, circumstances which at least tempt us to reach for such an explanation. The temptation would be completely incoherent if it were taken to be a matter of definition, or a logical necessity, that a cause must always precede its effect.

In grounding our family of causal concepts in the experience of agency, I believe it is vital to have one logically primitive concept that can be related directly to the basic experience of making something happen. Next, there is a need for a primitive modal concept, because the modal features of concepts such as causal necessity and possibility cannot be conjured up out of nothing. Lastly, an asymmetrical relation will be required to fill the role of the ordering relation in causal processes or chains of causes. For these reasons, I do not believe it would have been possible to make do with anything less than the three undefined concepts I have selected. But if those three can be shown to be derived from experience in a way that will satisfy the demands of an empiricist program in epistemology, then we can say that we have succeeded in the task that Hume set for himself but found himself unable to accomplish.

(But admittedly our success will be due to having defined the task somewhat differently than Hume did.)

From the analysis of causality in terms of agency there emerges the conclusion that when it comes to the question of determinism and free will, the 'can' of human agency cannot be separated from the 'can' of causal possibility in the way that the doctrine of compatibilism would require. It follows that compatibilism is false, and soft determinism is ruled out as a solution to the free will problem. I personally am inclined to adopt the position that could be labeled "soft indeterminism", according to which the world is *not* completely governed by deterministic laws, and this *is* compatible with the existence of free will in the strong, libertarian sense. But there are immense difficulties in establishing anything beyond the bare logical possibility that such a theory is true.

In order to defend the libertarian view of free will, it is necessary to explain the sense in which free choices and free actions can be said to be caused. I submit that there is a sense of 'cause' which appears to be the oldest in the language, and in which it is utterly uncontroversial to say that free actions and free choices are caused. For this sense of 'cause' I have chosen the label "rational-agency causation"; it will be discussed more fully in Chapter 6. I distinguish it from what I call "nomic causation" – the concept we employ when considering the causes of events other than free actions and choices. As the name implies, the analysis of nomic causation involves laws of nature.

The two notions of causation have in common the idea of efficacy – causes bring about their effects – and the asymmetrical relation of causal priority: causes are in this special (non-temporal) sense antecedent to their effects. But they differ when it comes to the causal modalities. Whereas nomic causation involves laws that are causally necessary – in a sense defined ultimately in terms of the 'can' of ability – rational-agency causation is to be analyzed in terms of counterfactual conditionals that are not in any sense necessarily true. Some philosophers have proposed that all singular causal judgments be given such an analysis;[3] I see it as the correct analysis of rational-agency causation, but I submit that nomic causation calls for a different account incorporating the idea of causal necessity.

I do not wish to imply that free actions and choices are exempt from nomic causation. Human actions are events in the physical world; the choices from which they proceed I presume to be identical to physical events in the brain and nervous system; the mental processes that produce those choices are likewise to be identified with neural processes. Neural events and processes, as such, result from causally prior conditions in accordance with the laws of physics and chemistry. So human actions and choices are indeed caused in the sense of nomic causation. It is just that in the case of free actions and freely made choices, the laws linking them to their physical causes will not be laws of a deterministic kind; they will be laws which do no more than assign a certain probability to the effect.

The historical background

The account of causation that will be elaborated and defended in these pages has evolved historically from John Locke's examination of the idea of power.[4] In Book II of *An Essay Concerning Human Understanding,* Locke wrote:

> *Power* also is another of those simple ideas which
> we receive from sensation and reflection. For, ob-
> serving in ourselves that we can and do think, and
> that we can at pleasure move several parts of our
> bodies which were at rest; the effects, also, that

natural bodies are able to produce in one another,
occurring every moment to our senses, – we both
these ways get the idea of power...[5]

But yet, if we will consider it attentively, bodies,
by our senses, do not afford us so clear and distinct
an idea of active power, as we have from reflection
on the operations of our minds. ... The idea of the
beginning of motion we have only from ourselves;
where we find by experience, that, barely by willing
it, barely by a thought of the mind, we can move the
parts of our bodies, which were before at rest. So
that it seems to me, we have, from the observation
of the operation of bodies by our senses, but a very
imperfect obscure idea of *active* power; since they
afford us not any idea in themselves of the power to
begin any action, either motion or thought.[6]

Locke's view was directly criticized by David Hume, who
claimed that our idea of power, like that of causal connection, is
derived from the experience of regularity in sequences of events,
together with the "new sentiment" of expectation which the iterated experience of constant conjunction will engender in us. In *A
Treatise of Human Nature* Hume asserts:

All ideas are deriv'd from, and represent impressions. We never have any impression, that contains
any power or efficacy. We never therefore have any
idea of power.[7]

In a section of the Appendix to the *Treatise* written to be inserted
at that point in the text, he adds:

> Some have asserted, that we feel an energy, or power, in our own mind; and that having in this manner acquir'd the idea of power, we transfer that quality to matter, where we are not able immediately to discover it. The motions of our body, and the thoughts and sentiments of our mind, (say they) obey the will; nor do we seek any farther to acquire a just notion of force or power. But to convince us how fallacious this reasoning is, we need only consider, that the will being here consider'd as a cause, has no more a discoverable connexion with its effects, than any material cause has with its proper effect. ... In short, the actions of the mind are, in this respect, the same with those of matter. We perceive only their constant conjunction; nor can we ever reason beyond it. No internal impression has an apparent energy, more than external objects have.[8]

The nub of the position I will be concerned to defend is that Locke was on the right track, and Hume's objections can be answered.

I will refer to the view of power and causality deriving from Locke as the "agency" view, since Locke sees these ideas as originating in our experience of agency. Hume's view I will call the "regularity" view, since Hume traces these same ideas to our experience of regularity, or the constant conjunction of phenomena of different kinds. (Not that Hume's theory of the nature of cause and effect is anything like a simple regularity theory.)

In the years following the death of Hume, the agency view underwent some significant developments at the hands of the Scottish "philosopher of common sense", Thomas Reid, and the French empiricist Pierre Maine de Biran.

Reid's contribution is found in his *Essays on the Active Powers of the Human Mind*. Early in the first essay, "Of the Notion of Active Power", Reid makes the point that 'power' is something of which we have only a relative notion: our idea of the power to do *x* is relative to our idea of doing *x*. Now if we are concerned, as good empiricists should be, to find and specify accurately the experiences that give rise to our ideas, then we should focus on the experience of those actions that represent the exercise of our powers. It is the activity that is directly experienced through reflection or consciousness; the power is something whose existence is inferred from the experience of activity.

> Power is not an operation of the mind, and therefore no object of consciousness. Indeed every operation of the mind is the exertion of some power of the mind; but we are conscious of the operation only, the power lies behind the scene; and though we may justly infer the power from the operation, it must be remembered, that inferring is not the province of consciousness, but of reason.
> ... [S]trictly speaking, I am not conscious that I have *power*.[9]

Reid concludes from this that "our having any conception or idea of power is repugnant to Mr. Locke's theory, that all our simple ideas are got either by the external senses, or by consciousness",[10] and makes this the basis for some highly critical remarks about Locke's work. But whether or not Reid's criticisms hit their mark will depend upon what, exactly, we mean by a simple idea's being "got" from sensation or reflection. For Locke it could be a process that brought in a whole range of other experiences, and also included some inferences. Indeed, Locke gives the show away at the very opening of the chapter in the *Essay* devoted to the idea of power: he acknowledges *both* that an inference is involved *and* that the experience of constant conjunction, to which Hume attached such great significance, is part of the journey to acquiring the idea of power:

> The mind being every day informed, by the senses, of the alteration of those simple ideas it observes in things without; and taking notice how one comes to an end, and ceases to be, and another begins to exist which was not before; reflecting also on what passes within itself, and observing a constant change of its ideas, sometimes by the impression of outward objects on the senses, and sometimes by the determination of its own choice; and *concluding from what it has so constantly observed to have been, that the like changes will for the future be made in the same things, by like agents, and by the like ways, –* considers in one thing the possibility of having any of its simple ideas changed, and in another the possibility of making that change; and so comes by that idea which we call *power.*[11]

Beyond all doubt Reid advances the empiricist project of tracing our ideas to their sources in experience by insisting on a tighter link between an idea and the experience from which it has been "got". Locke, here as elsewhere, uses philosophical terms with excessively broad meanings, although it is plain that he does so from a desire to be faithful to actual experience. But the conclusion I would draw from this is that Reid has refined and improved upon Locke's version of the agency view, not refuted it.

In the course of his critical comments on Locke, Reid makes the further point that in order to observe any change in the external world or within ourselves, we are obliged to make use of memory as well as simple sensation and reflection:

> Every idea, therefore, that is derived from observing changes in things, must have its origin, partly from memory, and not from the senses alone, nor from consciousness alone, nor from both together.[12]

Combining the observation concerning memory with Locke's admission that an inference is involved in arriving at the idea of power, Reid concludes:

> Thus, I think, it appears, that the account which Mr. Locke himself gives of the origin of our idea of power, cannot be reconciled to his favourite doctrine, that all our simple ideas have their origin from sensation or reflection; and that, in attempting to derive the idea of power from these two sources only, he unawares brings in our memory, and our reasoning power, for a share in its origin.

So the position Reid has brought us to, at this point in his argument, is that the idea of power is (1) a simple idea – as opposed, presumably, to a composite idea – yet (2) is relative to the idea of activity, which is got directly from experience, and (3) is derived somewhat indirectly from experience by a process that involves memory and inference.

He leaves us in no doubt that this is a reaffirmation of the agency view first expressed by Locke:

> But in certain motions of my body, and directions
> of my thought, I know, not only that there must be
> a cause that has power to produce these effects, but
> that I am that cause; and I am conscious of what I
> do in order to the production of them.
>
> From the consciousness of our own activity,
> seems to be derived, not only the clearest, but the
> only conception we can form of activity, or the ex-
> ertion of active power. ...
>
> And of the manner in which a cause may exert
> its active power, we can have no conception but
> from consciousness of the manner in which our
> own active power is exerted.[13]

Yet Reid does not here subject the idea of activity, or exertion of power, to a close examination; that task was left for the likes of Pierre Maine de Biran.

Neither does he see any opportunity for humans to know of the exercise of active power by other, non-human creatures in the natural realm, although his words do not rule out the bare possibility:

> With regard to the operations of nature, it is suf-
> ficient for us to know, that, whatever agents may
> be, whatever the manner of their operation, or
> the extent of their power, they depend upon the
> First Cause and are under his controul; and this
> indeed is all that we know; beyond this we are left
> in darkness.[14]

Here he is claiming ignorance, not conceptual impossibility.

In the fourth essay in the collection, however, Reid makes the claim that an exertion of active power in a manner that does not involve consciousness is, to us, a conceptual impossibility, although we do find it possible to enlarge our notion of active power to cover the case of the Deity:

> It is certain that we can conceive no kind of active power but what is similar or analogous to that which we attribute to ourselves; that is, a power which is exerted by will and with understanding. Our notion, even of Almighty power, is derived from the notion of human power, by removing from the former those imperfections and limitations to which the latter is subjected.[15]

In what follows I will urge that, Reid to the contrary notwithstanding, it would be possible to construct a concept of a non-conscious, non-human agent – even that of an inanimate agent. The procedure would be to *subtract* the elements of consciousness and deliberation from the conception of agency that we derive directly from our own experience.

Reid does not consider such a possibility; instead, he notes that in primitive cultures, the sun, moon, stars, and other (to us) inanimate objects are believed to be living, conscious agents. He credits speculative intellectuals with making the advance to a scientific account of the world in which such natural objects are viewed as "inanimate" and "inactive".[16] But he claims that in making this advance, such thinkers abandon the search for the causes of natural phenomena, and content themselves with unearthing the regularities that are to be found in nature:

> Those philosophers seem to have had the justest views of nature, as well as the weakness of human understanding, who, giving up the pretence of

> discovering the causes of the operations of nature,
> have applied themselves to discover by observa-
> tion and experiment, the rules, or laws of nature
> according to which the phenomena of nature are
> produced.[17]

There is an obvious affinity here with Hume's position that we cannot know the "secret powers" by which natural phenomena are produced, but only the observable regularities that are evident to our senses, and our own subjective reactions to the constant conjunctions of types of phenomena. Unlike Hume, Reid makes no move to redefine cause and effect in terms of those observable regularities and the feelings and expectations they engender in our minds. He simply notes that the word "cause" has come to be used with a multitude of different meanings.[18]

Pierre Maine de Biran made his contribution to the development of the agency view of causation by undertaking the very same kind of quest that his fellow empiricists Locke and Hume had undertaken: a search for the origin in experience of the idea of causation – more accurately, of the cluster of ideas having to do with causation. With a self-conscious attention to issues of philosophical method that reminds one of Descartes, Biran sets out the characteristics of the experiential datum he is seeking. It must, he says, be a *fait primitif* or primitive fact, since it is to play a foundational role, akin to that of the Cartesian *Cogito*, in his system of knowledge.[19] A primitive fact, Biran insists, must have three characteristics. First, it must be a *première connaissance*, or primal awareness, not arrived at by any learning process or inference. This would plainly rule out the complicated sequence of experiences and inferences from which Locke says we derive the idea of power. Secondly, a primitive fact will involve two terms: a conscious individual perceiver, and a perception that is distinct from, and in some sense opposed to, the perceiver. Both terms will fall within the sphere of consciousness. This would be consistent with Berkeley's account of consciousness, in which one is always simultaneously aware of ideas and of the conscious self by which they are perceived;[20] it is inconsistent with Hume's claim that "they are the successive perceptions only, that constitute the mind".[21] The third feature of a primitive fact, according to Biran, is permanence or persistence over a space of time. Biran takes this to be necessary for any fact that is to play the foundational role he has in mind for primitive facts. Hume's "perceptions, which succeed each other with an inconceivable rapidity, and are in a perpetual flux and movement",[22] would not qualify.

The one thing that does plainly exhibit the three essential characteristics of a primitive fact, according to Biran, is the ongoing experience of voluntarily moving or not moving our own bodies, and perceiving the greater or lesser resistance that the body offers to the will. Biran claims that this experience is present, to at least a minimal degree, throughout our waking lives: this is what gives it the persistence or permanence required to be a primitive fact. Whether or not one agrees with Biran that humans are aware of this primitive fact every waking moment, it is clear that he is focusing his attention on the experience that Locke identified as the source of our ideas concerning causation: "the *beginning* of motion". More precisely, he has seized on the experience of activity or exercise of power that Reid identified as the one from which we directly derive the fundamental notion of activity or efficacy (and indirectly, the idea of power).

Biran makes two central points concerning this all-important experience. First, it is a unified experience: at the actual moment of successfully executing a bodily movement, there is "a kind of felt necessary connection between the willing and the movements of the body".[23] Secondly, the two elements in the experience, the willing and the resistance, are experienced in different ways. Locke

had said of reflection, the second great source of ideas to be acknowledged along with sensation: "This source of ideas ... though
it be not sense, as having nothing to do with external objects, yet it
is very like it".[24] Biran, by contrast, stresses the difference between
the way the reflective experience of willing is *lived through* and the
way the sensation of bodily resistance is *presented to* consciousness
as an object.[25]

If Biran's account of the phenomenology of the exercise of
active power is correct, then any account which represents the
experience as a sequence of perceptions that are all presented to
consciousness in the same fashion will be radically and dangerously
mistaken. That is the nub of Biran's criticism of Hume. In treating
the experience of voluntary bodily movement as just one more
case of A followed by B, so that a constant conjunction of A-like
antecedents and B-like consequents will be required to establish
that A causes B, Hume has given a distorted account of the very
experience from which our most basic causal notions are derived.

Hume attempts to defend his view by noting that

> [a] man, suddenly struck with palsy in the leg or
> arm, or who had newly lost those members, fre-
> quently endeavours, at first to move them, and em-
> ploy them in their usual offices.[26]

The nasty surprise of discovering that he has lost the power to move
his limb, Hume contends, shows that "[w]e learn the influence of
our will from experience alone".[27] Biran's reply is to point out that
Hume has here turned his attention away from the primary experience of successfully executing bodily movements, from which
causal notions are initially derived, to the experience of a mature
person who remembers being able to move his leg, plans to do so
again, and discovers that his former power to move it has deserted

him.[28] Certainly such changes in our powers can only be discovered through experience, just as we must learn the limits of our powers by trying to produce certain effects and finding that it is beyond our ability to bring them about. But that does not refute Biran's fundamental claim that the experience of agency is the source of our ideas concerning causation.

From the wording of the relevant page in the Appendix to the *Treatise*, it would seem that Hume wishes to deny this claim outright. Yet the context indicates that he was not fully focused upon the task of discovering the origins of ideas in experience; he was, in addition, considering the theoretical issue of the proper definition of the essential features of mental and physical substances.

> [T]he will being here consider'd as a cause, has no more a discoverable connexion with its effects, than any material cause has with its proper effect. So far from perceiving the connexion betwixt an act of volition, and a motion of the body; 'tis allow'd that no effect is more inexplicable from the powers and essence of thought and matter.[29]

Biran's position is that we *do* perceive a connection between an act of volition and a motion of the body, and that this perception is a far more primitive and foundational experience than any theorizing about the essence of thought and matter.

> Biran was to retort: one does not try to "explain" an *experience* in a project such as ours, that of explicating terms by referring them to experience. One tries to find that appropriate experience and then tries to help others to do the same. That experience

is the terminal point of all elucidation, the "primary fact".[30]

One way of accounting for Hume's lack of single-mindedness in the pursuit of the source of our ideas concerning causation is to note that he was attempting to do two very different things at once: to trace those ideas to their source in experience, and to refute the rationalists' account of causation. The latter aim led him to think of power or necessary connection, not simply as that which distinguishes cause-effect sequences from trains of events in which causal connection is not present, but as something which would allow the occurrence of the effect to be inferred *a priori* from the occurrence of the cause. To think of causal connection that way is to invoke theoretical notions which have no place in the "historical, plain method" appropriate for the empiricist task of uncovering the experiential sources of our ideas.[31]

Biran, as Philip Hallie interprets him, adheres to the "historical, plain method" originally advocated by Locke[32] as long as he is investigating the origins of ideas in experience; he avoids mixing in concepts and arguments that belong to more sophisticated levels of knowledge. And the idea he arrives at as the most fundamental of all is the idea best expressed by the term *efficacy*. It is derived immediately – without any intervening steps – from the awareness that any conscious agent will have that *I did that*, when a bodily movement has been successfully executed.

The attribution of efficacy to oneself is straightforward; it is simply what is called for by the experience from which the very idea of efficacy has been gleaned. But it does not take us long to begin attributing efficacy to things other than ourselves. We start doing so, according to Biran, as soon as the limbs or other body parts we have set in motion come in contact with other physical objects which resist or cut short the movement we have initiated. As Hallie expresses it:

> [T]his experience of an invincible resistance con-
> trasted with the compliant resistance of one's own
> hands leads us by means of what was called a "pri-
> mary inductive inference" to a belief that there is
> an object exerting a force opposed to our willing.
> The hand once moved or arrested by one's own will
> is suddenly stopped, and one knows that it is not
> one's own will that is stopping it. On the basis of
> his experience of voluntary bodily effort, he makes
> his "primary inductive inference" to the effect that
> there must be some cause of this cessation of move-
> ment, since every previous cessation had a cause,
> namely his own willing. That the cause is not his
> own muscular inertia he knows by virtue of the
> pressure of the object felt against his hand, exterior
> to his hand.[33]

Biran might have added that the "primary inductive inference" to the existence of an efficacious agent that is not myself, when my hand encounters the resistance of a table top, might well have been facilitated and supported by the experience of pressing my two hands together, or slapping my thigh – cases in which I myself pro-vide the resistance to one of my bodily movements by performing a second bodily movement or deliberate non-movement. But to the best of my knowledge, Biran never made any such observation.

The so-called "primitive inductive inference" through which we come to believe in the efficacy of things other than ourselves is plainly an all-important step in the development of our knowledge of the world. Biran at first believed it to be unproblematic, and spoke of external causes being *known* on the strength of such inferences. But on the evening of October 30, 1816, he had a conversation with Ampère which brought him to the realization that there is a logical gap between the knowledge that *I* am not the cause of the experienced resistance to my will and the conclusion that some *other* efficacious agent must be present to provide the resistance:

> Between the "individual internal experience" and the "belief or universal necessary notion of causation" he found "an abyss that cannot be crossed by analysis alone, nor by analogy or inductive inferences". Between the expression "I am *not* the cause of this Impression now present", and the expression, "There *is* necessarily an external unperceived cause of everything that is presented without or against my willing", there is a gap.[34]

Biran's final position was simply that "[o]ne has a 'natural' tendency to think of the forces external objects exert on our organs as similar to one's own force".[35]

It might be disappointing to an empiricist who set out to establish sure foundations for empirical knowledge to find himself obliged to retreat to such a position, but a philosopher not committed to any form of foundationalism need feel no disappointment. We can say simply that humans have a natural tendency to form the *hypothesis* that we are surrounded by other agents whose efficacy is to be understood as analogous to our own, and which resist our efforts to shove them around.

To portray Biran's "primary inductive inference" as a process of hypothesis formation, rather than a true inductive inference, has several advantages. First, there will be no difficulty in framing the hypothesis concerning external agents so as to include some that are alive and conscious in the same way as ourselves (other people), some that are alive but possess a type of consciousness that is different from our own (animals), and some that are neither alive nor conscious. The bare notion of efficacy – making something happen – can still be attributed to external objects even when the other features of human agency have been stripped away. We humans enjoy great freedom in creating hypotheses to explain experience; it seems to me that if anyone wishes to maintain that we are unable to conceive of agents who possess efficacy but not consciousness, the burden of proof is on them.

A second advantage of portraying the "primary inductive inference" as hypothesis formation is that the door is then opened to seeing the support and verification of empirical knowledge as a sequence of hypothetico-deductive inferences – a far more crisp and comprehensible notion than Biran's rather obscure "primary inductive inference". Hypothetico-deductive inferences notoriously do not lead to conclusions that can be accepted as certain; but to one who is inclined to see empirical knowledge as fallible in any case, that is no difficulty.

Some concluding notes on epistemology

It will now be apparent that the claims and methods I aim to defend in this essay sit well with certain views on matters of epistemology. I acknowledge that I share these views – sometimes, perhaps, even presuppose their correctness. If I do not undertake to defend them in these pages, it is because I do not have anything to add to the arguments that have been offered elsewhere in their defence.

Thus I adopt the strategy, derived from the classical empiricists of the eighteenth century, of tracing the origins of ideas and concepts to very basic experiences, including some that we would have had as pre-verbal children. But any such philosophical strategy needs to be applied with an eye on the findings of the Gestalt psychologists. Their research leaves no room for doubt that the primitive, "foundational" sort of experience the empiricists hoped to uncover – and, if possible, employ as the evidential basis for *a posteriori* knowledge – will not take the form of "simple impressions" of sensation or reflection, such as Locke and Hume discussed. The most primitive sense experience of humans is, rather, awareness of a *figure* that is contrasted with a *ground*.[36] Lockean "simple ideas" must be viewed as the result of an analysis of perception by a reflective adult, and Locke's claim that simple ideas "enter by the senses simple and unmixed"[37] cannot be maintained.

But in any case, it has proved impossible to identify any kind of "pure", uninterpreted experience that will provide an indubitable foundation for our knowledge of the world. Empiricists have found themselves obliged, in the end, to accept Kant's insight that "intuitions without concepts are blind"[38] – i.e., sensory experience, if not structured and interpreted in terms of some conceptual scheme, is not capable of functioning as a perception or observation of anything. In the twentieth century this insight came to be known as the "theory-ladenness of observation". To the best of my knowledge the terms 'theory-laden' and 'theory-loaded' were first used by N.R. Hanson,[39] but it is possible to see antecedents of his view in the work of Kant and C.I. Lewis.[40]

Again, it will be evident that the views I will defend concerning causality and related matters fit well with the view of human knowledge that is associated with the name of Karl Popper. Popper notes that both in science and in pre-scientific inquiry, people learn by trial and error; by going through a series of "conjectures and refutations". Conjectures or hypotheses are thought up, consequences referring to observable entities deduced, and the conclusions compared with observation. A hypothesis is refuted if its consequences are at variance with observation; it is progressively corroborated if it survives repeated tests without being refuted.[41] (It has emerged, through the critical discussion of Popper's position, that both scientists and ordinary enquirers go through a complex sequence of choices in the process of deciding what hypotheses to believe; we do not always discard a hypothesis as soon as it is refuted by observation.[42] But I leave aside the details of that discussion because, once again, I have nothing novel to add to it.)

One important feature of this account of the growth and grounding of knowledge is the role it assigns to the creative and inventive faculties of the knower. When constructing concepts and framing hypotheses, we knowers are constrained only by the capacities of our brains and the limits of our imagination.[43] At the same time, it is important to acknowledge that the freedom to exercise our imagination is purchased at the price of an inescapable fallibility in our knowledge. Any item of empirical knowledge, no matter how well corroborated, might conceivably turn out to be false. It is even logically possible that the whole interconnected structure of hypotheses that makes up our conception of the universe around us is one vast illusion: that in fact is what certain mystics have been saying for centuries. While agreeing that our ordinary consciousness gives us a coherent experience of a world containing many separate things, which we seem to be able to know through perception and science, mystics have frequently claimed that that experience is at bottom illusory, and the true nature of reality is very different:

> The most important, the central characteristics
> in which all *fully developed* mystical experiences
> agree, and which in the last analysis is definitive of
> them and serves to mark them off from other kinds
> of experiences, is that they involve the apprehen-
> sion of *an ultimate nonsensuous unity in all things,*
> a oneness or a One to which neither the senses

nor the reason can penetrate. In other words, it entirely transcends our sensory-intellectual consciousness.[44]

That likewise is beyond the scope of this essay.

---

1   See Jean Piaget 1930, 1953 and 1955.

2   See David Hume, *Treatise*, Book I, Part I, Sec. I, pp. 3-5; *Enquiry Concerning Human Understanding*, Section II, pp. 17-20.

3   Notably Ardon Lyon, David Lewis and J.L. Mackie. See the discussion in Chapter 6, pp. 265-271.

4   For my own purposes I have not found a need to resort to the concept of 'power' to do any hard philosophical work. Anything I would have to say about power can be expressed by speaking of ability and efficacy.

5   John Locke, *Essay*, Book II, ch. vii, para. 8; Vol. I, p. 163.

6   Locke, *Essay*, Book II, ch. xxi, para. 4; Vol. I, pp. 311-313.

7   Hume, *Treatise*, Book I, Part III, Sect. XIV, p. 161.

8   Hume, *Treatise*, Appendix, p. 632.

9   Thomas Reid, *Active Powers*, Essay I, p. 6.

10 Reid, *Active Powers*, Essay I, p. 6. Evidently Reid here intends his terms "external senses" and "consciousness" to designate what Locke referred to as "sensation" and "reflection".

11 Locke, *Essay*, Book II, ch. xxi, para. 1; Vol. I, p. 308. Emphasis added.

12 Reid, *Active Powers*, Essay I, p. 24.

13 Reid, *Active Powers*, Essay I, p. 36.

14 Reid, *Active Powers*, Essay I, p. 37.

15 Reid, *Active Powers*, Essay IV, p. 270.

16 Reid, *Active Powers*, Essay IV, p. 275.

17 Reid, *Active Powers*, Essay IV, p. 279.

18 Reid, *Active Powers*, Essay IV, p. 280.

19 See Pierre Maine de Biran, *Oeuvres Complètes*, Vol. VIII, pp. 15-23, and Philip Hallie 1951, pp. 153-154.

20 George Berkeley, *Principles*, para. 2.

21 Hume, *Treatise*, Book I, Part IV, Section VI, p. 253.

22 Hume, *Treatise*, Book I, Part IV, Section VI, p. 252.

23 Hallie, 1951, p. 162.

24 Locke, *Essay*, Book II, ch. i, para. 4; Vol. I, p. 123.
25 See Maine de Biran, *Oeuvres Choisis*, pp. 118-120, and Hallie 1951, pp. 159-160.
26 Hume, *Enquiry*, Section VII, Part I, p. 66.
27 Hume, *Enquiry*, Section VII, Part I, p. 66.
28 Maine de Biran, *Oeuvres Complètes*, Vol VIII, p. 229; Hallie 1959, pp. 88-89.
29 Hume, *Treatise*, Appendix, p. 632.
30 Hallie 1959, p. 88.
31 See J.L. Mackie 1974, pp. 10-14.
32 Locke, *Essay*, Introduction, para. 2; Vol. I, p. 27.
33 Hallie 1959, pp. 98-99; Maine de Biran, *Oeuvres Complètes*, Vol. IX, p. 371.
34 Hallie 1959, p. 101.
35 Hallie 1959, p. 101; Maine de Biran, *Oeuvres Complètes*, Vol. XIV, p. 63.
36 The founders of the movement known as Gestalt psychology were Max Wertheimer (1880-1943), Kurt Koffka (1886-1941) and Wolfgang Köhler (1887-1967), although a pioneering article by Christian Freiherr von Ehrenfels (1859-1932) is acknowledged to have played a seminal role in the formation of its central ideas. See Ehrenfels 1890, Wertheimer 1912, Koffka 1935, Köhler 1947 and Ellis 1938.
37 Locke, *Essay*, Book II, ch. ii, para. 1; Vol. I, p. 144.
38 Immanuel Kant 1929, p. 93.
39 See N.R. Hanson 1958, pp. 19, 54ff., 59, 62, 64, 65.
40 See C.I. Lewis 1929, *passim*. Eric Dayton observes that "Lewis's account of inquiry offers both a non-metaphysical account of induction and an early version of the so called 'theory-ladenness of observation terms'". See the entry for C.I. Lewis in the *Internet Encyclopedia of Philosophy* (http://www.isp.utm.edu/lewisci/).
41 See "Science: Conjectures and Refutations" and "Three Views Concerning Human Knowledge", in Karl Popper 1962.
42 See Thomas S. Kuhn 1962, Imre Lakatos 1970, Hilary Putnam 1974, Popper 1974, Paul Feyerabend 1975, Larry Laudan 1977, and Popper 1983.
43 On this point see, e.g., Popper 1962, p. 117.
44 W.T. Stace 1960, pp. 14-15.

CHAPTER 2
Making Something Happen

M y aim in this chapter is to begin the process of setting out
a certain basic vocabulary in terms of which the range of
concepts having to do with causation can be expressed. After introducing each item of the basic vocabulary, I will note what contribution it makes to the total intricate web of our shared conceptual
scheme. I will not be aiming for anything like the standard of rigor
that would be expected of a logician spelling out the primitive
basis of a formal system, but the purpose is similar. These are to be
terms whose sense is given informally and discursively. They will
not, strictly speaking, be defined. But other terms will be defined
by means of them.

In adopting this procedure I am making several claims on behalf of the primitive terms and the ideas they convey. First, that
they *are* basic – that when we seek to analyze our stock of concepts
having to do with cause and effect, the search will end with some
such set of elementary concepts as this. There are none simpler in
terms of which these may be analyzed, which would still convey the
sense of the familiar and distinctive language of causation.

Secondly, I am claiming that this limited set of primitive expressions – three in number, as indicated in the previous chapter – is

sufficient for the purpose of rational reconstruction of the part of our conceptual scheme that is related specifically to causation. The richness and subtlety of the linguistic and conceptual resources that are available to us when we are coping with causal phenomena can be a hindrance, rather than an asset, when we turn to the task of philosophical analysis. Common language enshrines a wealth of distinctions and nuances, not all of which are helpful for the purposes of philosophy. Even the ones which are or could be helpful will tend to get in one another's way if we attempt to use too many of them in a single philosophical project. There is merit, therefore, in deliberately limiting our vocabulary – particularly our primitive, undefined vocabulary – when we are engaged in philosophical analysis and reconstruction. Very general claims, and especially the systematic connections between our claims, become clearer when the claims are stated with the minimum needed vocabulary. I view the vocabulary to be introduced in this chapter and the two following chapters as providing the necessary minimum for the purposes I have in hand.

The third and final claim I take myself to be making on behalf of the minimal undefined vocabulary is that by adopting it, we will go as far as we ought to go towards satisfying the demands of empiricists for a foundation for human knowledge grounded in sensation and introspection. The proposed primitive terms are ones which will connect, as closely as the subject matter allows, with *experience* in the classic Lockean sense of that term: sensation plus reflection. Hume was quite correct to enquire after the impressions of sense and/or introspection which give rise to our concept of necessary connection. I will argue, however, that while his strategy was correct in principle, he was thrown off the scent by his commitment to the maxim that ideas must be copies of the impressions from which they are derived, and by his commitment to the project of refuting the rationalist philosophers.

Causal efficacy: A brings it about that p

The first of the primitive terms I wish to introduce is the basic verb of agency and agent causation: A brings it about that p. The variable 'p' (to spell out what I hope is obvious) is a stand-in for an expression of sentential form describing a state of affairs. The variable 'A' ranges over agents – and it will be necessary to discuss which entities will be classified as agents. Finally, in the frequent cases in which the state of affairs A brings about is simply an action of A's, the suggested expression can be pressed into service by saying 'A brings it about that A does X' – where the variable 'does X' ranges over verbs designating the doings of agents.

The use of a clumsy two-verb expression to replace simpler expressions of the form 'A does X' is suggested simply as a means of having a single undefined expression, 'A brings it about that p', which can do duty for the whole range of cases in which we wish to speak of agency or agent causation. It is not meant to suggest that there are *two* actions involved, A's doing X and A's bringing it about that A does X. To some it may appear that we are now running the risk of getting ourselves trapped in an infinite regress. But if we do get trapped, it will be due solely to our own ineptitude. There is nothing in the phenomena to which this language applies which would generate a problem of the kind that leads to a regress.

The expression 'A brings it about that p' is designed to be applied to any situation in which that unique and familiar relation obtains between an agent and a state of affairs which we designate by saying that he or she or it *did that*. In practice, we most frequently use more specific and descriptive action verbs: a runaway car knocked over my newly planted sapling; Wendy raised her arm; the cat scratched Joe's face; the rain flushed the cobwebs out of the downspout. The agents involved in these transactions may be animate or inanimate, conscious or unconscious, moral agents or just plain agents: the basic notion of agency applies equally to them all.

Indeed, I see no difficulty in attributing agency to things that would be classified as events, facts, or states of affairs rather than substances. We speak of a low pressure system bringing stormy weather to part of the continent; the fact that it had snowed overnight, we say, made the roads slippery during the morning rush hour; there being ice on the highway made my car skid.

Out of the collection of philosophical terms which have been devised to apply to the phenomena of causation, the one which most exactly captures the notion I have in mind is *efficacy*: making something happen.

The experience, and the idea, of efficacy

The idea of efficacy – bringing something about or making something happen – is applied in the first instance to single episodes: *that* agent (or event or whatever) made *this* happen. There is no firm implication that the outcome was in any way necessitated: it is possible that what happened did not *have* to happen. There is certainly no implication that an outcome of the same kind will always occur in similar conditions. When Hume says that "the terms of *efficacy, agency, power, force, energy, necessity, connexion,* and *productive quality*, are all nearly synonimous",[1] he is guilty of an unfortunate confusion. There is some excuse for regarding some of the members of this list as being nearly synonymous; but by no means all. A power, according to the common understanding of the term, may exist even if it has never been exercised. But to describe an agent as efficacious is to claim something beyond possibly unfulfilled potential; efficacy involves actually making something happen. A force may be resisted by a countervailing force, with the result that nothing actually happens. But if nothing happens, the agent in question is not exhibiting any efficacy. Energy, likewise, may be expended without actually making anything happen. Necessity is a modal concept, which efficacy is not. And as for necessary connection, that is a relation between cause factors or causal conditions and their effects, of a sort that requires the modal concept of necessity for its analysis; whereas efficacy, in so far as it is a relational concept, represents a non-modal relation between a cause or agent and a state of affairs which that cause or agent brings about.

It is revealing that Hume wishes to sweep away all of these distinctions, and make do with a philosophical vocabulary in which they have no place. I have also committed myself to the use of a vocabulary which omits many of the concepts and distinctions available in ordinary language, but I do wish to make use of a number of resources that Hume chose to do without.

Hume's challenge to the validity of the idea of efficacy (and by the same token, the ideas expressed by those other terms he has deemed to be synonymous) is found on the same page of the *Treatise*:

> [S]ince reason can never give rise to the idea of efficacy, that idea must be deriv'd from experience, and from some particular instances of this efficacy, which make their passage into the mind by the common channels of sensation or reflection. Ideas always represent their objects or impressions; and *vice versa*, there are some objects necessary to give rise to every idea. If we pretend, therefore, to have any just idea of this efficacy, we must produce some instance, wherein the efficacy is plainly discoverable to the mind, and its operations obvious to our consciousness or sensation.[2]

To this challenge, Elizabeth Anscombe gives the direct and telling response:

> Nothing easier: is cutting, is drinking, is purring not 'efficacy'? But it is true that the apparent perception of such things may be only apparent: we may be deceived by false appearances. Hume presumably wants us to 'produce an instance' in which *efficacy* is related to sensation as *red* is. It is true that we can't do that; it is not *so* related to sensation.[3]

From what experience, then, would our idea of efficacy, of making something happen, have arisen? Obviously from the experience of making something happen, the experience of being an agent. We may, as Anscombe is careful to point out, be deceived by false appearances; but this is plainly a matter in which appearances can occasionally deceive us only because they do *not* deceive us in the great majority of cases. The experiences on which our attention should be focused, then, are experiences in which we correctly perceive ourselves to be making something happen.

There can be little doubt that one of the most basic experiences of this type is the experience of moving our own bodies, particularly our limbs. That is also among the very first experiences of efficacy in the life of a human being: babies start kicking while still in the womb, as any mother will tell you.

So this should be the experience we "consider with the utmost attention". And perhaps the first thing to be noted is that at this level, it is next to impossible to believe that appearances would in fact deceive us, save in the most extraordinary circumstances. When someone else raises my arm, and I simply remain passive and allow it to happen, it is perfectly plain to me that this is *not* a case of my making something happen. The other person is making it happen. Likewise when the doctor bangs my kneecap with a mallet and my foot shoots out in a reflex action. An observer might not be able to distinguish a voluntary jerk from an involuntary one; but I myself would be in no doubt that in the one case I had brought about the bodily movement in question, and in the other case I had not.

People do of course dream of making things happen which in fact are not happening, as for instance when someone dreams of running down the street while in truth doing no such thing. But in the central group of cases – wide-awake humans voluntarily moving their limbs – there is next to no possibility of error when we make such judgments as 'I did that; I made that happen' or 'I did not do that; it happened, but I did not make it happen'. These judgments, it seems to me, are no more prone to error than judgments about the content of our sensory fields.

Secondly, the experience of making something happen, of which voluntarily moving a limb is a ground-floor example, is a unified experience, although different elements in it may be distinguished. You do not try to raise your arm and *then* check to see whether or not you are succeeding; you just raise your arm. The experience of exerting whatever effort is needed is simultaneous with the sensory feedback which informs you that what you are making happen is in fact happening. The two are, indeed, not merely simultaneous, but tightly bound together by the links of long-established association. Pierre Maine de Biran, as we have noted, went so far as to think in terms of "a kind of felt necessary connection between the willing and the movements of the body".[4] Yet the empiricists' division between sensation and reflection runs right through the center of this unified experience. It is through receiving impressions of sensation that I am aware that my arm is rising or my lower leg is being extended. But the impressions through which I am aware that *I* am making it happen would be classified as impressions of reflection, "that notice which the mind takes of its own operations". It would follow that on Locke's or Hume's principles, the idea of making something happen would be a compound idea, since the experience which gives rise to it is composed of at least two distinct impressions.

I have no quarrel with this conclusion. It matters little, for my purposes, how philosophers carve up the flux of experience into countable impressions. But two observations are in order.

First, Hume apparently assumed that the impression of efficacy or power or necessary connection or whatever, if he were lucky enough to find it, would be a single, simple impression – hence, an impression of sensation *or* an impression of reflection. After his initial allusion, in the *Treatise*, to the "impression or impressions" from which the idea of necessary connection might be derived, he regularly refers to its "impression", in the singular. He treats necessary connection as one of the simple ideas into which the complex idea of causation is to be broken down, and attempts no analysis of it into yet simpler ideas. Since he held that simple ideas have to be copies of simple impressions, it would stand to reason he was convinced that the impression of efficacy or necessary connection, if there were such a thing, would have to be a single, simple impression. This conviction would go a long way towards explaining his failure to appreciate the significance of the everyday experience of voluntary movement.

Secondly, the conceptual construct 'A brings it about that p' can still be a fundamental and logically primitive building block in our conceptual scheme – not defined in terms of anything else – even though the experience which gives rise to it is an experience composed of more than one impression – indeed, more than one type of impression.

In saying that I am following the lead of Maine de Biran, who held that the experience of voluntary bodily movement – in particular, movement in which a willed effort is experienced as overcoming the inertia or resistance of our own bodies – is a primitive fact (*fait primitif*) than which nothing is more basic in the scheme of human knowledge. He held, in fact, that its complex internal makeup, consisting of a conscious subject relating itself to a datum being presented to it, is one of three characteristics which make it fit for a foundational role in an empiricist-style reconstruction of empirical knowledge. (The other two characteristics are that it is unlearned, and that it persists as long as we are conscious. Hume's impressions, on the other hand, have only one of the three desired characteristics. Like the primitive experience of willed effort, they are unlearned. But they are transitory, not persistent; and they lack a subject/object structure. Biran concluded that Humean bundles of impressions could not possibly provide an adequate foundation for empirical knowledge.)[5]

Now when I suggest that the experience of voluntary movement is the outstanding candidate for the role of the experience which gives rise to our idea of causal efficacy, I cannot possibly claim to be breaking fresh ground. This philosophical path is already well trodden, as the survey of eighteenth- and nineteenth-century empiricists in the previous chapter will have shown. And the experience of efficacy in the context of voluntary bodily movement is indeed, as Hume says, an experience of the constant conjunction, and delicate correlation, of volition and result. The correlation gets established in the very dawn of awareness, and holds with such constancy that an association of the strongest sort comes to hold between the element of voluntary effort, perceived as an impression of reflection, and the sensory feedback that informs us of our success. The whole comes to be felt as a single experience.

In order to find examples in which the association is sundered, we need to look beyond routine waking life. In my sleep I may dream that I am dancing, or on the other hand I may kick my spouse without forming any conscious volition to do so. Examples involving fully conscious subjects will arise only when the organism's normal control and feedback mechanisms have been somehow disrupted or damaged. Hume himself used the example of a man "suddenly stricken with palsy in the leg or arm"[6] to drive home the point that our expectation of success in moving our limbs when we try to do so is based upon past experience – not upon any special, infallible insight that some might have supposed us to enjoy as a consequence of having an awareness of power. I would say, on the contrary, that healthy people do have an experience of efficacy when they successfully move their limbs, but the man suddenly struck with palsy would not – precisely because efficacy entails success. The palsied man would have had the experience of trying to move a limb and not succeeding – a most unnerving surprise, if he had had no prior inkling of his diseased condition.

A more challenging class of examples is provided by amputees who feel "phantom limbs" following their surgery. Some have been known to have the illusion of actually moving their missing limbs, even wiggling their phantom toes. They are thus having the experience, through impressions of reflection, of trying to move their limbs; they are also having an illusory experience of success, by way of non-veridical bodily sensations. Only visual feedback or further experimental behavior (e.g., trying to stand on an amputated leg and falling over) will serve to uncover the sensory illusion. These I take to be examples of the false appearances of efficacy of which Elizabeth Anscombe warned us. Examples of this type might be troubling to a philosopher who wished to regard the unified experience of voluntarily moving a limb as part of an infallible foundation for empirical knowledge. But as long as we are not committed to that type of foundationalism, we can cheerfully agree with Hume on several points concerning the experience of efficacy in voluntary action. It is not a source of *a priori* knowledge. It is not an insight into a secret connection between cause and effect. It *is* an experience of constant conjunction and correlation between volition, known through reflection, and results known through either reflection or sensation. And beyond all doubt, our certainty concerning the reality, and the limitations, of our control over our bodily movements and our mental acts is the result of many years of experiencing that constant conjunction and correlation.

If I admit to being in agreement with Hume to that extent, where then do I part company with him? I can think of no better way to answer that question than to return to the point made by Elizabeth Anscombe: Hume apparently expected to come up with an example in which *efficacy* would be related to sensation in the same way as *red*; but this is an error, because it is not so related to sensation.[7]

My contention will be that Hume misclassified the experience of volition and of being an agent, acting or attempting to act. This aspect of self-knowledge certainly comes to us through reflection, "that notice which the mind takes of its own operations". It is even acceptable to say that the experience is made up of impressions of reflection, provided that the term 'impressions' is not taken in too narrow a sense. But it *is* a mistake to suppose that those particular impressions can be treated on the same footing as the impressions that constitute an experience of passively observing some phenomenon.

The point applies even to phenomena involving my own body, of which my awareness is constituted in part by internal bodily sensations. If I bang my fist on the table, it is perfectly evident to me that this is something *I* am doing. If another person takes hold of my fist and bangs it on the table, while I merely allow this to happen, it is equally evident to me that what is going on is not something I am doing – even if this is not evident to an outside observer. A theory of knowledge that ignores the importance of this difference between being active and being passive is bound to go off the rails when it comes to dealing with causation. Of course Hume is not so blind as to overlook the difference entirely; but he does ignore its importance.

I am well aware that I am not the first student of Hume to make such a charge. Antony Flew was the one who made it in perhaps the most pointed fashion:

> [I]t is significant that Hume presents 'cause' as an
> *observer's* not as an *experimental enquirer's* or an
> *agent's* concept: his might irreverently be called a
> paralytic's eye view. Only after the main business
> of showing that causal necessity is no sort of log-
> ical necessity does he go on, more or less as after-
> thought, to offer 'Rules by which to judge of causes
> and effects' and to note that causes offer levers. . . .
> But even these 'Rules' . . . are formulated for an *ob-
> server* not for an *experimenter.* [8]

What should we do, then, to carry out fairly the task that Hume set for himself and his fellow enquirers – the task of tracing the experiential basis of our concepts related to causation? If our aim is to carry out Hume's strategy, and apply his empirical method, then the thing to do is to examine "with the utmost attention" an experience following which we are prepared to say 'I did that', and compare it with one which leaves us ready to say only 'So-and-so occurred, but I didn't do it'.

Here I find I must resort to the classic tactic of the eighteenth-century empiricists, and invite each reader to try the experiment for himself or herself. What *do* you experience when you bang your fist on the table, which is missing when someone else picks it up and bangs it on the table?

It is certainly not a sensation like the sensation of red; Elizabeth Anscombe was surely correct to say that efficacy is not related to sensation as red is. I will not object to calling it an impression of reflection, provided that is not taken to imply that it can be set alongside other impressions (especially impressions of sensation) and contributes to the total experience in an exactly analogous fashion. It is not one more brushstroke on the scenery in the theatre of the mind; it is much more like a current of energy zipping across the stage.

Elusive though it is when one struggles to describe it, its presence in unproblematic cases of voluntary bodily movement and voluntary direction of attention is quite unmistakable. It comes as no surprise to learn that the efferent nerves form a distinct system which is not in play when we are passively observing the scene, but that those nerves are busily transmitting impulses when we are engaged in voluntary bodily movement. Indeed, the distinctive experience of being physically active could be viewed as a perception of this distinctive neural activity. (But the point must not be pressed too far, because our sensory experience of the world around us should certainly *not* be viewed as a perception of the activity of our afferent nerves.) Physiology, as well as introspection, supports the view that Hume was guilty of a consequential category mistake when he failed to recognize the distinctive role of the experience of agency in the tissue of experience on which empirical knowledge is founded.

I have brought physiological considerations to bear upon the argument; Hume does so as well. He argues in the *Enquiry*:

> We learn from anatomy, that the immediate object
> of power in voluntary motion, is not the member
> itself which is moved, but certain muscles, and
> nerves, and animal spirits, and, perhaps, something

> still more minute and more unknown, through
> which the motion is successively propagated, ere
> it reach the member itself whose motion is the im-
> mediate object of volition. ... How indeed can we
> be conscious of a power to move our limbs, when
> we have no such power; but only that to move cer-
> tain animal spirits, which, though they produce at
> last the motion of our limbs, yet operate in such a
> manner as is wholly beyond our comprehension?[9]

If awareness of our power or efficacy as agents involved foreknowl-
edge of what we will accomplish, or insight into the many side
effects of our actions, Hume's point would be well taken. But it
does not. When I raise my arm, I am aware of my efficacy in raising
my arm; the arm raising, described as such, is the thing I know I
made happen. There is then a more detailed story to be told about
the nerves and muscles and tendons and bones. Included in this
detailed story will be a description of chains of causes in which
the efficacy of nerves and muscles themselves will be mentioned.
Thus in relating the detailed story, we will have occasion to apply
to our body parts the concept of efficacy which originates in our
awareness of our efficacy as undivided organisms. On the level of
the organism, raising an arm is characteristically perceived as a
single action. This is the level which is *epistemically* basic, the level
at which the primitive materials of empirical knowledge are to be
found. It makes no difference that when the sciences of anatomy
and physiology were developed to a high degree of sophistication,
a simple arm-raising was found to be a complex physiological process whose description involved the application of those epistemic
materials, at the microscopic level, to entities which are sub-parts
of the organism.

I have focused almost exclusively on voluntary bodily movements as the context of the experience which gives rise to our idea
of causal efficacy, and our awareness of ourselves as agents. But
Hume (and many others) regarded mental acts as equally germane
examples of the exertion of the powers of the will. I do as well,
although it must be admitted that it is impossible to specify any
particular impression of reflection which must be part of the experience of a particular mental act, such as doing an addition in one's
head. There are typical bodily sensations that let me know when
I have raised my arm, but no sensations of any kind which are essential to my being aware that I have added 77 and 50. There is the
further point that provided I am not struggling against fatigue or
distraction etc. to focus my attention, I do not experience resistance
to my effort to carry out a simple mental addition: I think of the
problem, and there is the answer: 127.

This is to be contrasted with the slight (or not so slight) feeling
of resistance that is always present when we attempt to make a
bodily movement. To Maine de Biran, that feeling of resistance,
or something like it, was essential to any experience which was
to qualify as a foundational *fait primitif*.[10] But the effortlessness
of certain mental acts, the absence of resistance – which is itself
something we directly experience – is sufficient to show that the
overcoming of resistance is not an essential element in the experience, or the idea, of making something happen. It merely accom-
panies the experience of making something happen in the earliest
and most significant class of cases, executing bodily movements.

This might pose something of a problem for a foundationalist
such as Biran, since it suggests that the foundations of empirical
knowledge might not have been correctly characterized, and has
the unfortunate result that effortless mental acts will now be arbitrarily excluded from those foundations. It is not a problem for
the version of the agency theory being developed here; I look to

the experience of voluntary bodily movements and mental acts as the source of ideas related to causality, but not as a uniquely important evidential foundation supporting the edifice of empirical knowledge.

This is perhaps a good time to explain what I understand by an experience providing a source for an idea, or an idea's being derived from a certain experience. In the first place, I have been using the term 'idea' to stand for a concept that may or may not be accompanied by a corresponding mental image. This usage is consistent with Locke's very broad understanding of the word: "whatever it is which the mind can be employed about in thinking".[11] It is different from Hume's understanding of the term: he used it to stand for those perceptions of the mind which are faint copies of the more vivid impressions of sense or reflection. He then claims that impressions and ideas are the only two kinds of perceptions we have.[12] As is well known, Hume held that simple ideas always resemble the simple impressions from which they have been derived, whereas complex ideas may be constructed out of simple ideas in ways that do not wholly resemble any complex impression that one has actually experienced.[13] And he understands the process by which ideas are derived from impressions as a process of copying:

> An impression first strikes upon the senses, and makes us perceive heat or cold, thirst or hunger, pleasure or pain of some kind or other. Of this impression there is a copy taken by the mind, which remains after the impression ceases; and this we call idea.[14]

It would follow that when we verify that a certain idea has been derived from a certain impression, we need to make certain that a process of copying took place, and that the resulting idea resembles the original impression. If on the other hand we conceive of the idea as a concept rather than a mental image, we need to make certain that a process of conceptual construction took place, and that the resulting concept is unequivocally *instantiated* by the object that was experienced.

Applying the idea of efficacy to nature

Before we turn to the way in which we apply the concepts of agency and causal efficacy to objects in nature, it is important to take note of a particular type of context, other than voluntary behavior, in which we become aware of our own efficacy and our role as agents making things happen in the world. Compare the case in which I deliberately crush an eggshell by stamping on it with my foot, with the case in which I lose my balance and fall on the eggshell, crushing it with whatever part of my anatomy happens to make contact. I will claim, as does Biran, that the first is an example of the kind of experience which is the prototype for our basic idea of efficacy; an experience of being an agent and deliberately making something happen. But the second is worthy of attention. In that case also, I have plainly made something happen, in that it was the sudden arrival of my body in the vicinity of the ground which crushed the eggshell. If we are supposing that I am conscious throughout this little misadventure, we may suppose that I receive sufficient sensory feedback to make me aware of what is going on, and of my role in the eggshell crushing process. Yet, if it is plain that in falling on the eggshell I have made something happen, it is equally plain that something important is missing in the second case that was present in the first: the element which we designate by calling the act of stamping on the eggshell deliberate or intentional.

Now some philosophers have wished to reserve the language of action for the case of full-blown, deliberate, intentional acts. If we were to adopt their way of speaking, we would say that when I crush an eggshell by accidentally falling on it, the crushing is not an act of mine. There is certainly a lot to be said for this suggestion: the element of deliberation and control, when it is present, is beyond all doubt a significant part of our grounds for feeling and saying 'I did that'. At the same time, we need to recognize the element in the accidental eggshell crushing which makes it appropriate to say, in that case also, that I did it (although not deliberately or intentionally). Common language handles these cases, not by abandoning the verbs of action as some philosophers might appear to be suggesting, but by retaining the use of the action verbs while inserting some qualifying adverb, such as 'accidentally' or 'inadvertently', to signal that this is action in something less than the full-blown sense.

I have no wish to dispute about words. But it is vital to take note of our common practice of employing verbs of action in a way that imputes agency to ourselves and to others in a less-than-full-blown sense. We do this when we see that *in fact* agency is present in less than the full-blown sense; that some, but not all, of the features of full-blown deliberate action are present.

It is helpful to note that we apply a reduced or qualified notion of agency to ourselves and other persons in certain conditions, because it makes it clear that we habitually scale down what we intend and imply by our verbs of action, in cases where we are not dealing with paradigm examples of deliberate behavior. The scaling-down process is carried further when we apply verbs of action, and with them the underlying idea of causal efficacy, to entities and processes in nature. Imagine that it is not a person but a large, heavy icicle falling from the roof which crushes the eggshell that is lying on the ground. We still use the same action verb: we say that the icicle crushed the eggshell. But in this case, we not only withhold any attribution of deliberate intent; we take it for granted that the icicle is not conscious, unlike a falling person who crushes an eggshell.

At this point it is necessary to consider once more the claim advanced by Locke and challenged by Hume: "we feel an energy, or power, in our own mind; and ... having in this manner acquir'd the idea of power, we transfer that quality to matter, where we are not able immediately to discover it".[15] The most basic idea I have said we acquire from the experience of our own agency is the idea of efficacy, as expressed in the phrase 'A brings it about that p', and I am in fact claiming that we apply this idea to matter when we say such things as 'The falling icicle crushed the eggshell'. But it is of the utmost importance to notice that the idea of efficacy we apply to an inanimate entity such as an icicle is not the entire, full-bodied idea that we acquired from the experience of our own agency. It is a stripped-down version devoid of any implications of life, personality, intention or consciousness. Stripped of such connotations, the bare idea of efficacy is nothing more than the simple notion of making something happen. The icicle does what I did when I *fell* on the eggshell – only the icicle has no awareness of what is happening. If this point is not appreciated, an account of causality incorporating the notion of efficacy that we have been discussing will come across as a rather silly kind of vitalism that no adult in an advanced culture would entertain as a basic belief.

It is known that some primitive cultures have an animistic view of everything in nature, and it is at least logically possible that the animistic approach might be carried to the extent of applying the entire concept of personal agency to such agents as icicles. The Swiss psychologist Jean Piaget has amassed substantial clinical evidence to the effect that children in our own Western culture begin by believing every physical object has personal characteristics, and only gradually discover which of these characteristics are missing from those things that come to be classified as non-human, non-conscious, and non-living.[16]

Atomism versus a *Gestalt* approach

I have represented the full-blown idea of personal efficacy as one that can be analyzed into different parts or elements, in such a way that we are then able to ascribe some but not all of these elements to inanimate objects in nature. Thus, to use the terminology of the classical empiricists, I have portrayed the idea of personal efficacy as a complex idea that may be broken down into simpler ones: personal efficacy equals bare efficacy plus consciousness plus intention etc.

Now in discussing ideas and impressions, the classical empiricists adopted what may be described as an atomistic approach: the simple elements were assumed to be available as building blocks for a philosophical account of the structured whole. It is one thing to take an atomistic approach of this sort when carrying out a rational reconstruction of our knowledge, paying no regard to the antecedent processes of learning and concept formation. But the classical empiricists were committed to the "historical, plain method" pioneered by Locke;[17] and when practising any such philosophical method, it is of the essence to trace the origins of ideas and give an account of how concepts are formed. Logical analysis thus gets combined with developmental psychology, and the simple ideas must be so conceived that they are fitted to play a role in this hybrid enterprise. There is but one way to do so, and that is to suppose that simple ideas are present, separate and distinct from one another, at the earliest stages of the learning process.

The supposition must be maintained even if experience tells us that simple ideas of sense (what Hume calls simple "impressions") do in fact arrive in clusters which we are obliged to regard as complex ideas. Locke makes the move that his methodological atomism requires, and declares that simple ideas of sense are distinct from the beginning:

Though the qualities that affect our senses are, in the things themselves, so united and blended, that there is no separation, no distance between them; yet it is plain, the ideas they produce in the mind enter by the senses simple and unmixed. For, though the sight and touch often take in from the same object, at the same time, different ideas;– as a man sees at once motion and colour; the hand feels softness and warmth in the same piece of wax: yet the simple ideas thus united in the same subject, are as perfectly distinct as those that come in by different senses.[18]

Naturally, Locke has chosen examples that serve the purpose of the argument he has in hand. But in a later chapter of the *Essay*, devoted to "our complex ideas of substances", he gives the following example:

[T]he idea which an Englishman signifies by the name swan, is white colour, long neck, red beak, black legs, and whole feet, and all of these of a certain size, with a power of swimming in the water, and making a certain kind of noise, and perhaps, to a man who has long observed this kind of birds, some other properties: which all terminate in sensible simple ideas, all united in one common subject.[19]

As a logical analysis of a mature person's conception of a swan, this is fine (given that it antedates the discovery of black swans in Australia). But if we are required to suppose that all the simple ideas which go to make up the complex idea of a swan must have "entered by the senses simple and unmixed", even in a case when seeing a swan is among a young child's earliest encounters with wildlife, then this is plainly false to the fact. It is by now well established that many ideas which Locke would need to regard as simple ideas do not in fact "enter by the senses simple and unmixed". What is perceived in the first instance is a unified *Gestalt*; only later, if at all, is this unified perception differentiated into subparts and perhaps – but not necessarily – into ultimate Lockean simples.[20]

I have been attempting a kind of analysis that follows in the footsteps of the classical empiricists, yet takes account of the findings of Gestalt psychology. For the purposes of logical analysis and the rational reconstruction of empirical knowledge, I am taking the bare idea of efficacy, as expressed in sentences of the form 'A brings it about that p', as one of the logically primitive expressions in terms of which causal concepts will be defined. It is, in that sense, a "simple idea", although it has subparts and an internal structure: subject, verb, 'that'-clause.

Concerning this idea, which I have labeled "bare efficacy", I have posed the classic question of the empiricist philosophers: what experience would have given rise to this idea? And I have concurred with the answer offered by Locke, Reid and Biran: it is the experience of voluntary action, of which the most elementary example is voluntary bodily movement. But in voluntary action we experience more than bare efficacy. There are the further aspects of consciousness and intention – aspects that we do not, as adult members of an advanced culture, wish to attribute to all of the objects in nature to which we are willing to ascribe bare efficacy. Nevertheless, I do not wish to say, as Locke would have been obliged to say, that the idea of voluntary efficacious action is a complex idea, whose simple elements enter our consciousness "unmixed". Beyond doubt what we experienced in the earliest days of our lives were actions – kicking of legs, waving of arms, rolling of head – each perceived as a unified *Gestalt*. Between the original experience and the stripped-down idea of bare efficacy lies a long process of differentiation and subtraction.

Not that we complete the entire process, to the extent of being able to use the abstract philosophical concept of efficacy, before starting to *apply* the concept of bare efficacy to objects around us. It is rather a matter of applying action verbs and causal concepts to particular agents and processes that we perceive as analogous – in certain ways, not in every way – to ourselves and to our own voluntary behavior. Being *acted upon* – by other humans, animals and inanimate things – gives us a range of experience that is of great significance in this process.

So we end up viewing the world as a system of causal processes, and substances with characteristic causal powers. We think that we actually perceive causal connections. When not inhibited by philosophical scruples, we will say that we saw Lou Pasaglia kick a field goal, implying that we saw him *make* the football sail through the air and go between the goalposts. Before reading Hume we were prepared to say that we could see one billiard ball *make* another one move by striking it, and hear that it makes a noise.

Perceiving causation

The Belgian psychologist Albert Michotte, after an extensive and exact study of the conditions in which subjects will say that they seemed to perceive a causal connection between phenomena, in the end endorsed the commonsensical view of the matter. Michotte devoted several chapters of his book, *The Perception of Causality*, to what he called the "Launching Effect" *(l'effet lancement)*, in which one object is perceived to bump into another and set it in motion while coming to a halt itself. (A rolling boxcar coming up to a second boxcar, making contact, and pushing the second one off down the track, would be a clear, everyday instance. Hume's billiard balls provide a classic example of what Michotte calls launching-by-striking.) Summarizing his results, he writes:

> From the experiments described so far there is suf-
> ficient evidence to show clearly that the Launching
> Effect (in the case of launching-by-striking) must
> be considered as a perceptual Form (Gestalt). It is
> characterised by a specific internal structure, and
> occurs when there are certain definite conditions
> of stimulation and reception. ...
>
> It is therefore quite out of the question to re-
> gard the causal aspect of the Launching Effect as
> due to an "act of interpretation" on our part, or
> to suppose that, under the influence of past ex-
> perience or in some other way, we ourselves in-
> vest certain basic impressions of movement with
> a "meaning". On the contrary there is actual *per-
> ception* of causality, in the same sense that there is
> perception of shapes, movements, and so on. These
> expressions are logically similar; and in each case
> it is a question of specific phenomenal data, whose
> appearance is linked with the action of a particular
> system of sensory stimulation.[21]

It is worth noting that Michotte's subjects, when they reported the circumstances in which a perception of causality was forced upon them, were not looking at railroad trains or billiard balls. They were looking at patches of color projected on a movie screen. When they saw one patch of color approach another and "launch" it, they themselves would have been aware that the process which was stimulating the irresistible perception of causality was not itself a genuine causal process. It was what Wesley Salmon would classify as a pseudo-process.[22] An image on a screen does nothing towards producing the image that succeeds it, or determining its qualities; each image is in fact being produced by a genuine causal process operating through the projection device. But of course a pseudo-process consisting of a series of images may be used to *depict* a genuine causal process; any ordinary movie provides an example of this. So it was causal connection in the process being depicted, not in the process actually being observed, that Michotte's subjects felt they were perceiving. There is nothing particularly strange about this – after all, our everyday perceptions of genuine causal processes depend upon the occurrence of pseudo-processes in various parts of our sensory systems, from the retina to the eardrum to the perceptual centers of the brain. The fact that Michotte had his subjects looking at pseudo-processes actually helps to reinforce his point that causality is a perceptual Form (or *Gestalt*) triggered by certain patterns of sensory stimulation.

Michotte, as we have seen, insists that laboratory subjects, when presented with the appropriate sequence of stimuli, actually perceive the efficacy of one object acting upon another, and the necessary connection between cause and effect, in the same way as the shapes and movements of the objects are perceived. This, as he is well aware, is radically different from what Hume had claimed to see when he wrote:

> [U]pon the whole, there appears not, throughout all nature, any one instance of connexion which is conceivable by us. All events seem entirely loose and separate. One event follows another; but we never can observe any tie between them. They seem *conjoined*, but never *connected*. [23]

Michotte's response is to say that Hume had adopted an "analytical attitude" which is appropriate for a scientific observer, and which is apt to *prevent* the formation of an impression of causality.[24]

Michotte takes himself to be dealing with the popular idea of causality rather than a scientific one, and avers:

> If Hume had been able to carry out experiments such as ours, there is no doubt that he would have been led to revise his views on the psychological origin of the popular idea of causality. He would probably have appealed in his explanation to the 'causal impression' rather than to habit and expectation. This causal impression, however, would have been for him, as for Malebranche, nothing but an illusion of the senses, as is shown by his views with regard to the feeling of effort. Moreover it is probable that his philosophical position would not have been affected in the least.[25]

In an apparent effort to minimize his disagreement with Hume, Michotte points out that Hume acknowledged the significance of the experience of voluntarily moving our bodies with regard to the popular notion of power, as contrasted with the strict, scientific notion:

> Hume admitted that the impression of effort against resistance can enter into the popular inaccurate idea of power or cause; but he denies that it has anything to do with power in the strict sense, which implies necessity.[26]

He proceeds to quote a footnote from Hume's *Enquiry:*

> It must, however, be confessed, that the animal
> *nisus*, which we experience, though it can afford no
> accurate precise idea of power, enters very much
> into the vulgar, inaccurate idea, which is formed
> of it.[27]

Michotte, as an experimental psychologist, was investigating the perception of causality – or the causal impression, as he frequently called it – as a psychological phenomenon occurring in subjects who had not got themselves into the "analytical attitude" that Hume achieved. Insofar as such an impression might supply a source or a support for an idea of causation, it would be a "popular inaccurate idea", rather than one which would stand up to critical scrutiny. And he acknowledges that the impression itself will fail to occur if one persists in an analytical attitude towards one's perceptions. This amounts to conceding Hume's point that we do not truly have an impression of efficacy or necessary connection.

For myself, I do not wish to concede quite so much to Hume. I have defended the central claim of the agency view of causality, namely, that we derive an idea of causal efficacy – making something happen – from the experience of executing bodily movements against resistance. I have claimed that we incorporate this idea into the *hypothesis* that objects in the external world possess causal efficacy, by means of which they have effects upon us and upon one another.

Now is the time to remind ourselves of the point made by recent philosophers of a pragmatist persuasion that is summed up in the phrase "the theory-ladenness of observation".[28] The point is that there is no such thing in human experience as a sensory observation entirely innocent of any structuring or interpretation in terms of some theory that says *what* kind of thing is being observed. All our perceptions and observations are perceptions and observations *of* things and processes whose characteristics are specified in some ontology – some general, overall theory of what's out there – which the observer has consciously or unconsciously embraced.

So the next important claim of the agency theory of causality is this: subconsciously, from a very early stage in our lives, we structure our perceptions in accordance with the hypothesis that the world around us is filled with agents possessing causal efficacy. It takes a combination of epistemology and experimental psychology to uncover the course of the process and the content of the onto-logical theory with which our everyday observations thus become laden.

This claim is consistent with Michotte's findings concerning the perception of causality: the loading of observation with a par-ticular ontological theory is not the same as an act of interpreta-tion through which an observation is imbued with meaning after the fact. Nor is it the same as the operation that Kant claimed we humans all accomplish: the synthesis of the manifold of sensa-tions in accordance with the categories of the understanding.[29] The Kantian operation consists of an application of concepts not derived from anything in experience; it is a purely *a priori* exercise, albeit unconscious. It presupposes a vision of nature as an arena of events and processes ordered by laws of cause and effect. This adds up to a great deal more philosophical baggage than is required to account for the theory-ladenness of perception. All we need to suppose at this stage, I am suggesting, is that we take the concept of causal efficacy derived directly from our experience of agency in our own activity, and incorporate that concept into the hypotheses in terms of which we structure our perceptions. No elaborate *a pri-ori* machinery is called for. A similar approach, referring back to our familiar experience of agency, will serve to ground other members of our family of causal concepts, including the concept of a law of nature and that of necessary connection between cause and effect.

In recent years the line of enquiry opened up by Michotte has burgeoned into a very active field of experimental investigation, with many researchers undertaking painstaking observations of the behavior of children and infants as young as two months. Varying hypotheses have been advanced concerning the process by which infants begin to develop the cognitive capacities that will eventually blossom into causal concepts, and it is not yet clear what sort of scientific consensus will eventually be arrived at. What is already clear, however, is that the infant's awareness of its own agency, and the attribution of agency to perceived objects and to humans and animals, plays a central role.[30]

It seems to me that what has been said here is also in harmony with the findings of Paul Churchland, who approaches the topic from the very different perspective of a neuroscientist tracing the process of learning in the neural networks of the human brain and nervous system. He puts his finger on a neural counterpart to the mysterious cognitive act of hypothesis formation alluded to by philosophers:

> [The] capacity for leaping from partial data to a complete representational interpretation, called *vector completion*, is an automatic processing feature of any well-trained compression network. ... Though it does not make a leap from one *proposition* to another (but rather from one *activation pattern* or *vector* to another), vector completion is clearly a form of *ampliative inference*, no less than abduction, or hypothetico-deduction, or so-called 'inference-to-the-best-explanation.' Specifically, the accuracy of its representational outputs is not strictly guaranteed by the contents of its representational inputs. But those outputs are deeply

and relevantly informed by the past experience of
the network, and by the residue of that experience
now resident in the structure of its well-trained
middle-rung activation space. Accordingly, it is at
least tempting to see, in this charming capacity
for *relevant* vector completion, the first and most
basic instances of what philosophers have called
"inference-to-the-best-explanation," and have
tried, with only limited success, to explicate in linguistic or propositional terms.[31]

I am confident, therefore, that the philosophical position I have
adopted will prove to be consonant with the picture of human
concept formation that emerges from the efforts of researchers in
infant psychology and neurophysiology. In any case, the decisive
evidence will come from experiment and observation far more than
from further philosophical analysis.

Skepticism versus common sense

Once we see the causal efficacy of things around us as a hypothesis with which our perceptions are typically laden, it becomes
apparent that we can, without logical absurdity, suspend belief in
any such hypothesis. Then all events will indeed seem loose and
separate – conjoined, but never connected. That of course is the
skeptical position envisaged by Hume in the most skeptical passage
of the *Enquiry*, and it is worth recognizing that it took nothing less
than a genius of the first order to achieve such a stance in defiance
of ordinary patterns of thought. For most of the human race, the
course of our physical and mental development, combined with the
culture in which we are immersed, makes it impossible to attain the
detachment of a philosophical skeptic – unless of course we have

the help of a thinker of outstanding originality and independence of mind, such as Hume. Even then it is not an easy task.

It would be possible to accept the agency view of causality as an analysis of commonly employed causal concepts, and as an account of their genesis, while remaining skeptical about the ontological hypothesis that applies those concepts to the world we perceive. But the agency view will undoubtedly have a greater appeal to those who do not desire to be skeptics, but instead are inclined to endorse the hypotheses underlying common knowledge. Such people might well be willing to accept those hypotheses – while acknowledging that they can be denied without logical absurdity – in the same spirit in which Thomas Reid accepted what he called the "first principles" of common sense:

> All reasonings must be from first principles; and for first principles no other reason can be given but this, that, by the constitution of our nature, we are under a necessity of assenting to them. Such principles are parts of our constitution, no less than the power of thinking. . . .
>
> How or when I got such first principles, upon which I build all my reasoning, I know not; for I had them before I can remember; but I am sure that they are parts of my constitution, and that I cannot throw them off. . . . That our sensations of touch indicate something external, extended, figured, hard or soft, is not a deduction of reason, but a natural principle. The belief of it, and the very conception of it, are equally parts of our constitution. If we are deceived in it, we are deceived by Him that made us, and there is no remedy.[32]

Despite Reid's emphatic words, it is necessary to exercise caution in accepting any hypothesis in this commonsensical spirit. Reid himself gave a list of principles that he assented to on this basis, and the list reflects the convictions of an eighteenth-century man. He takes it as a first principle that every proposition is either true or false; he appears to endorse Euclid's axioms as first principles in geometry; he even believes there are common principles of taste in aesthetics: "I never heard of any man who thought it a beauty in a human face to want a nose, or an eye, or to have the mouth on one side".[33] To us, familiar as we are with three-valued logic, non-Euclidean geometries and the paintings of Pablo Picasso, these convictions appear quaint as well as simply untrue.

The conclusion to be drawn, I think, is that we humans are fallible even in committing ourselves to beliefs which we find it practically impossible to "throw off", and for which there seems to be no conceivable alternative. Whether this position of fallibilism represents a capitulation to the philosophical skeptics is a question I will leave to one side.

Be that as it may, there have been both philosophers and experimental psychologists who have endorsed the agency view of causality, and insisted that people would never arrive at the idea of causation if it were not for their experience of being agents. Thomas Reid himself was a philosopher who made this claim. He wrote:

> It is very probable, that the very conception or idea
> of active power, and of efficient causes, is derived
> from our voluntary exertions in producing effects;
> and that, if we were not conscious of such exertions,
> we should have no conception at all of a cause, or
> of active power, and consequently no conviction of
> the necessity of a cause for every change which we
> observe in nature.[34]

A representative empirical psychologist would be the aforementioned Jean Piaget, who carried out a thorough study of the development of children's thought patterns. Piaget was emphatic in concluding that the experience of agency is of central importance in the evolution of our ideas concerning causality, and that it would be a grave mistake to become trapped in what Flew called a "paralytic's eye view":

> The most definite conclusion from our analysis of the beginnings of mental assimilation . . . is that ever since the first contacts with the external environment, the child is active. . . . Nothing is further removed from psychological truth than the image proposed by classical empiricism of a ready-made universe gradually impressing itself on the sensory organs to engender fixed associations and thus to constitute causality.[35]

R.G. Collingwood expressed the point even more bluntly:

> For a mere spectator there are no causes. When Hume tried to show how the mere act of spectation could in time generate the idea of a cause, . . . he was trying to explain how something happens which in fact does not happen.[36]

On the nature, and the occasional observability, of the causal relation

We have so far examined only the first and most basic of our notions having to do with causality. Yet it is not too early to draw some conclusions about the status of causal claims.

First, I would conclude that efficacy is indeed essential to the causal relation, and that it is to be attributed to single instances of causation: this agent or event brings about this outcome; makes it happen. Nothing is here implied about general laws or conditional statements or necessitation. The philosopher who, in my view, has perceived this point most clearly is Elizabeth Anscombe, who in this context speaks of the derivativeness of effects from their causes:

> There is something to observe here, that lies under our noses. It is little attended to, and yet still so obvious as to seem trite. It is this: causality consists in the derivativeness of an effect from its causes. This is the core, the common feature, of causality in its various kinds. Effects derive from, arise out of, come of, their causes. ... Now analysis in terms of necessity or universality does not tell us of this derivedness of the effect; rather it forgets about that. For the necessity will be that of laws of nature; through it *we* shall be able to derive knowledge of the effect from knowledge of the cause, or vice versa, but that does not shew us the cause as the source of the effect. Causation, then, is not to be identified with necessitation.
>
> If A comes from B, this does not imply that every A-like thing comes from some B-like thing or set-up or that every B-like thing or set-up has an A-like thing coming from it; or that given B, A had to come from it, or that given A, there had to be B for it to come from. Any of these may be true, but if any is, that will be an additional fact, not comprised in A's coming from B. If we take "coming from" in the sense of travel, this is perfectly evident.[37]

Secondly, I would be ready to reach a conclusion on the pair of issues that C.J. Ducasse named in the title of a celebrated article: the nature and the observability of the causal relation.[38] If the nature of the causal relation is that causes bring about their effects, and we humans have direct experience of bringing about our own voluntary bodily movements and mental performances, it follows that the causal relation is directly observable by us in exactly that class of cases. In other cases, a judgment about what is causing what involves forming and believing some hypothesis in which agency or efficacy is ascribed to something other than oneself – another human, or some animate or inanimate thing. In such cases, the causal relation is *not* directly observed, although our perceptions can become so loaded with the "theory" that causal efficacy is everywhere that it will seem absurdly uncommonsensical to deny we see causal processes taking place.

J.L. Mackie reached a similar position in *The Cement of the Universe*, except that he took the acceptance of counterfactual conditionals, rather than hypotheses about efficacy, as the key intellectual move involved in a judgment about the cause of an observed phenomenon. I find it worthwhile to cite his words at some length:

> If I see someone else peel a potato, I see the relative movement of the potato and the knife, I see the gradually lengthening strip of peel come up from the surface of the potato, each new portion coming up just as the leading edge of the knife reaches it; but as Hume would still rightly protest, I don't *see* the knife *making* the peel come up. And what I most obviously fail to *see*, though I do *judge*, is that each bit of peel would not have come up if the knife had not moved in there. But what if I peel the potato myself? Then in addition to seeing all that has been mentioned, I

feel my fingers pressing on the knife and the potato, and I may guess that the knife is also pressing on the potato and the potato on the knife. ... [T]here is force here as well as motion. But to feel forces, and even to transfer them, in thought, from one place to another (from the finger-knife and finger-potato surfaces to the knife-potato surface) is still not to perceive a counterfactual conditional. ... It sounds absurd to say, in the spirit of Hume, that I do not perceive myself peeling a potato, but only imagine this, even in the most favourable circumstances. But it is not absurd, but true, to say that an element either of imagining or of discursive thinking enters into what we would ordinarily call my knowledge that I am peeling a potato. ...

Admittedly we can, in the most ordinary sense of 'see', see a stone break a window. But this seeing, like almost all seeing, includes an element of interpretation. And, of course, we *might* be wrong. It might be that a vacuum somehow suddenly produced on the inside of the window made it collapse a tenth of a second before the stone arrived. The point of mentioning such fantastic possibilities is not to promote scepticism, not to recommend the conclusion 'Perhaps the stone did not really break the window' on some perfectly ordinary occasion, but merely to bring out the fact that something which we can call interpretation is involved, and to leave room for a further inquiry into its nature ...[39]

The Cement of the Universe: A Study of Causation CLLP by J.L. Mackie (1980), pp. 133-4. Reproduced by permission of Oxford University Press.

I have maintained that the *indispensable* element of the interpretative thinking that goes into seeing a stone break a window is the formation and acceptance of the hypothesis that the mass and motion of the stone was efficacious in bringing about the breaking of the window. An average observer would, of course, also come to believe that if the stone had not hit the window, the window would not have broken. But this judgment, I wish to say, involves more complex conceptual equipment than we have examined so far. Those in possession of these richer intellectual resources – including the notion of a law of nature – will be able to marshal past experience, and, if need be, creatively assemble new experience through a process of experimentation, in order to amass evidence to support the hypothesis that it was the stone that broke the window. What goes for a change in the situation, like the breaking of a window, will apply equally to what Ducasse, following Charles Mercier, calls "unchanges"[40] – the persistence of a condition or state of affairs, as when one sees that a vase of flowers remains in place because it is being supported by the table.

Before leaving the topic of our capacity to observe a causal connection, one very different type of example needs to be mentioned. When we perceive, by introspection, that a certain reason or motive was the reason (the *real* reason, not a rationalization) for a choice that we have made or an action we have taken, then we are perceiving that that reason or motive was the cause of the choice or the action in question. It is another instance of a perception of causal efficacy. In such a case as this, the kind of causing that is going on will need to be understood as rational-agency causation; although if the reason amounted to a truly irresistible urge, it could be viewed, at the same time, as an example of nomic causation of a deterministic sort. (If there is no irresistible urge and the action or choice is a free one, we will have an example of nomic causation of a probabilistic sort.) Unlike the case of seeing a stone break a window, the insight we have through introspection into the causes of our choices and actions is notoriously fallible: people all too readily believe the phony rationalizations they invent to explain their conduct. Yet here, as in the case of seeing a stone break a window, wholesale skepticism is not called for. It would be absurd to suggest that humans never correctly understand what is causing them to act as they do.

In so far as there is a perception of causal efficacy here, it is a perception of *being acted upon,* not an awareness of our own efficacy. Hence the aptness of saying that we are 'moved', 'nudged', 'prodded' or 'goaded' by the motives that cause our behavior.

---

1   Hume, *Treatise,* Book I, Part III, Section XIV, p. 157.

2   *Treatise,* Book I, Part III, Section XIV, pp. 157-158.

3   G.E.M. Anscombe 1971; in Sosa 1975, p. 69.

4   Hallie 1951, p. 162; see above, ch. 1, p. 16.

5   Maine de Biran, *Oeuvres Complètes,* Vol. VIII, p. 23; Hallie 1951, p. 154.

6   *Enquiry,* Section VII, Part I, p. 66.

7   Anscombe, *ibid.*

8   Antony Flew 1954, pp. 49-50.

9   *Enquiry,* Section VII, Part I, pp. 66-67.

10   Hallie 1951, pp. 154-156; Hallie 1959, pp. 32, 37.

11   Locke, *Essay,* Introduction, Sec. 8; Vol. I, p. 32.

12   See *Treatise,* Book I, Part I, Section I, p. 1; cf. *Enquiry,* Section II, pp. 17-19.

13   See *Treatise,* Book I, Part I, Section I, p. 3; cf. *Enquiry,* Section II, pp. 18-19.

14   *Treatise,* Book I, Part I, Section II, pp. 7-8.

15   Hume,*Treatise,* Appendix, p. 632.

16   Piaget 1929, ch. v.

17   Locke, *Essay,* Introduction, Sec. 2; Vol. I, p. 27.

18   Locke, *Essay,* Book II, ch. ii, Sec. 1; Vol. I, p. 144.

19   Locke, *Essay,* Book II, ch. xxiii, Sec. 13; Vol.I, p. 405.

20   See above, ch. 1, pp. 22-23, and note 36.

21   Albert Michotte 1963, p. 87.

22   See Wesley Salmon 1984, pp. 142-147; also Milton Rothman 1960.

23 Hume, *Enquiry,* Section VII, Part II, p. 74.

24 Michotte 1963, p. 8 and p. 256.

25 Michotte 1963, p. 256.

26 Michotte 1963, p. 9.

27 Hume, *Enquiry,* Section VII, Part I, p. 67, n. 1.

28 See above, ch. 1, p. 23, and nn. 39, 40.

29 See Michotte's critical footnote on Kant's philosophy in Michotte 1963, p. 270, n. 6.

30 See Susan Carey 2009 for a major contribution to this research, with many references to other contributors.

31 Churchland 2012, pp. 66-67.

32 Reid, *Inquiry into the Human Mind on the Principles of Common Sense,* (1764), chap. V, section VII; Reid 1967, p. 130.

33 Reid, *Essays on the Intellectual Powers of Man* (1785), Essay II, chap. X; Reid 1967, p. 285.

34 Reid, *Essays on the Active Powers of the Human Mind* (1788), Essay IV, chap. II; Reid 1969, p. 270.

35 Piaget 1955, p. 225. See also Piaget 1930 and Piaget 1953.

36 Collingwood 1938, pp. 93-94.

37 Anscombe, pp. 67-68.

38 See Curt John Ducasse 1926.

39 Mackie 1974, pp. 133-134.

40 See Ducasse 1926, p. 60, n. 8, Ducasse 1960, p. 5, n. 1, or Sosa 1975, p. 117, n. 7.

CHAPTER 3
Necessity, Possibility, and Laws of Nature

What ideas concerning cause and effect can be taken as logically primitive, and from what experiences are they derived? In the last chapter we attacked the first and most basic aspect of this question; I argued that the fundamental idea of causal efficacy – making something happen – is derived from our experience of successfully carrying out bodily movements, the rock-bottom first-hand experience of being an agent.

We must next consider the origin of the family of causal concepts that exhibit a modal character: causal necessity, contingency, possibility, impossibility. It is a standard procedure in modal logic, when such a family of concepts is to be defined or elucidated, to take one member of the family as primitive or undefined, and define the others in terms of that first member, in accordance with one of the following formulae:

It is possible that p $=_{df}$ Not necessarily not-p
It is not possible that p (or, p is impossible) $=_{df}$
Necessarily not-p

Necessarily p =$_{df}$ It is not possible that not-p

p is contingently true =$_{df}$ p and it is possible that
   not-p

The argument to be set forth in this chapter will end by proposing an account of causal impossibility – it is not causally possible
that p – which will justify taking that as the relatively primitive
term to be used in defining the other members of the family. I say
"relatively primitive" because the notion of causal impossibility will
not be left completely undefined: it will be defined in terms of two
other concepts having to do with agency that *will* need to be taken
as logically primitive or undefined, although an informal explanation of their meaning will be offered. These two are the concept of
a natural agent, and a modal term connected with agency. For the
modal term, I will offer the rather artificial expression 'It is possible
to A at t that p', or 'M(A,t)p', where A is an agent and t is an instant
or an interval of time. We will find that the negative employment
of this term – "It is *im*possible to A at t that p" – has a special role
to play in relating causal concepts to experience in a way that will
meet the demands of an empiricist theory of knowledge. 'N(A,t)p'
will be used as an abbreviation for 'It is necessary to A at t that p'.

As I indicated in the previous chapter, I do not think of the
fashioning of an idea derived from experience as the making of a
copy that resembles the experience, but as the creation of a concept
that is unequivocally instantiated by the experience.

'I can'

Since the artificial modal term 'It is possible to A at t that p' is not
going to be, strictly speaking, defined, its meaning needs to be
informally explained with great care. As a starting point we may

take note of J.L. Austin's remarks about the different uses of the verb 'can' that are applied to (human) agents.

> We are tempted to say that 'He can' sometimes means just that he has the ability, with *nothing said* about opportunity, sometimes *just* that he has the chance, with nothing said about ability, sometimes, however, that he really actually *fully can* here and now, having both ability and opportunity. ...
> The only point of which I feel certain is that such verbs as *can* and *know* have each an all-in, paradigm use, around which cluster and from which divagate, little by little and along different paths, a whole series of other uses.[1]

The "all-in" sense connotes that the agent A has the ability, the means and the opportunity to do X, and is furthermore *able* to exercise the ability in the circumstances prevailing at the time. Alice wants to take some pictures of the solar eclipse that will be visible in her home town on Monday. She has the ability – she is a skilled and experienced photographer. She has the means: a working camera with fresh batteries. But if the weather is cloudy, she will not get the opportunity. If the skies are clear on Monday, then when the eclipse is occurring, and only then, it will be correct to say of her that she *can*, in this sense, take her pictures – but only on condition that she is not, for example, seized by an irrational panic which makes her unable, for the moment, to press the shutter release. 'I can now raise my arm' is an English sentence which has been uttered countless times by persons engaged in philosophical discussion who wished to give an example of this all-in use of 'can'. Don Locke has called it "the 'can' of being able", and distinguishes it, quite properly, from the 'can' of ability.[2]

J.L. Austin was entirely right, I think, to identify this as the basic use, in terms of which the other uses of 'can' having to do with agency should be explicated (although it was Don Locke who first noted the point about being *able* to exercise an ability). Yet it was a mistake on Austin's part to characterize the all-in 'can' as a "paradigm use, around which cluster and from which divagate, little by little and along different paths, a whole series of other uses" – as though the 'can' of ability and the 'can' expressing opportunity were uses which more or less *approximated* to the central, all-in use. The relationship of the derivative uses to the basic one is rather this. We are aware that certain conditions must obtain if an agent A is to be able, in the all-in sense, to do X. Some of these conditions are capacities and dispositions of the agent himself; others consist in his having the necessary possessions and resources at his disposal; still others consist in being in appropriately disposed circumstances. Conditions of the first group are called abilities; in the second case, we speak of having the means; in the third, of having opportunity. (In connection with abilities, there is a further refinement to be noted. We say that Venus Williams is a tennis player of great ability, and we say this of her even at times when she is asleep, suffering from 'flu, or otherwise temporarily disabled. She possesses her ability as a tennis player in the fullest sense, however, only at times when she could (all-in sense) exercise it, provided she had means and opportunity, and was not disabled by panic etc.) The three derivative uses of 'can' are correlative to one another. The ability to do X is always understood to be the ability to do X when means and opportunity are present, and to describe a situation as an opportunity to do X is to note that the conditions are right for an agent who has the means to exercise his ability to do X.[3]

Statements employing the 'can' of being able make claims about the whole interval needed to complete the act in question. They are, to this extent, future-infected. To characterize the conditions prevailing in an interval preceding t as an opportunity for A to do X is to imply that it is possible the conditions will remain favorable long enough for A to finish doing X. If I and the building in which I am preparing dinner are pulverized by an atomic explosion when I am half way through the process, and if causally sufficient conditions for the explosion obtained well before I started, then it will have been false to say that in the interval preceding the moment I began I was able to prepare dinner, in the all-in sense we are here concerned with. I had the ability and the means, but was never going to get the opportunity. A dramatic scene along just these lines occurs at the conclusion of Nicholas Freeling's novel *Gadget* : the President of the United States stands up to make a speech, but is blown to pieces by a terrorist's nuclear bomb before he has uttered so much as the first syllable.[4]

At any time t when an agent A can, in the all-in sense of being able, do X, we have a case that instantiates the artificial modal concept I have in mind, and we could say 'It is possible to A at t that A does X'. Applying this thought to oneself, one would say 'I can, here and now, do X'.

How and when would one say such a thing of oneself on the basis of experience? Plainly the experience of going ahead and doing X at t would be sufficient grounds for saying 'I can'; but it is equally plain that it would be an error to make this a necessary condition. Actually doing X is not part of what is meant by saying one *can* do X. So 'can' or 'possible' are even further removed than 'efficacy' or 'making something happen' from the possibility of being related to sensation the way 'red' is. The expression 'I can do X' is designed for use by an agent who remembers doing X, imagines himself doing X again, and would expect to succeed in doing X if he tried. At whatever age we become capable of such memories, imaginings and expectations, we acquire the experiential basis for deriving the concept 'can'. I take it to be beyond controversy that normal human children reach such a stage of development *before* learning to use language, so that language acquisition, when it takes place, is carried out by a creature that already has the appropriate experiential structures ready for labeling.

'Can' and time

The aspect of temporality and tense in the expression 'It is possible to A at t that p' calls for several observations.

First of all, there is a large class of cases in which the possibility of doing X at t co-exists with the possibility of refraining from doing X at t, right up to the time t at which the action commences – a point that is of major significance for the free will problem. But once you have started doing X it is no longer possible for you completely to refrain. So the possibility of doing X commencing at t must be thought of as existing in an interval of time ending at t. In the cases when we would say 'A can do X here and now', the interval will be a very short one.

How short? Common sense leaves this indefinite, and I would prefer to do the same. But the interval will be measured in seconds or fractions of a second. Any attempt to bring more precision into the matter will have to begin with a stipulation of just what constitutes the commencement of the act. There are, for instance, devices designed to measure the rapidity of a person's voluntary responses. A light comes on, a buzzer sounds, and the timer starts to run. As soon as you see the light, and/or hear the buzzer, you touch a button. As soon as your finger contacts the button, the timer stops. A response time of one-quarter of a second is average; those who manage to stop the clock in less than one-fifth of a second go away congratulating themselves.[5] But when does the act of touching the button truly begin: when the finger makes contact with the button? or when the finger first moves? or when the efferent nerves are first activated? These events will be separated from one another by intervals measured in hundredths of a second. A detailed scientific account of what happens in the quarter-second that the timer is running would be needed to provide the proper background for judging when, precisely, the act of touching the button really began – supposing that someone insisted on making such a judgment. Still more such scientific background would be needed to make precise sense of, let alone to answer, the question of the length of the interval preceding t_1 in which an agent is able to do X commencing at t_1.

But now a different objection may be launched, on behalf of common sense, against the proposed analysis. Granted that being able to do X commencing at t_1, and likewise being able wholly to refrain from doing X commencing at t_1, are conditions which obtain in an interval preceding t_1, and granted that if I do start doing X at t_1 I no longer am able wholly to refrain, is it not, nevertheless, perverse to suggest that while I am in the middle of doing X I am not able to do X?

I do not think that this objection is fatal. Consider the following example. Let X be pushing a heavy table across the room, and suppose this will take me ten seconds, pushing as hard as I can. At t_1 I begin to do it. Let $t_2 = t_1 + 2$ seconds. At t_2 I can stop doing X, and I could then be said to have refrained from doing X in the sense that I aborted the action before completing it. I will not have pushed the table across the room; I will only have pushed it part way. But I certainly started to push it across the room; at t_2 it is too late for me to *refrain wholly* from doing X, i.e., not carry out any part of the action. The ability wholly to refrain from doing X existed, we may suppose, in an interval preceding t_1; it cannot have lasted longer.

It follows that it can only be in an interval preceding t_1 that I am able to do X commencing at t_1, and also able, in the same sense, wholly to refrain from doing X commencing at t_1. The sense of 'able' which I am interested in analyzing is a sense in which it is sometimes possible to say that an agent was able to do X and also able wholly to refrain from doing X.

The sense in which I am able, in the short interval preceding t_2, to do X commencing at t_1, is the following. I did commence doing X at t_1, which satisfied one necessary condition for having done X commencing at t_1. I am able, by continuing to do X after t_2, to complete the act of doing X which I commenced at t_1: this will satisfy the sole remaining condition which is necessary for having done X commencing at t_1. In this perfectly good sense I may be said, while in the middle of doing X, to be able to do X. But this perfectly good sense does not require, for its analysis, any basic ability term other than the one already given. Common sense would not require us to say that in the short interval preceding t_2, while in the middle of pushing the table, I was able to *start* pushing it at t_1: quite the contrary.

For any agents who exist in time, the expression 'It is possible to A at t that p' will have to be understood with this result in mind: if p comes to be the case at t, then the possibility to the agent exists in an interval preceding t. (Common sense would not conceive of the possibility as continuing to exist after t; but there are systematic reasons for concluding that it does which will be addressed later.)

But on the other hand, there are cases in which that interval will end before t. When I was having breakfast in Winnipeg early one morning, I was able, in the all-in sense, to be in Toronto for lunch: I had the ability, means and opportunity, and nothing made me unable to exploit them. I was not, of course, able to be in Toronto then and there; but I was able to take steps then and there which would bring it about that I was in Toronto for lunch. An essential element in the opportunity I had to be in Toronto by lunch time was the Air Canada flight which left Winnipeg at eight-thirty and arrived in Toronto at noon. I do not know what would have been the last possible moment to leave for the airport; but unless the flight was delayed, my opportunity to keep a luncheon date in Toronto evaporated some time between seven and eight. In other cases, we speak of an opportunity's not arising until a certain juncture. Stephanie will have an opportunity to go to Princeton when, and only when, the admissions committee accepts her application. If the committee has not yet met, there is nothing Stephanie can do here and now to bring it about that she goes to Princeton, although she could do something here and now to ensure that she does not, viz., withdraw her application.

The necessity of the past

With the artificial expression 'It is possible to A that p' available to us, we may articulate the well established (and very commonsensical) doctrine of the necessity of the past; only we shall also find that we are obliged to qualify one of the commonsensical results expressed in the preceding section. If p is the case at t_1 and t_1 is earlier than t_2, then it will not be possible to any agent at t_2 that p not be the case. Applying the third of the definitions listed at the beginning of the chapter, we may conclude that it is *necessary* to any agent at t_2 that p be the case. The past is necessary in the sense that it is unalterable by any agent.

Now it was my intention that the expression 'It is possible to A at t that p' should be applied in accordance with an alethic modal logic of a very unexceptional sort, so that 'necessarily p' entails 'p' and 'p' entails 'possibly p'. Hence 'necessarily p' entails 'possibly p'. So if it is necessary to an agent A at t_2 that p (as would be the case if p had occurred at an earlier time t_1), then it is also *possible* to A at t_2 that p. Applying this formula to the table-pushing example, we would have to conclude that at t_2, when I am in the middle of pushing the table across the room, it is possible to me to start pushing it at t_1. Possible, because I did so, and the past is necessary, and what is necessary must be possible. This is contrary to the common-sense view that at t_2, while in the middle of pushing the table across the room, I am not able to start doing so at t_1.

It is worth pointing out once again that having started to push the table across the room at t_1, I am no longer able to refrain completely from doing so. The joint possibility of starting to push it and not starting to push it vanishes at t_1 when I either do or do not start pushing. And it appears that people of common sense are interested in talking about what an agent *can* do only so long as there is the possibility of not doing it; once the deed is done, common sense focuses on the fact that it cannot be undone, so that it seems odd to bring up the weaker point that the deed still can be done (though not of course done over again). But in the interest of being able to apply a standard modal logic to the expression 'It is possible to A that p', I am prepared to say that actual past deeds and past states of affairs are possible to us.

We may in fact formulate two different versions of the metaphysical platitude that the past is unalterable. The first, weaker version is the claim that if a state of affairs p obtains at t_1, no agent is able to act at a later time t_2 to bring it about that $\sim$p obtains at t_1:

$$[p(t_1) \bullet (t_1 < t_2)] \supset (A) \sim M(A, t_2)[A \text{ acts at } t_2 \text{ to} \\ \text{bring it about that } \sim p(t_1)].$$

Note that this, while it rules out altering the past, does not rule out bringing about the past: it leaves open the possibility of some agent A acting at t_2 to bring it about that p obtains at t_1, so long as p *did* obtain at t_1. Causes that work backward in time, and actions which have effects before they are performed, are thus not ruled out *a priori*; this, I think, is as it should be.

The second, stronger, version of the principle that the past is unalterable, holds that if p obtains at t_1, there is no possible world in which an agent A has the abilities, means and opportunities he does have, at a later time t_2, and in which ~p obtains at t_1:

$$[p(t_1) \bullet (t_1 < t_2)] \supset (A)\text{-}M(A,t_2)\text{-}p(t_1)$$

This stronger version, unlike the weaker one, implies that if the past were different in any way, the abilities, means or opportunities enjoyed by each agent would be different. If Prince Philip had not told the Queen a certain joke last week which he did in fact tell, the range of what I am able to do in the present would be different from what, in fact, it is. Now to be sure, I find it a strain to come up with any way in which the royal family's private conversations have substantially affected what I am able to do. I am forced to fall back on some such candidate as this: I am now able to drink a toast to a reigning monarch whose subject I am, and whose husband told her a certain joke in the past seven days, whereas I am unable to drink a toast to a reigning monarch whose subject I am, and whose husband never told her any such joke. The artificiality of this stems from the fact that I would have been able to toast Queen Elizabeth anyway, and in the same words. As things are, I am able to perform this action under a description which otherwise could not have been applied to it, and I am *unable* to perform it under a description which otherwise *could* have been applied to it; but the act, considered in itself, is the same in every respect. But despite the silly tactics one must adopt, in such circumstances, to produce concrete instances of the principle, I do not find the principle itself objectionable. One must simply recognize that it represents a substantial limitation on what an agent A is able to do at a certain time t only in those cases in which p is causally relevant to the abilities, means and opportunities which A enjoys at t. The artificiality of some of the things we end up saying is the price we pay for having a symbol that can be manipulated with the machinery of a sophisticated modal logic.

However, I do not mind having to assert things which, in the eyes of common sense, it is silly to assert, so long as these are true things and not falsehoods.

Another way of reading the stronger principle is this: given the abilities, means and opportunities of agents as they are at the present time, there are no alternatives to the past as it in fact occurred. Now it is good common sense to suppose that there *are* alternative futures – that it is within the power of humans and other agents to determine, within limits, the future course of events – yet there are no alternative pasts. There were, of course, alternatives that we could have pursued in the past, though we did not; but these alternatives remained open to us only so long as they lay in the future. Once the appropriate time for action has come and gone, such alternatives are, as we say, forever closed off to us – that is, they have ceased to be real, available, alternatives.

Thomas Aquinas was, I believe, making a similar point when he wrote that "whatever is said about the past, if true, is necessary; for, since it has been, it cannot not have been".[6] This cannot be viewed as a simple application of the law of non-contradiction. If we do regard it that way, we fall straight into the trap of the logical fatalist, who offers the parallel argument: "Whatever is said about the future, if true, is necessary; for, since it will be, it cannot not be going to be". We need to come up with a sense of 'necessary' in which all statements about the past, if true, are necessary, but some true statements about the future are not necessary.

It is no easy matter to specify what the appropriate sense of 'necessary' might be, if one's only resources are those found in a modern philosophy textbook. Plainly it is both logically and causally possible that the past might have been different than it in fact was. Even the most hard-nosed determinists grant that past events are causally contingent – they would have been different if the initial conditions had been different. Nor will it do to introduce a notion of relative logical or causal necessity, and say that the past is logically or causally necessary-given-the-fact-that-the-present-is-as-it-is. It is *logically* possible for the past to have been other than it in fact was, and nevertheless to have been succeeded by the present as it in fact is. And to say that such a sequence would have been causally impossible is to commit oneself to the view that each state of affairs E is preceded in time by a set of conditions C such that it is causally necessary that if not-C, then not-E. This is not determinism, as that doctrine is commonly understood, although it is entailed by the stronger thesis known to many as Laplacean determinism – the thesis that, given the state of the universe at any time t, and a complete set of physical laws, it is possible to deduce the state of the universe at any other time t', whether t' be earlier or later than t.[7] The thesis of determinism, as most people have understood the term, claims that every event or state of affairs E is related to a set of conditions C such that C is causally sufficient for E; it leaves open the possibility that the present state of the universe might have been brought about in more than one way. (In *this* sense, it is also good common sense to think that there are alternative pasts.)

I count it a virtue of the modal analysis of 'able' that it offers a way of seeing Aquinas's dictum as an obvious, even platitudinous truth of common sense. The sense in which all truths about the past are necessary truths, is an agency sense of 'necessary', related to the 'can' of agency by the definition which is standard in modal logic: Necessarily p $=_{df}$ It is not possible that ~p. Thus Aquinas was saying exactly what our stronger principle says.

John Thorp, in his book on free will, introduces the useful concept of "the necessity of past and present fact".[8] To believe in such a thing is to believe that whatever is *now* the case, or is *now* occurring, is necessary in exactly the same way that the past is necessary. Aristotle held this view: "There is no contingency in what has now already happened", he writes;[9] "what is necessarily is, when it is, and what is not necessarily is not, when it is not";[10] "it is not possible that what has come to pass not come to pass".[11] Thorp argues – successfully, in my estimation – that Aristotle never departed from this opinion, although there is a passage in *De Caelo* which seems, on the surface, to suggest that he did.[12]

I have said that being able to do X at time t is a condition that obtains in a short interval preceding t. This feature of the present analysis makes it natural and easy to incorporate the Aristotelian thesis about the necessity of past and present fact, in the same way that we incorporated Aquinas's point about the necessity of the past. Past and present fact is necessary in the sense of 'necessary' which is related to the 'can' of agency. Just as there are no alternative pasts, there are no alternatives to that which is the case at the present moment. There are only alternative futures, starting a very short time, perhaps an infinitesimally short time, from now.

The principle of the necessity of past and present fact has been stated by applying the sense of 'necessity' that is related to agency. But the principle will apply to any *logically* possible agent; it is therefore appropriate to build it into the tensed modal logic that will govern the 'can' of agency and the other modal terms derived from it.

A logic for the 'can' of agency

In the present essay, none but the most basic and uncontroversial modal inferences will be made with the operator 'M(A,t)'. For the immediate purposes of the argument in hand, therefore, I do not believe I need to specify a particular system of modal logic as *the* correct one for the handling of modal inferences involving the 'can' of agency. But the question that has here been raised is a question of major theoretical significance. It will be worth digressing for a few pages to attempt an answer, because in so doing we will be spelling out just what the modal analysis of the 'can' of agency amounts to.

I have indicated that when a statement of the form 'M(A,t) p' is asserted to be true at some world W_1, the meaning is that p is true in at least one world W_2 in which A has the same abilities, means and opportunities, in the short interval preceding t, as he, she or it enjoys in W_1. The sameness of A's abilities etc. during that interval constitutes the accessibility of W_2 from W_1 for the purpose of applying the modal operator 'M(A,t)'. Now it seems plain that the relation between W_1 and W_2 expressed by saying 'A has the same abilities etc. in W_2 as in W_1 ' is an equivalence relation: reflexive, transitive, and symmetrical. So once the values of 'A' and 't' are fixed, the accessibility relation between worlds invoked by our modal operator 'M(A,t)' will likewise be an equivalence relation. Now whenever this is true of the accessibility relation between worlds, the appropriate modal logic to employ is S5 – more accurately, a member of the S5 family of modal systems.[13] We are thus led to the conclusion that as long as we are talking about a particular agent at a particular time, it is correct to adopt S5 as our system of rules of inference.

The distinctive feature of S5 is that it contains the implication

$$Mp \rightarrow NMp$$

Translated into talk about the abilities of an agent A during a particular interval t, this would be

$$M(A,t)p \rightarrow N(A,t)M(A,t)p$$

which says in effect, "If p is possible to A in the interval t, then it is necessarily so: he is powerless to avert its being possible to him at that time".

At first glance this may seem rather too strong for a logic that is supposed to reproduce the common-sense concept of ability.

But such appearances are deceiving; this formula is expressing nothing more than the necessity (in the agency sense) of past and present fact – which of course must embrace present facts about what agents are able to do.

We saw that if we accept the logical platitude about the unalterability of the past in its more sweeping form – i.e.,

$$[p(t_1) \bullet (t_1 < t_2)] \supset (A) \sim M(A,t_2) \sim p(t_1)$$

we may conclude that if the past had been the slightest bit different, the present abilities of all existing agents would be different. From this it follows that the only possible worlds in which the abilities etc. of a given agent A, during a given interval t, are the same as in a given world W_1, are worlds whose histories up to the moment t are identical with the history of W_1. It is obvious that the class of worlds whose histories up to a certain moment t are identical to that of a given world W_1 will be an equivalence class. Once this is perceived, there will cease to be any appearance of strangeness in the applicability of S5 to inferences employing the operator 'M(A,t)', so long as t remains fixed. (It will be otherwise if we begin to reason about the abilities of agents at different times.)

One consequence of the point which has just been made, is that if we accept the principle of the unalterability of the past in its stronger form, the reference to agent A in the subscript of the modal operator 'M(A,t)', becomes redundant. If the only possible worlds in which *I* now have the precise collection of abilities, means and opportunities *I* now enjoy, are those worlds in which the past has been exactly as it was in the actual world, then that set of worlds is equally the set in which *you* now have the precise collection of abilities, means and opportunities *you* now enjoy; and similarly for any other agent in existence. In any theory, therefore, which incorporates the thesis that the past is unalterable, in the stronger sense, the reference to a particular agent in the subscript to the modal operator 'M(A,t)' may be eliminated. So in place of

$$M(A,t)p$$

we will have simply

$$M(t)p$$

and in place of

$$M(A,t)[A \text{ does } X \text{ commencing at } t]$$

we will have

$$M(t)[A \text{ does } X \text{ commencing at } t].$$

The remaining reference to agent A in the last formula is sufficient to make that formula an acceptable rendering of the all-in 'can' of agency: the fact that A *can* do X commencing at t, in the all-in sense of 'can', is equivalent to the possibility (in our generalized sense) that A *does* do X commencing at t.

I expect that to the discerning reader, this point will have been evident all along; but it eluded me until I was composing the third draft of the text you are now reading. Rather than eliminate the older, more awkward notation 'M(A,t)' entirely, I have presented the argument in the form which is now before you, in order to draw attention to the role of the principle of the unalterability of the past. We will now, however, bid goodbye to 'M(A,t)' and its substitution instances, and make use of the more elegant 'M(t)'.

Abilities that change over time

What now of those occasions when we concern ourselves with what is or will be possible to certain agents at different times? Here it seems that we commonly engage in patterns of reasoning which are accurately captured by taking the relevant accessibility relation between possible worlds to be fully reflexive and transitive, but not symmetrical.

Suppose that Cynthia is a highly talented and well trained musician who plays the clarinet and the trumpet with distinction, but has never, as yet, played the oboe. She now has the means and the opportunity to take oboe lessons. We would say

> (1) It is now possible that she take oboe lessons –
> i.e., there is a world W_1, accessible from the actual world at the present time, in which Cynthia takes oboe lessons, starting now.

Given our knowledge of her talents, we should have good reason to go on to say

> (2) In world W_1 it is possible that Cynthia will be playing the oboe at a professional level in eighteen months' time – i.e., from W_1 a world W_2 is accessible in which she does so.

The important question is whether we would then be prepared to *infer*

> (3) It is now possible (in the actual world) that Cynthia be playing the oboe at a professional level in eighteen months' time.

If so, we are treating the accessibility relation between possible worlds as transitive, and will consequently need a modal logic with the resources of S4 to represent our pattern of inference.[14]

Needless to say, our everyday thinking about what people can do is not carried on in terms of possible worlds or by means of a rigorous modal logic. But in making the attempt to devise rigorous modal concepts which correspond in outline to everyday patterns of thought, I find myself very much inclined to say that the inference of (3) from (1) and (2) exhibits a pattern which is always legitimate when dealing with the all-in 'can' of agency. It presupposes the validity of the principle

$$M(t_1)M(t_2)p \rightarrow M(t_1)p, \text{ where } t_1 < t_2$$

which is a tensed version of the distinctive thesis of S4,

$$MMp \rightarrow Mp$$

On the other hand, we would not infer, from the fact that it is *now* possible for Cynthia to be playing the oboe at a professional level in eighteen months' time, that this will still be possible in eighteen months' time. To illustrate this point for us, Cynthia need only drop her oboe lessons next month and take up the saxophone instead. So we do *not* have

$$M(t_1)M(t_2)p \nrightarrow M(t_2)p, \text{ where } t_1 < t_2$$

as a principle whose validity is assumed in our everyday modal reasonings.

The system TA

Putting together the points made in the last few pages, we find that what has been said about the formalized 'can' of agency gives us the elements of a modalized, tensed propositional logic. I will call it System TA (for Temporal Agency). The primitive basis of System TA may be stated as follows.

We begin with an axiomatization of the classical propositional calculus which incorporates Modus Ponens and a rule of uniform substitution as its primitive rules of inference (for example, the system PM of Hughes and Cresswell).[15] To this we add, as primitive vocabulary, the modal operator 'M', and an infinite list of time indicators (t_i), (t_j), . . ., which can be arranged in a well-ordered series. As additional formation rules we have

> F1. If A is well formed and has no final time indicator, then $A(t_i)$ is well formed.

> F2. If A is well formed, $M(t_i)A$ is well formed.

We now define the necessity operator in a way in which conforms to the standard procedure:

> D1. $N(t_i)A =_{df} {\sim}M(t_i){\sim}A$

The sole additional transformation rule that will be required is the principle of necessitation:[16]

> R1. If A is provable, then for any time indicator (t_i), $N(t_i)A$ is provable.

The axioms, or rather axiom schemata, are as follows:

A1. For any time indicator (t_i),
$$N(t_i)[p \supset q] \supset [N(t_i)p \supset N(t_i)q]$$

A2. For any time indicator (t_i),
$$p \supset M(t_i)p$$

A3. For any time indicator (t_i),
$$p(t_i) \supset N(t_i)p$$

A4. For any pair of time indicators $\{(t_i),(t_j)\}$ such that $i < j$,
$$N(t_i)p \supset N(t_j)p$$

A5. For any pair of time indicators $\{(t_i),(t_j)\}$ such that $i < j$,
$$M(t_i)M(t_j)p \supset M(t_i)p$$

A6. For any time indicator (t_i),
$$M(t_i)p \supset [M(t_i)p](t_i)$$

A1 through A6 must be regarded as axiom schemata, each of which yields an infinite set of axioms as different members of the set of time indicators are substituted for '(t_i)' and '(t_j)'.

I have deemed it preferable, for the purposes of the present informal discussion, to state some of the axiom schemata in a form incorporating the defined symbol 'N'. If a formal metatheoretic treatment were to be attempted, it would be desirable to replace 'N' with the definiens, using only the primitive symbols 'M' and '~'.

The axiom schemata A1 and A2 correspond to the two axioms used in the standard treatment of tenseless modal logic to generate the weakest of the familiar modal logics, the one known as System M or System T.[17] A2 is the Axiom of Possibility, which says that whatever is actually the case is possible; the impossible never happens.

Given the intended interpretation of the time indicators, A3 will express the necessity of present fact: everything that occurs is necessary *when* it occurs. It is assumed here that the internal structure of p will make it plain that p designates an event or state of affairs which obtains at the time or during the interval (t_i), and that the time indicator need not, therefore, be repeated in the consequent of A3.

A4 expresses the point that whatever is necessary now will forever *remain* necessary; together with A3 this gives us the necessity of past fact. A5 embodies the S4-like principle illustrated by the story of Cynthia the future oboe player: if it is now possible that next year it will be possible that next year Cynthia will be playing professionally, then it is now possible that next year Cynthia will be doing so.

Last but not least, A6 is an innocuous-looking axiom schema which says merely that p's being possible during the interval (t_i) is something which itself obtains during the interval (t_i). But together with A3 it yields the following theorem:

T1. For any time indicator (t_j),
$$M(t_i)p \supset N(t_i)M(t_i)p$$

This is nothing other than the S5-like principle, discussed earlier, that what is now possible is now necessarily so. That it is derivable from A3 and A6 makes it plain that it is simply a natural extension of the principle of the necessity of present fact.

'Can' versus 'can at will': J.L. Austin at golf

The fact that a standard modal logic is being used at all to represent inferences involving the 'can' of agency means that a distinction must be made between 'It is possible for agent A to do X' and 'A can do X *at will*'. The latter, stronger claim I take to mean two things: first, that it is possible for A to do X, and secondly, that A's attempting to do X is a causally sufficient condition for his doing X. (Thus the stronger claim can only be made about an agent to whom it makes sense to attribute *attempts* to act.) We may call this the strong all-in 'can'. The weak all-in 'can', on the other hand, would be the use of 'can' to mean simply 'It is possible for A to do X', in the sense of 'possible' which we have been engaged in analyzing by means of the formal operator 'M'. But frequently, when someone says simply 'A can do X', the stronger claim is intended. This has led to no end of confusion over the question whether 'A can do X' is equivalent to 'A will do X if he tries'.

A feature of any standard alethic modal logic is the Axiom of Possibility:

$$p \supset Mp$$

A tensed version of this principle was built into our system TA as axiom schema A2. Construing the all-in 'can' by means of the logic of system TA, we obtain the result that whatever I *do* do is something I *can* do.

Very well. Once during a game of ping-pong I was reaching to return a mean and well calculated shot from one of my children, and I struck the ball in such a way that it sailed upward toward the ceiling, rebounded off the light fixture, and dropped neatly into the cat's water dish. From the fact that I performed this extraordinary feat, it follows by the Axiom of Possibility that I was able to do it at the time, in the sense of 'able' expressed by our formal operator 'M(t$_i$)'. But of course I was not able to do such a thing at will. When the children screamed "Let's see you do that again, Daddy", their intention was quite consciously humorous.

John Thorp, who does not distinguish the strong and weak senses of the all-in 'can', finds himself obliged to deny that the Axiom of Possibility applies to the 'can' of human agency at all:

> [I]n the logic of human ability *ab esse ad posse non valet consequentia:* from the fact that I *do* hit the bull it does not follow that I *can* hit it. ... [F]rom the fact that I cannot hit the bull it does not follow that I do not hit it, for I may hit it by luck.[18]

If this were true of every sense of 'can' having to do with human agency, there would be no hope of finding a straightforward connection between the logic of human ability and any system of alethic modal logic. Fortunately, distinguishing a strong and a weak sense of the all-in 'can' provides a way out of this dead end.

In between the kinds of thing we can do dependably at will, such as steering the car into the garage, and freaky, unrepeatable deeds such as my improbable ping-pong shot, there lies a range of cases in which the attributing of an ability to do X implies only that the agent will succeed in doing X on a certain proportion of the occasions when he makes the attempt. A Vancouver Canucks fan will declare stoutly that the Canucks *can* beat the Toronto Maple Leafs, citing as proof the fact that the Canucks won two of the last eight games in which the two teams met.

Sports of all kinds involve performances at the ragged edge of human competence. Their capacity to hold our interest depends on this. Life would be hair-raisingly exciting, but nasty and short, if we could be no more certain of steering our cars accurately than of scoring field goals. Not surprisingly, it was an example from sport that provided a focus for the philosophical discussion of abilities that sometimes fail to secure success:

> There is some plausibility . . . in the suggestion that 'I can do X' means 'I shall succeed in doing X, if I try' and 'I could have done X' means 'I should have succeeded in doing X, if I had tried'.
> Footnote: Plausibility, but no more. Consider the case where I miss a very short putt and kick myself because I could have holed it. It is not that I should have holed it if I had tried: I did try, and missed. It is not that I should have holed it if conditions had been different: that might of course be so, but I am talking about conditions as they precisely were, and asserting that I could have holed it. There is the rub. . . .
> But if I tried my hardest, say, and missed, surely there *must* have been *something* that caused me to fail, that made me unable to succeed? So that I *could not* have holed it. Well, a modern belief in science, in there being an explanation of everything, may make us assent to this argument. But such a belief is not in line with the traditional beliefs enshrined in the word *can:* according to *them,* a human ability or power or capacity is inherently liable not to produce success, on occasion, and that for no reason (or are bad luck and bad form sometimes reasons?).[19]

What Austin refers to as "a modern belief in science" might better be described as a belief in determinism. He astutely observes that "the traditional beliefs enshrined in the word *can*" do not entail or presuppose determinism. Equally astutely, he refrains from claiming that those beliefs actually entail indeterminism; for he has given no grounds for such a claim. The common-sense beliefs to which he refers constitute nothing more than a recognition that there are limits to the precision with which we are able to control our bodily movements. We cannot, therefore, control the movements of golf balls nearly so well with golf clubs as we could with our bare hands. It is this that lends such fascination to the activity once cynically described as "inserting small balls into smaller holes with instruments singularly ill designed for the purpose". It follows that different attempts by the same golfer to sink short putts in identical circumstances may meet with differing success, even if it seems to the golfer himself that he does exactly the same thing each time. The fact that he lacks the capacity to control each molecule of his body individually means that there will be considerable variations, of which he himself is unaware, in the bodily movements he executes on different occasions when he attempts to do the very same thing.

Professor Austin's skill as a golfer was presumably such that he succeeded in sinking short putts the great majority of the time. Hence, when he missed one, he would kick himself, because he could have holed it – i.e., his attempt had had a high probability of eventuating in success. (Putting, like other performances at the limits of human skill, must be viewed as a superficially random process, like many disease processes: while we may assume that the underlying physical processes are subject to deterministic laws, our knowledge of the initial and surrounding conditions is not sufficiently precise to enable us to predict the outcomes with any exactitude. We can only give the probabilities of different classes of outcomes.) The self-inflicted kick was doubtless a good method of releasing inner tensions brought on by rage and disappointment at his ill luck. But unless he had failed to exercise his customary care and attentiveness when putting, he would have had no reason to reproach himself.

I will not attempt a review of the substantial literature that was generated by the debate over Austin's celebrated golf ball. Instead, I will go straight to a contribution in which the authors, Winston Nesbitt and Stewart Candlish, try to assess where Austin has left the issue of determinism and people's ability to do otherwise than as they actually do.

> Austin has shown . . . that 'He can do otherwise' does not entail 'He will do otherwise if he tries'. However, for all that is shown by his example, it can still be claimed that the reverse relationship holds – that 'He will do otherwise if he tries' entails 'He can do otherwise'. (And similarly for the different tenses of the two sentences.) This would not be enough to save the claim that the two sentences have the same meaning; but it would be enough to save the claim that determinism is consistent with our having the ability sometimes to do otherwise than we do. . . . Of course, it may not be true that 'He would have done otherwise if he had tried' entails 'He could have done otherwise'. But as we have pointed out, Austin's example in no way shows that it is not true; and moreover, it is highly plausible to suggest that it is in fact true, since to say 'I would have done so if I had tried, but nevertheless I could not have done so' is to give a strong impression of contradicting oneself.[20]

I have analyzed the strong all-in 'can' as a conjunction of two elements – the weak all-in 'can' expressed by the modal operator

'M(t)' plus the causal conditional 'He would have done so if he had tried, or attempted, to do so'. This analysis would be incorrect, or at best contain a redundancy, if, as Nesbitt and Candlish suggest, the second conjunct entails the first. But in fact no such entailment holds. This is plain from the fact that there are such things as voluntary actions which are plainly not exercises of free will. The behavioral items that provide the clearest illustrations of this point are actions that are performed as a result of truly irresistible impulses or desires.

There was once a mother who arrived home to find that the apartment building in which she lived was on fire. She believed her children were inside. Despite the fact that firefighters were already at the scene, she ran for the building, and would have rushed in to hunt for the children, putting her own life at risk, if she had not been physically restrained by her neighbors.

More than once serious accidents have occurred on the New Jersey Turnpike because of bands of fog settling across the highway. Drivers who suddenly find themselves enveloped in fog tend to jump on the brake, even though they have no reason to believe there are any vehicles ahead of them, and every reason to believe that they are likely to be hit from behind as a result. Can they help what they do?

The drowning person who clutches at a would-be rescuer, with the result that two people are then in danger of drowning; the child who pushes away the dentist's hand; the starving man who seizes food from another starving man; anyone who runs in terror from danger; the prisoner who gives in to torture; the leper who scratches an unbearable itch; a person paralyzed by fear who stands rooted to the spot; even, perhaps, a person who jumps for joy on hearing a piece of good news – all these illustrate the type of action I have in mind, if we assume the desires or impulses in question to be, for those individuals in those circumstances, irresistible.

Regardless of one's metaphysics, these must be termed unfree actions. Actions they certainly are: they are items of voluntary behavior; operants, not reflexes. Although they are somewhat removed from the central paradigm of "action in the full-blooded sense", it would be contrary to standard usage to deny them the title of action, and perverse to insist that they are actions only in an anemic or a mongrel sense. We have no trouble producing, or understanding, the *rationale* for an act of this kind.

At the same time, they fail to qualify as free acts in even the minimal sense of that term. Not only would one withhold blame and responsibility; one would say that in the circumstances, the agent was unable to do otherwise.

The mother who ran towards the burning apartment building, upon realizing that her children were inside, was quite incapable of doing otherwise. The impulse was irresistible; she was not able, in the weak all-in sense, to stand still, or even to *try* to stand still. Yet it is true that if she had tried to stand still, she would have stood still. I think it is merely the relative rarity of unfree voluntary acts which gives the formula 'I would have done X if I had tried, but nevertheless I could not have done X' its superficial air of self-contradiction.

Some of the formal and epistemological features of the concept of possibility relating to temporal agency – 'It is possible to A at t that p' – will, I hope, be apparent by now. The concept is grounded in our experience of being agents and knowing that we *can*, from moment to moment, do certain things (in Don Locke's sense of being fully able). Yet the ability to carry out a certain action – 'It is possible to A at t that A does X' – is only a special case of the generic possibility 'It is possible to A at t that p', which in turn may be supplanted by the yet more generic 'It is possible at t that p' provided we accept the doctrine of the necessity of past and present fact in its strong form. What an agent is able, at a given moment, to do, may then be seen as defining a set of possible worlds: each world in the set has, as an initial segment, the actual world up to time t, and each represents one of the multitude of possible future courses of events branching out from the actual state of the world at t.

'I can't'

We observed that the experience to which it would be fitting to apply the words 'I can do X' would of necessity be the experience of an agent who remembered doing X, imagined doing it again, and expected to succeed if he tried. (The agent in question might, however, be an animal or a human infant; and if so, the sense of those verbs imputing mental activity would have to be suitably qualified.) In any case, it is not an experience whose characteristics could be specified in terms of the sensible qualities of either public objects or private sensations. Hence the wrong-headedness of Hume's search for a sensory impression from which the idea of power or necessity could have been copied.

This is yet more strikingly apparent if we ask after the experiential basis of the negative use of the 'can' of agency – the experiences that would prompt a person to say or think, for the first time in his or her life, 'I can't, as of now, do X'.

There must, one feels, have been an experience of trying to do X and failing (whether or not the agent expected to succeed) in either the very recent past or the more remote past. There may or may not have been times when agent A did X; there *will* typically have been an occasion when A did *not* do X.

Yet even this much is philosophically instructive. If I try to do something and fail, I will have had an experience that may have included elements of both sensation and reflection, but will certainly include the latter. If the thing I was trying to do was thread a needle, then it will be my outward sense of sight that informs me I have not succeeded. But it is only through reflection – "that notice which the mind takes of its own operations"[21]– that I could have known what I was trying to do in the first place. On the other hand, if what I was trying to do was recall my great-aunt's birthday, the trying and the lack of success would both have been perceived through reflection.

But if that is the required experiential background for saying or thinking 'I can't do X', at the point when one first acquires the idea, the actual gist of the thought cannot be *identified* with the background experience. The gist of the judgment 'I can't' is that there is no possible course of events branching out from the present state of the actual world in which I do whatever it is.

Such a judgment plainly does not follow either deductively or inductively from the facts of the background experience. It is best viewed as a hypothesis invented by the agent to interpret or explain the experience of failure. The development of ordinary self-knowledge can then be understood as a series of conjectures and refutations that ends in a finely articulated awareness of our abilities and their limits. We can do A but not B; we can do Z by doing X but not by doing Y; we can do F or G but not both; we can do D but only in conditions of type C. G.E. Moore had abundant evidence for his claim that on a certain day he could have walked a mile in twenty minutes, but could not have run two miles in five minutes, although he had not in fact done either of those things.[22]

The concept of a natural agent

Having discovered that some things are impossible for *me*, and some but not all of those things are impossible for fellow humans who are stronger or cleverer or more nimble than I, it is only natural for me to think that perhaps there are some deeds which no agent in the universe could do, no matter how strong or clever or nimble he, she or it might happen to be. I thus arrive at two all-important concepts: the general concept of a natural agent, and the concept of an action that is absolutely impossible in the sense that no natural agent would ever, under any conditions, be able to perform it. Similarly, an absolutely impossible state of affairs is one that no natural agent would ever be able to bring about. Here, I will maintain, is the primitive modal causal concept: the causally impossible is what is absolutely impossible in this natural-agency sense. (The *logically* impossible is a proper subset of the causally impossible: this very special way of being absolutely impossible is a way whose distinctive features one remarks at a later stage of one's mental development.)

The idea of a natural agent, like the modal concepts connected with agency, should be regarded as a product of creative thinking, rather than an idea copied from or directly modeled on any perception of sense. The concept of a natural agent, once invented, is employed in the construction of hypotheses as to what things are absolutely impossible.

Informally speaking, a natural agent is any agent, human or non-human, animate or inanimate, whose powers are limited by the laws of nature. (Formally speaking, I plan to *define* 'law of nature' in terms of the abilities of natural agents, so the term 'natural agent' needs to be taken as logically primitive.) It is to natural agents that we ascribe causal efficacy: natural agents make things happen. To those who are alive and conscious and rational, such as our fellow humans, we ascribe life and consciousness and rationality as well as bare causal efficacy. We take it that these epistemic peers of ours are the subjects of the same sort of experience that enabled us to acquire the concept of causal efficacy ourselves. But to those natural agents that are inanimate and unconscious, such as stars, snowstorms and falling rocks, we attribute nothing beyond the stripped-down form of causal efficacy, with no implication of life or consciousness. But we do nevertheless say that those natural agents make things happen: a star attracts other objects by means of gravitation; a snowstorm will deposit a blanket of snow on the countryside; a falling rock may dent the roof of a car. These and many other verbs in the active voice are used to impute agency and causal efficacy to inanimate things, processes and events. And by the use of 'can', 'possible', and the other modal terms connected with agency, we extend the talk of being *able* to make things happen to agents of all kinds.[23]

Since a natural agent is thought of as one whose powers are limited by the laws of nature, the term 'natural agent' does have a significant opposite: a *super*natural agent is one whose powers are not so limited. When, for instance, it is said that God would have been able to create a universe with different physical laws, it is implied that God is a supernatural agent (but it is not implied that exceptions to the laws of nature occur in the actual world).

We are now in a position to define the modal concepts having to do with causality – including causal possibility, necessary connection, and the idea of a law of nature – in terms of the primitive concept of a natural agent and the modal term $M(t)p$.

From agency to causality

Having hit on the idea of a natural agent, and the thought that some things might be beyond the capacity of *any* natural agent, a person would be in a position to define the notion of causal impossibility thus:

> p is causally impossible $=_{df}$ for any natural agent A
> and any time t, $\sim M(A,t)p$.

The rest is easy. A causally necessary connection is one that is causally impossible to break. A law of nature is a universal generalization that is causally necessary.

The way we gather evidence of a necessary connection between A and B is by repeatedly trying, in various ways and under various conditions, to bring about A without B and/or B without A, and discovering that we are never able to do it. The fact that we have been fortunate enough to discover limits on our powers which are systematic, and not subject to arbitrary variation, makes it reasonable to extrapolate the laws which limit *our* abilities, and draw conclusions about the limits on the powers of natural agents in general. We confidently calculate what force would be required to knock Jupiter out of its orbit, although it is beyond the capacity of any human being to do this.

We also find it easy to say what distinguishes the conditionals expressing causally necessary or causally sufficient conditions. Such conditionals are causally necessary statements; that is all there is to it. So of course they have counterfactual force, and will sustain counterfactual conditionals: they do so in a fashion that is parallel to logically necessary conditional statements.

Every experiment intended to procure evidence in support of a hypothesis about a causally necessary connection must therefore be viewed as an attempt to bring about a counter-instance. We test the theory that Fs are necessarily accompanied by Gs – $N_c(x)$ $[Fx \supset Gx]$[24] – by attempting to bring it about that there is an F not accompanied by a G – $(\exists x)[Fx \bullet \sim Gx]$. If we succeed, the theory is refuted; if we fail, it is confirmed in some degree. We are thus led to a view of experimental enquiry that is very much akin to the view propounded by Karl Popper.[25] Antony Flew makes a similar point:

> What better evidence indeed could we offer to warrant our belief that a real causal connection lies behind a constant conjunction between X's and Y's than the failure of attempts to break that

conjunction, and our success in producing (or preventing) Y's by producing (or preventing) X's?[26]

This is not to imply, of course, that an experimenter who is investigating what he suspects may be a necessary connection between
Xs and Ys must always think of himself as trying to produce a
counter-example. Frequently the description he would give of his
intentions is, rather, "to bring about an X and see what happens".
The very essence of experimental enquiry was expressed by Wesley
Salmon in the folksy little recipe: "You wiggle something over here
and see if anything wiggles over there".[27] I would maintain, however, that what ultimately convinces us that there is a *necessary*
connection between the two wiggles is that it proves *impossible* to
wiggle something over here *without* something wiggling over there.

In a way it was unfortunate that the first empirical science to
reach a high state of theoretical development was astronomy. The
result was that when philosophers sought examples of scientific
knowledge other than mathematics, they were continually led to
contemplate a branch of enquiry in which the active, manipulative
role of the experimenter is reduced to the very minimum. When
investigating the heavenly bodies, we are in no position to wiggle
anything. All we can *do* is get ourselves and our telescopes into
the appropriate posture for observing certain far-off events; we
are quite unable to manipulate or control the objects of our study.

More commonly, however, we *are* in a position to manipulate
things; and in that situation the experience of trying to control the
objects we observe, and sometimes failing, gives rise, over time,
to the idea of natural necessity. Some early experience of trying
and failing would have been the occasion for forming the initial
idea 'I can't', the idea by which I distinguish the things beyond my
power from the things I *can* do. When generalized to apply to the
whole class of natural agents, this becomes the idea of the causally

impossible. Later, in the context of experimental enquiry, the experience of trying and failing fills a different role: it constitutes the evidence that justifies the ascription of natural necessity to the connection between a cause and its effect.

I would not be prepared to claim, positively, that every human being comes by the concept of causal connection in the manner outlined above. Such a claim would have to be tested empirically, and this poses daunting problems of experimental design. The clinical work of Jean Piaget is of major significance in this connection.[28] Nevertheless, two points can now be made with confidence. First, we have arrived, by way of a plausible story about the genesis of our concept of necessary connection, at an account of how that concept functions in the thinking of grownups. This functional account is one that can be verified in its own right by an examination of our logico-semantic principles and linguistic practices. It need not be founded upon evidence stemming from research in the area of infant psychology. It is the story about function, not the story about genesis, that is essential for philosophical purposes. As Antony Flew remarks in the course of his examination of Hume,

> The questions, 'How do we learn the meaning of the word?' or 'How would we teach it?' are often philosophically illuminating. They look pedagogical and psychogenetic. But they are relevant to philosophy insofar and only insofar as the answers help to throw light on the functional issues: 'What is its use, what does it mean?'[29]

Secondly, the mere fact that the account I have given might *possibly* be true of *some* individuals, is sufficient to refute Hume's contention that the idea of necessary connection cannot be rooted in experience.

Besides Antony Flew, whose words I have already quoted, there are other contemporary philosophers who have come close to such a view of causation, without quite hitting it. Thus, for instance, Douglas Gasking explains the cause-effect relation in terms of the "producing-by-means-of" relation: "one says 'A causes B' in cases where one could produce an event of the A sort as a means to producing one of the B sort".[30]

But of all the philosophical discussions of this matter with which I am familiar, the one that comes closest to the view here espoused is that of Georg Henrik von Wright. Von Wright, however, attempts to define causal connection strictly in terms of human agency, and reaches a counter-intuitive result:

> The idea of causation which I have been discussing could be termed *manipulative* or *experimentalist* causation. It is an idea which sees an essential connection between causation and (human) action. ...
>
> That two states are causally connected means that we can influence the one by manipulating the other. (We must not say that *because* they are causally connected we can influence the one by manipulating the other.)[31]

The thing which, on von Wright's view, we must not say, is something which sensible people very much wish to say. Defining causation, not in terms of human agency alone, but by means of the broader concept of a natural agent, permits us to say it. By pushing down on *his* end of the teeter-totter, Jack influences Jill's end: she sails upward. Jack is able to do this *because* the state of his end is causally connected to the state of Jill's end. The connection is such that any natural agent who exerts a sufficient downward force on

Jack's end will thereby raise Jill's end. Jack is a natural agent with the ability to exert the requisite downward force; this, together with the causal connection spelled out in terms of natural agency, explains his ability to raise Jill's end. The 'because' indicates a truncated explanation in which only the causal connection is expressly mentioned. What Jack can do is explained by being deduced from a generalization about what any natural agent with the requisite ability could do.

More impressive yet is the negative side of the case. No human could exert a downward force of 80 pounds on Jack's end of the teeter-totter, in these circumstances, *without* thereby raising Jill's end; and that is because of the necessary connection which obtains in these circumstances between the state of Jack's end and the state of Jill's end. Spell out the meaning of 'necessary connection' in terms of natural agency, and this statement is seen to be asserting that no human can do it *because* no natural agent can do it: a clear case of explaining one regularity by subsuming it under a more comprehensive one.

If von Wright errs in one direction by limiting himself to the idea of human agency, Stephen Toulmin errs in the opposite direction. He writes:

> Wherever questions are asked about causes, some event ... has a spotlight turned on it: the investigation of its causes is a scrutiny of its antecedents in order to discover what would have to be different for this sort of thing to happen otherwise – what in the antecedent God or man would need to manipulate in order to alter the spotlighted event.[32]

This is jumping from the frying pan into the fire. While we need to avoid limiting our consideration to human agents, it is a most unfortunate error to bring God into the picture at this precise juncture. God is to be thought of as a supernatural agent, who would have been able to create a universe with different laws of cause and effect, had he so chosen. To bring God's powers into the analysis of causality, therefore, is to extend the scope of the analysans beyond the limits of what is in fact causally possible. An account of causality in which the causally impossible is entertained as a possibility would quickly dissolve into incoherence.

Moderate modal realism

J.L. Mackie groups the questions connected with causality under three heads: factual, conceptual, and epistemic:

> It is one thing to ask what causation is 'in the objects', as a feature of a world that is wholly objective and independent of our thoughts, another to ask what concept (or concepts) of causation we have, and yet another to ask what causation is in the objects so far as we know it and how we know what we do about it.[33]

The Cement of the Universe: A Study of Causation CLLP by J.L. Mackie (1980), p. ix. Reproduced by permission of Oxford University Press.

When all is said and done I will contend that our concept of causation, while being uniform in most ways across different contexts, is best viewed as having two variant forms: one that we apply to the actions and choices of rational agents, whose behavior is explained by setting out the rationale for their conduct, and another applying to causal processes unfolding in accordance with laws of nature. I call the two variant concepts, respectively, rational-agency causation and nomic causation. What the two have in common is the fundamental notion of causal efficacy, the asymmetrical relationship between cause and effect, and the grounding in ideas connected to agency. The one significant difference between them concerns the interpretation of the conditional statements describing causally necessary and sufficient conditions.

The examination of rational-agency causation will be undertaken in Chapter 6; in the present chapter I have been engaged in setting out and defending a certain view of *nomic* causation. It should be seen as an interconnected set of answers to Mackie's three questions. To the conceptual question, I answer that our concept of causal necessity is the concept of systematic limitations upon what natural agents are able to do. Our concept of causal priority (to be explained in the next chapter) is likewise a concept of what is and is not within the powers of natural agents. Other causal concepts can be explicated in terms of these two, together with the basic notion of causal efficacy. To the epistemological question, I answer that it is above all by experimentation that we discover the limits upon *our* powers, and these discoveries provide us with evidence for broader hypotheses about the limits on the powers of natural agents in general. These hypotheses can, of course, be further tested and confirmed by the observation of processes that we cannot ourselves manipulate or control.

To the factual or ontological question about what causation "in the objects" really *is,* I have no difficulty in answering that causes *really do* bring about their effects, and a causal law *really is* a systematic set of restraints limiting the powers of whatever natural agents there may happen to be. There is, I submit, no reason to doubt that causation, as a wholly objective feature of the world, is anything different from what our concept of causation would have it be. By saying this I mean to endorse, as factually correct, our instinctive belief in the existence of something "out there" corresponding to our concept of causation.

That there are limits of a systematic kind to what we are able to do, is as hard, objective, and well confirmed a fact as any that experience informs us of. Just try to get a volume of gas to behave in a way that is contrary to Boyle's Law. Or try to get water to boil at a temperature other than 100 degrees Celsius, in standard pressure. You can't, and it isn't all in your mind. Nor is it due to the frailty of your physical constitution. Your inability to perform these feats is an instance of the *systematic* limitations on the abilities of *all* natural agents that we call laws of nature. The fact that such limits on our powers are a well confirmed feature of "a world that is wholly objective and independent of our thoughts", if anything is, puts paid to Hume's contention that "necessity is something, that exists in the mind, not in objects".[34]

To be sure, there is nothing in the *actual* world corresponding to our concept of a causally necessary connection, over and above *de facto* constant conjunction. Likewise, there is nothing in the actual world corresponding to our concept of a causal law, over and above regularities and statistical correlations. But, shocking as this may seem to regularity theorists, what there is in the actual world does not exhaust what there is to be known about reality. Not only is it the case that things are as they are; it is furthermore the case that among the many ways things did *not* actually turn out, some were, as a matter of objective fact, open possibilities, and others were impossibilities. This is modal talk. To claim objective truth for it is to claim that in order to say all there is to be said about the actual world – and in particular, to give an account of what caused what – it would be necessary not only to recount all the occurrences *in* this world, but also to say what other logically possible worlds were in fact *causally* possible alternatives to it.

As for the existence of logically possible worlds other than the actual world, I have nothing very novel to say. I am in agreement with the "moderate modal realism" of Robert Stalnaker,[35] a position that accepts modal talk as primitive and irreducible, so that "the concept of a possible world is a basic concept in a true account of the way we represent the world in our propositional acts and attitudes".[36] Yet while affirming that possible worlds are "more than just a convenient myth or a notational shortcut",[37] Stalnaker denies that non-actual worlds are entities resembling the actual world: the actual world is the totality of everything there is. One may thus picture the world as being set in a logical space of possibilities that are objectively real *qua* possibilities, without being obliged to infer that there *are* worlds in which these possibilities are realized.

As conscious agents, we have a way of knowing by experience what things it is possible for us to bring about, and what things impossible. This is nothing less than empirical knowledge, not just of the actual world, but of sets of possible worlds. Admittedly we only ever observe events in the actual world; but what we have observed in the actual world is evidence for statements about sets of possible worlds, in much the same way as what we have observed in the past is evidence for statements about the future. We know some things about non-actual worlds with just as much certainty as we know the date of the next solar eclipse. Yes, Virginia, there is such a thing as natural necessity, and we have empirical knowledge of it.

A critique of actualist accounts of causality

This, of course, is the very conclusion that regularity theorists and actualists, who regard themselves as the intellectual heirs of Hume, have been at pains to avoid. It would be well beyond the scope of this essay to survey all of the various paths by which they have sought to avoid it; but I will comment on two of the most ingenious attempts. I have selected these two for their brilliance, their thoroughness, and their sensitivity to the intricacies of the concept of causation. The two philosophers in question are Hans Reichenbach and J.L. Mackie.

(a) Hans Reichenbach

Reichenbach applies the modal term 'physically necessary' to laws of nature, but then attempts to explicate physical necessity along actualist lines. He might, therefore, be called an actualist in modal realist's clothing. He wrote two different accounts of his theory of physical necessity, the second being a refined and elaborated version of the first.[38] The earlier version is found in his book *Elements of Symbolic Logic*. There, the key terms are defined as follows:

> p is physically necessary =df 'p' is a nomological statement. ...
>
> By 'nomological' we mean here 'nomological in the wider sense'. ...
>
> A statement 'p' is a nomological statement in the wider sense if it is derivable from a set 'a₁ ... aₙ' of original nomological statements. ...
>
> By 'derivable' we mean here deducible, i.e., derivable by means of deductive operations, excluding inductive inferences. ...
>
> An original nomological statement is an all-statement that is demonstrably true, fully exhaustive, and universal. ...
>
> By the phrase 'demonstrable as true', we mean that there is a method, of the deductive or the inductive kind, proving the statement to be true. (Footnote: We include here a verification as *practically true*, since inductive methods never lead to absolute truth.) The word 'demonstrable', therefore, does not presuppose the definition of possibility to be given below; such procedure would be circular. We do not require, however, that the proof be

actually given. If it is given we shall know that the statement is nomological; but there may be nomological statements that are not known to be such. In requiring that the statement be not only true but also demonstrable as true, we exclude statements that are true but that cannot be proved to be true. Thus the statement 'all gold cubes are smaller than one cubic mile' may be true; but since we cannot prove it as true it is no nomological statement. We thus exclude statements that are true by chance.[39]

By 'universal' Reichenbach means a statement containing no references to individuals. The requirement that original nomological statements be "fully exhaustive" is designed to avoid the paradoxes stemming from the Boolean interpretation of all-statements. Reichenbach's technical term 'exhaustive' is so defined that a true statement of the form 'All F are G' – $(x)[Fx \supset Gx]$ – would be excluded if it owed its truth to the fact that there are no Fs, or to the fact that everything is G. Such a statement could not, therefore, be an original nomological statement.[40]

Despite his ingenuity, and despite the complexity of the formal machinery he has developed for the task, Reichenbach has failed to give a criterion that is either necessary or sufficient for the target notion of physical necessity. That it is not a necessary condition may be seen as follows. Imagine that in the physics laboratory of the University of Manitoba, a heavy radioactive element, which exists nowhere in nature, is synthesized from elementary particles. With becoming pride in their achievement, the researchers christen the new element Manitobum. It proves to be unstable stuff: the small quantity that they have synthesized decays into lighter elements within a matter of minutes. The same thing occurs on the few subsequent occasions when they synthesize additional small quantities of it. Then some social catastrophe, such as world war or a drastic cut in funding for basic research, forces them to abandon their experiments, and Manitobum is never synthesized again. Unbeknownst to the Manitoba research team, Manitobum has an interesting dispositional property: when placed in conditions of type C, it does D. But this property is not deducible from physical theory – now, or, we may suppose, in the future. And of course, the Manitoba team never got around to placing a quantity of Manitobum in conditions of type C in order to observe what would happen.

I take it that our pre-analytic notion of physical necessity would require us to say that it is physically necessary that Manitobum have the chemical properties it does, in fact, have. The statement 'All Manitobum does D when placed in conditions of type C' – (x) $[(Mx \bullet Cx) \supset Dx]$ – expresses a law of nature – one of those laws which the human race, unfortunately, never learns of. Yet according to Reichenbach's criterion, it fails to qualify as a nomological statement. The statement is true in the actual world; but since it is also true that no Manitobum was ever placed in conditions of type C – $\sim(\exists x)[Mx \bullet Cx]$ – the statement is not fully exhaustive. Hence it is not an original nomological statement. Since *ex hypothesi* it cannot be deduced from any original nomological statement in the corpus of present or future science, it cannot be a nomological statement at all, according to Reichenbach. We thus have a logically possible situation in which Reichenbach's explication of physical necessity is at odds with our pre-analytic understanding of the concept.

But if we adopt a "frankly modal" analysis of the concept which is not a disguised form of the regularity theory, we can avoid flying in the face of our pre-analytic notions. On a "frankly modal" analysis, $(x)[(Mx \bullet Cx) \supset Dx]$ is a law if and only if it holds true in every physically possible world. If it so happens that in the actual world this disposition of Manitobum never manifests itself in any concrete occurrences – well, so what?

There might, then, be lawful dispositions of physical things which never have a concrete manifestation in the actual world. And on the other hand, it is possible, although very unlikely, that some of the seemingly lawful regularities we have observed in the actual world are not in fact instances of genuine laws of nature – laws, that is, which hold in all physically possible worlds. Some of them might, instead, be nothing but "cosmic coincidences". That this is most improbable is due, not solely or even principally to circumstances beyond our control, but to our own activity of experimentation. By actively manipulating the world in order to find out how it works, *we* determine, in some respects, which physically possible world gets actualized. And when we are engaged in experimental enquiry, we make the choices we do make about which world shall be actualized, precisely with a view to actualizing a world which will *not* mislead us concerning the laws of physics.

Nevertheless, we cannot rule out the bare logical possibility that we have been misled. Perhaps one or more of those universal truths which hold *de facto* throughout the actual world, and which we believe, on good experimental evidence, to be laws of nature, really are not. That this is a logical possibility shows that Reichenbach has not given us a sufficient criterion for physical necessity either. For it means that there could be an all-statement that was demonstrably true of the actual world, in Reichenbach's sense of 'demonstrably true', yet did not hold true in all physically possible worlds.

Reichenbach virtually admitted as much when he noted that his sense of 'demonstrably true' would take in statements verified as *practically true*, "since inductive methods never lead to absolute truth". The sentence exhibits a deplorable confusion of semantic and epistemological concepts. Once we tidy up that particular confusion, we see that Reichenbach wishes to include, as nomological statements, those whose truth is practically certain, since inductive methods never lead to absolute certainty. Now the cat is really out of the bag.

Reichenbach's later treatment of these matters is found in the book *Nomological Statements and Admissible Operations*, first published shortly after Reichenbach's death, and reissued some twenty-two years later under the title *Laws, Modalities, and Counterfactuals*. Here the philosophical craftsmanship is even more impressive, the conceptual gadgetry even more intricate and refined, than in the earlier work.[41]

In order to allow for the possibility of physical laws which forever escape the notice of human investigators, Reichenbach adopts an extended sense of 'verifiably true'. He begins with the system S_0 of scientific laws and theories that are demonstrably or verifiably true in the original, narrower sense: these are the ones which are or will be inductively supported by observations that people actually make.

> The term *physically possible* then refers to any occurrence not excluded by a nomological statement, i.e., not excluded by a statement of S_0 . . .
>
> Furthermore, the system S_0 leads to definitions of kinds of physical objects and quantities, such as temperature, voltage, wave length, etc.; but also including such things as trees, planets, human beings, cats, etc. For the observation of such objects we have developed *observational procedures*. For instance, looking at a cat is an observational procedure to ascertain the color of its skin, but unsuitable to ascertain the content of its stomach; directing a telescope to the night sky is an observational procedure for the observation of stars, but

unsuitable for the observation of radio waves. The result of an observational procedure is an *observational datum*. There are actual and possible observational data; for instance, the temperature of a certain room during a certain night is an actual or a possible observational datum, depending on whether observations by means of a thermometer were made.[42]

Now it is possible for Reichenbach to speak of the class R_1 of possible observational data: R_1 is much larger than the class R_0 of *actual* data on the basis of which the statements in S_0 are deemed to be demonstrably true. We may thus envisage a much larger class S_1 of nomological statements that is verifiable on the basis R_1; and it is this large class S_1 which will answer to the concept "all existing laws of nature".

This goes about as far as a regularity theorist can go in constructing definitions which approximate to our actual concept of causal necessity. Just a step or two further, and he might succeed in giving a correct analysis of the concept, and by the same token cease to be a regularity theorist. Indeed, Reichenbach may already have fallen off the Humean bandwagon at this stage of his argument. What we need to ask ourselves is this: Does the class R_1 represent a set of possible observations of the *actual* world? If so, then the objections I have urged against Reichenbach's earlier definition of physical necessity will hold with equal force against the later version. 'All Manitobum, when placed in conditions of type C, does D' would still be ruled out as a nomological statement, in the circumstances imagined; and the actual world might still exhibit some cosmic coincidences, as a result of which some non-nomological statements would wrongly be included in S_1.

The phrase 'possible observation of the actual world' is more than a little odd. If certain possible observations of the rings of Saturn, which in fact were not made, *had* been made, then it would not have been *this* world that was actualized after all, but a slightly different world – viz., a world in which a certain astronomer got to work and made those observations, instead of lingering over her midnight snack.

But I do not think it would be fair to press this line of objection against Reichenbach. His project was to give an explication of physical necessity expressible in the metalanguage while utilizing an extensional object language. Now to J.L. Mackie's three questions about causality – factual, conceptual, and epistemic – there correspond three questions on the narrower topic of physical necessity: what is our concept of it, what is there in objective reality corresponding to that concept, and how do we know about it? Reichenbach, if I understand him correctly, wished to answer the conceptual question by saying that our concept of physical necessity, though characteristically expressed in modal language, is the concept of a certain kind of *de facto* regularity. This is what makes him a regularity theorist. To the factual question, he will say that there *are* regularities in the actual world corresponding to the concept of physical necessity, as he has analyzed it: this makes him an actualist as regards the ontology of physical laws. When it comes to the epistemic question, he will answer that it is by inductive inference from observations of the actual world that we arrive at knowledge, practically but not absolutely certain, of the laws of nature.

Now if we cannot, in practice, observe the world without disturbing it, and cannot *actually* make certain *possible* observations without having an effect upon which possible world becomes actual, this is no objection in principle to Reichenbach's project. We could allow him to speak of true *statements* concerning observable states of affairs, leaving aside the whole question of the activities of actual and possible observers. R_1 may then be thought of as a set of statements about observables, rather than a set of possible observational data.

Now if R_1 is a set of statements about the actual world, Reichenbach's revised account is vulnerable to the objections raised earlier; if it includes statements about the whole set of physically possible worlds, he has abandoned the regularity theory, i.e., he has conceded that the explication of the concept of physical necessity will require a modal, or intensional, object language.

I said that the construction of the class R_1 of possible observational data went about as far as a regularity theorist can go without adopting an intensional object language for the analysis of physical necessity. Yet Reichenbach, with his almost inexhaustible ingenuity, attempts to go one step further. In the final paragraph of the chapter we have been examining, he continues:

> If the class S_1 appears not comprehensive enough, an iteration of the definition may be employed. We can speak of the class P_1 of observational procedures which it is logically possible to construct for S_1 and R_1, and then define in terms of R_1, P_1, S_1 a class R_2 of possible observational data and a class S_2 of nomological statements, repeating the form of definition used before. This iteration may be continued. Are we allowed to speak of the joint class S (union) of all the classes S_1, S_2, . . . ? This is presumably permissible. However this may be, the statement 's is a law of nature' may be interpreted as meaning, 'in the series S_1, S_2, . . . there is an S_i which includes s'. And the term 'verifiably true in the wider sense' may then be interpreted as meaning, 'there is a basis R_i on which it is logically possible to verify the statement'. For all practical

purposes, the class S_1 is a sufficient approximation
to the concept 'all existing laws of nature'; and the
concept 'verifiable on the basis R_1' to the concept
'verifiably true in the wider sense'.[43]

Reichenbach is surely right to say that his form of the regularity
theory, even without his final refinement, can give us an approximation to the concept 'law of nature' which is sufficient for all practical purposes. But never mind "all practical purposes"; this is metaphysics. Either the actual world is thought of as *given*, and the class P_1 of logically possible observation procedures represents a set of methods for arriving at different sets of true statements about that world – in which case the objections about Manitobum and cosmic coincidences can be iterated; or, alternatively, different observation procedures can be thought of as actualizing different possible worlds – in which case the essential point has been conceded. Either way, Reichenbach cannot succeed in explicating the concept of physical necessity without resorting to an intensional object language.

(b) J.L. Mackie

A regularity theorist answers J.L. Mackie's conceptual question by saying that our concept of causality is the concept of a certain kind of regularity. Characteristically, he would then proceed to answer the factual or ontological question by saying that causality in the objects is nothing more than a set of regularities corresponding to that concept; this position on the ontological question is what I have termed "actualism". Reichenbach's account of physical necessity proceeds along these lines. So do the attempts by Reichenbach and others to give an actualist account of causal priority, the other key element in causation, in terms of asymmetrical statistical relationships.[44]

I have insisted, *per contra*, that only a frankly modal analysis will accurately represent our concept of causation; and I have maintained that causation in the objects is a phenomenon which corresponds to *that* concept. This answer to the ontological question is the central claim in the position I refer to as "modal realism".

I suspect that Mackie may have been led to formulate his very helpful distinction between the conceptual question and the ontological question because of the fact that on the level of ontology, he is attracted to the theory of actualism, yet when it comes to the analysis of our concept of causation, he recognizes the inadequacies of the regularity theory. The result is a tension between his view of our concept of causation and his view of causation as it is in the objects: he does not, in fact, believe that the latter corresponds to the former. Rather than simply urging the abandonment of the concept of causation we now have, Mackie attempts to resolve the tension by adopting a form of instrumentalism. He concludes that our causal judgments are never, strictly speaking, true (though 'C caused E' would be quite strictly and straightforwardly false in the event that either C or E did not occur); their significance is to be found in the fact that we employ them in order to perform certain intellectual acts and make certain conversational moves.

When we make the judgment that a causal connection obtains between two events C and E, certain counterfactual conditionals will be essential to the analysis of that judgment. Counterfactual conditionals, in turn, are just one species of non-material conditionals. This much is hardly controversial. Mackie then proceeds to give an instrumentalist account of non-material conditionals in general.

The function of an open conditional 'If P, Q', he says, is not to describe a state of affairs in the actual world or in any other possible world; it is, rather, to make the conditional *assertion*, 'Suppose that P; on that supposition, Q'.

This account holds for all non-material conditionals; a counterfacutal adds to this the suggestion that the antecedent does not hold in the actual world. ...

Statements of singular causal sequence involve in their analysis counterfactual conditionals which on the present showing are not capable of being true; so the singular causal statements cannot be true either. ... [T]hese counterfactual conditionals ... are concerned with suppositions and their consequences or accompaniments, they do not describe what actually occurred, let alone what was observed to occur, in the actual individual sequence. They state what would have happened, not what did happen.[45]

The Cement of the Universe: A Study of Causation CLLP by J.L. Mackie (1980), p. 54. Reproduced by permission of Oxford University Press.

The making of a conditional assertion may be warranted by empirical evidence; and in such a case, the methods that take us from the evidence to the justifiability of the conditional assertion will be the familiar methods of induction.

Thus the counterfactual conditionals which emerge from the analysis of causal statements, though not themselves true, are surrogates for clusters of statements which can be true.[46]

The Cement of the Universe: A Study of Causation CLLP by J.L. Mackie (1980), pp. 229-30. Reproduced by permission of Oxford University Press.

This provides Mackie with a way of accounting for the celebrated capacity, possessed by laws of nature but not by accidental generalizations, to warrant or sustain the assertion of counterfactuals. He sees a law of nature as a universal generalization which enjoys an appropriate type of inductive support; it warrants or sustains the assertion of a counterfactual by transferring the authority of the evidence on which *it* rests to the act of asserting, or accepting, the counterfactual. But that act is nothing other than the act of conditionally asserting, or accepting, the consequent, on the supposition that the antecedent is the case.

> Regularity statements, if inductively supported, will sustain the conditionals which an initial analysis of causal statements brings to light. The meaning of causal statements is given by the conditionals, but their grounds may well include the corresponding regularities.
>
> ... And there is no need to introduce the mystery of a special *sort* of regularity, a 'nomic universal', to account for the ability of causal laws to sustain counterfactual conditionals.[47]

The Cement of the Universe: A Study of Causation CLLP by J.L. Mackie (1980), p. 60. Reproduced by permission of Oxford University Press.

Statements of many other kinds – e.g., the singular statement 'Bizet was French' – can warrant the assertion of a counterfactual; but accidental generalizations cannot, because the kind of evidence upon which they characteristically rest is undercut or set aside by the belief-contravening supposition expressed by the antecedent of the counterfactual. Suppose that we check each individual in the room, and by this means establish the truth of the accidental generalization 'Everyone in this room understands Italian'. This fails to lend any support to the assertion of the counterfactual 'If Mr. Chou En-Lai were in this room, he would understand Italian' – not because of any obscure logical property of the accidental generalization, but because of the nature of the evidence which has led us to accept it.

> Since our sole ground for believing this universal was the enumerative check, that ground collapses as soon as we add the supposition that someone *else* is in the room; someone who – as the counterfactual form concedes – is not in fact in the room and whose understanding of Italian has therefore not been checked by this enumeration.[48]

The Cement of the Universe: A Study of Causation CLLP by J.L. Mackie (1980), p. 115. Reproduced by permission of Oxford University Press.

Mackie's analysis of the concept of causation departs from Hume's regularity theory in three distinct ways. First, as we have seen, he sees counterfactuals as being indispensable to the analysis of the concept. Secondly, he insists that causal priority, the asymmetrical relation between cause and effect, is something over and above regularity, and distinct from temporal succession. Thirdly, he recognizes that not any universal regularities will count as causal laws or laws of nature; and like Reichenbach he seeks to formulate a criterion which will mark off lawful regularities from accidental ones.

To do this, he begins with a definition of natural or physical necessity proposed by Karl Popper, taking care to note that Popper himself had "considerable reservations both about its accuracy and about the importance of definitions anyway, as contrasted with ideas":

> A statement may be said to be naturally or physi-
> cally necessary if, and only if, it is deducible from a
> statement function which is satisfied in all worlds
> that differ from our world, if at all, only with re-
> spect to initial conditions.[49]

Mackie then contrasts pure laws of working with universal collocations – the latter being the subject of true accidental generalizations, including true generalizations about initial conditions
in our universe. Laws such as Kepler's laws of planetary motion,
which are a consequence of the laws of mechanics together with the
conditions prevailing at the formation of the solar system, Mackie
classifies as "mixed laws".

> [W]e can sort out pure laws of working – some
> basic, some derived – from both mixed laws and
> collocation statements. We can do this in practice
> only where we take it that we fully understand
> how the system in question works, as we do with a
> Newtonian mechanical system.[50]

The Cement of the Universe: A Study of Causation CLLP by J.L. Mackie (1980),
p. 211. Reproduced by permission of Oxford University Press.

This criterion, while more vague than Reichenbach's, does succeed in keeping the conceptual question – what we understand by
cause and effect – separate from the epistemological question –
how we know what causes what. To be sure, it will be on the basis
of empirical evidence that we sort out pure laws of working from

mixed laws and collocation statements; but the three classes of statements have been distinguished without reference to episte-mological considerations.

Pure laws of working, says Mackie, govern the changes that occur in the universe, in so far as those changes are caused; and they make those changes orderly and intelligible by being "forms of partial persistence".[51] An object that changes in accordance with one of these laws is in some intelligible sense going on do-ing the same thing. A process which, as it unfolds, instantiates a pure law of working, will exhibit a spatio-temporal or qualitative continuity that joins its different phases into an unbroken "rope of causation".[52] Such continuities and partial persistences "consti-tute the long-searched-for link between individual cause and effect which a pure regularity theory fails, or refuses, to find".[53]

The Cement of the Universe: A Study of Causation CLLP by J.L. Mackie (1980), pp. 228-9. Reproduced by permission of Oxford University Press.

I have said that when it comes to the ontological question – the nature of causation as it is in the objects – Mackie is attracted to the theory of actualism. But he does not adopt a simple Humean form of actualism; he does not claim that causation in the objects just is reg-ularity. In the first place, not all regularities are causal regularities; a causal sequence is an instance of a pure law of working. Secondly, the causal nexus is present in the individual case, and an individual case cannot of itself be, or exhibit, a regularity; it can only instantiate a regularity. What constitutes the link between cause and effect in the individual case, according to Mackie, is the presence of those continuities and partial persistences which are called for by the pure laws of working. Thirdly, causal priority is a feature of causation in the objects; a cause is, as a matter of objective fact, prior to its effect.

Thus, contrary to the Humean view, there is more
in objective causation than regularity, but contrary
to the traditional rationalist view, this extra element is nothing like logical necessity. ...

... [O]ur continuity ... is an empirical counterpart of the rationalists' logical or near-logical
necessity. ...

... There is also a direction of causation, an
asymmetry between cause and effect which is not
simply temporal order, though it is related to this.[54]

The Cement of the Universe: A Study of Causation CLLP by J.L. Mackie (1980),
pp. x, 228, ix. Reproduced by permission of Oxford University Press.

While the theory of causality offered here is far more complex than
Hume's, Mackie definitely intends it as an actualist answer to the
ontological question concerning causation in the objects. This is
plain from the emphatic rejection of modal realism with which he
prepares the ground for his own, instrumentalist account of the
causal conditionals:

Why do causal laws entail or sustain counterfactuals whereas accidental generalizations do not?
Does this fact show, as is widely believed among
philosophers, that causal law statements include,
in their meaning, something stronger than merely
factual universality? Do these statements implic-
itly assert the existence of some sort of 'natural
necessity' in the events themselves? Is there some
special virtue either in causal law statements, or
in the objective laws which they report, which enables them to entail counterfactuals, mysterious

truths that hold beyond the actual world and govern the realm of possibilities as well?

My contention is that this way of asking the questions is thoroughly misleading. Counterfactual conditionals are not to be taken literally as truths about possible worlds, but as a species of human procedure. They are just non-material conditionals plus a hint that their antecedents are unfulfilled, and non-material conditionals merely express the asserting of something within the scope of some supposition. ...

... Simple truth, truth in the strict sense, can belong only to descriptions of what is actual. ...

... Possible situations, or possible worlds, just because they are not actual (or may not be actual) do not stand on their own, do not exist independently. We must come back in the end to something like a speech-act analysis of statements about possible situations, and hence of the conditionals which were initially analysed in this way. People can consider possibilities; but the possibilities exist only as the contents of such considerings.[55]

I turn now to an assessment of Mackie's theory. Little needs to be said here about the treatment of causal priority in *The Cement of the Universe*, although I profited a great deal from reading it, since Mackie has apparently abandoned the position he adopted in that book. It was searchingly criticized by a number of reviewers, notably J.A. Foster.[56] Subsequently, Mackie has written of causal priority, "I have tried more than once to analyse it, but with less than complete success"[57] and "the objective asymmetry is, I admit, obscure and elusive".[58]

The Cement of the Universe: A Study of Causation CLLP by J.L. Mackie (1980), p. ix. Reproduced by permission of Oxford University Press.

I must agree that it is amongst the most obscure and elusive aspects of the whole subject; but I will state in the next chapter what I believe is the correct account of the matter, and for now will pass on to other parts of Mackie's theory.

It is worth noting that Mackie's version of actualism does *not* fall prey to the first of the two objections I advanced against the actualism of Reichenbach. That objection concerned a supposed law of chemistry – "All Manitobum, when placed in conditions of type C, does D" – for which no inductive evidence was available. We supposed that in the actual world, no Manitobum ever *was* placed in conditions of type C. By Reichenbach's criterion, the statement would not then count as law-like, contrary to our pre-analytic understanding of the matter. But Mackie could perfectly well allow it to count as a pure law of working, despite the fact that it would remain forever uninstantiated. Thanks to his careful separation of ontological and epistemological questions, Mackie is not obliged to say that a statement counts as law-like only if inductive evidence for it is available in the actual world.

The second objection to Reichenbach concerned the logical possibility that one or more of the regularities we believe, with good reason, to be laws of nature, are in fact just cosmic coincidences. In this connection Mackie's theory runs into difficulties. Suppose there were such a deceptive regularity R, which held without exception in the actual world, and which constituted a form of continuity or partial persistence in certain physical processes, yet was in fact a cosmic coincidence. Naturally *we* would take R to be a pure law of working. Common sense would say that we were mistaken in so doing, and commonsensical philosophers would add that as long as our knowledge of nature is based upon inductive evidence, it is obvious that such mistakes are theoretically possible. But what could Mackie say? He could not say that there are causally possible worlds in which exceptions to R occur, and mean the words literally, as a modal realist would. Nor would it be plausible for him to say that in taking R to be a pure law of working, we have not understood nature aright; for what, on his theory, could we possibly have misunderstood? *Ex hypothesi,* R describes a form of continuity or partial persistence to which there are no exceptions in the actual world; but to a thoroughgoing actualist, that is all there is to being a pure law of working.

This, then, is the actualist position toward which Mackie's argument is leading: pure laws of working are regularities of continuity and partial persistence to which there are no exceptions in the actual world; and conversely, all regularities of continuity and partial persistence to which there are no exceptions in the actual world are pure laws of working. But although Mackie's argument is leading to this conclusion, Mackie does not expressly draw it. And it is not hard to see why a cautious and sensitive philosopher would shrink from drawing such a conclusion: baldly stated in this way, it all too plainly invites the objection I have posed in terms of regularity R.

Actualism, then, when thought through, leads one to deny the possibility of regularities such as R, which appear on the surface to be laws of nature, and escape being unmasked despite the efforts of scientists armed with rigorous inductive methods. But this flies in the face of the commonsensical view of inductively based knowledge.

It was an age-old objection to the regularity theory that it failed to distinguish between laws of nature and cosmic coincidences. Mackie has successfully countered this objection at the level of conceptual analysis with his explication of our causal concepts. But the age-old objection was equally an objection to the ontology of actualism, and at this level Mackie has failed to get around it. His distinction between collocations and pure laws of working fails to classify the goings-on *in the objects* in the appropriate way, as the example of regularity R has, I hope, made clear. It is of course perfectly true to say, as Mackie does, that in practice we do not make up our minds about which regularities are pure laws of working until we think we fully understand the system we are studying. But this merely underlines the conceptual point, and adds the innocuous observation that we do normally apply our concepts consistently.

While Mackie might well wish to avoid embracing a bald and thoroughgoing form of actualism, it is hard to see how he *could* avoid it without retracting other claims he has made. He would need to say, "All, and only, the *suitable* regularities of continuity and partial persistence to which there are no exceptions in the actual world, are pure laws of working", and then find a criterion of suitability which did not turn his theory into a form of modal realism. I very much doubt that this could be done.

The trouble has sprung, in part, from the fact that Mackie makes use of Popper's definition of the *concept* of physical necessity, which is one that would please any modal realist, but will not take its modal character seriously when it comes to talking about causation as it is in the objects. In this he draws encouragement from Popper himself, mentioning a passage in which Popper dismisses 'necessary' as a "mere word".[59] Such a procedure is of a piece with Mackie's treatment of causal conditionals: giving a sensitive analysis of their meaning, and then denying that they are ever literally true.

The modal realism of common sense

This brings me to what I believe to be the central and most serious difficulty with Mackie's philosophy of causation: more even than the ontology of actualism, Mackie's instrumentalism flies in the face of common sense. People do, of course, entertain suppositions without necessarily taking them to be true, and use the expression

'If P, Q' to make a conditional assertion of Q on the supposition that P. Mackie's account has added greatly to our understanding of what goes on in such situations. But when the theory results in the conclusion that judgments about one event causing another are never literally true, and that nothing in objective reality corresponds to our distinction between the physically impossible and the contingently non-actual, then something has gone very badly wrong.

But G.E. Moore, I believe, got it right. In the passage that leads up to his well-known remarks on the meaning of 'I could have, if I had chosen', we find these words:

> It is impossible to exaggerate the frequency of the occasions on which we *all* of us make a distinction between two things, neither of which *did* happen – a distinction which we express by saying, that whereas the one *could* have happened, the other could *not*. No distinction is commoner than this. And no one, I think, who fairly examines the instances in which we make it, can doubt about three things: namely (1) that very often there really is *some* distinction between the two things, corresponding to the language which we use; (2) that this distinction, which really *does* subsist between the things, is *the* one which we mean to express by saying that the one was possible and the other impossible; and (3) that this way of expressing it is a perfectly proper and legitimate way. But if so, it absolutely follows that one of the commonest and most legitimate usages of the phrases, 'could' and 'could not' is to express a difference, which often really does hold between two things *neither* of which did actually happen. Only a few instances need be given. ... [T]o take an

instance which concerns an inanimate object. Some ships *can* steam 20 knots, whereas others *can't* steam more than 15. And the mere fact that, on a particular occasion, a 20-knot steamer *did* not *actually* run at this speed certainly does not entitle us to say that she *could* not have done so, in the sense in which a 15-knot one *could* not. On the contrary, we all can and should distinguish between cases in which (as, for instance, owing to an accident to her propeller) she did not, *because* she could not, and cases in which she did not, *although* she *could*. Instances of this sort might be multiplied quite indefinitely; and it is surely quite plain that we all of us do *continually* use such language: we continually, when considering two events, neither of which *did* happen, distinguish between them by saying that whereas the one *was* possible, though it didn't happen, the other was *impossible*. And it is surely quite plain that what we mean by this (whatever it may be) is something which is often perfectly true.[60]

Moore then proceeded to analyze statements containing the modal terms 'could' and 'possible' in terms of conditionals. This approach ultimately leads nowhere, as the intervening decades of debate have amply demonstrated. It turns out that the conditionals in question have to be non-material conditionals, and the quest for the feature that will distinguish them from material conditionals brings us right back to the study of the modalities.

Yet Moore knew exactly where to start the inquiry: with the ideas and beliefs of common sense. And right at the beginning he notes that it is not simply a matter of explicating a common-sense distinction; we have also to take account of the common-sense *belief* that this distinction "really *does* subsist between the things". Common sense, in short, is committed to some form of modal realism.

Given that this *is* the position of common sense, philosophy may do any one of three things: accept it, refute it, or explain it away. If, as philosophers, we accept it, we have to tackle the difficult problem of formulating it in a precise way and defending it against skeptics. If we are to refute it, this will have to be done by means of *a priori* argument or empirical research, or both. For this there is ample precedent: both these means have served, many times, to refute things that had long passed as "common knowledge". J.L. Mackie takes the third route. He attempts to explain away the instinctive modal realism of common sense, by giving an instrumentalist account of our common habits of thought and speech, while maintaining that this is compatible with an actualist ontology.

I doubt that anyone would think it preferable to explain away an inherently sensible and widely held belief, if the problems involved in accepting it could be satisfactorily solved. So while I have noted some reasons for thinking that Mackie's combination of actualism and instrumentalism cannot succeed on its own terms, my main arguments against Mackie are the *positive* arguments in favor of modal realism.

These arguments have been given above; I will now add a concluding comment about how they should be interpreted. In discussing the "possible worlds" account of conditionals, Mackie poses the fair and penetrating question:

> There *are* no possible worlds except the actual one: so what are we up to when we talk about them?[61]

Anyone who is out to defend modal realism must answer this question, and do so without losing what Bertrand Russell called "a robust sense of reality".

The position I have taken with regard to the causal modalities amounts to treating talk about possible worlds as an organized way of talking about the powers of natural agents, and the ineluctable limits within which we find those powers to be constrained. Another way of putting it – which I take to be equivalent – is to say that although things in the world are as they are, they have a certain *potential* for being different; but this potential is not unlimited. The cold water in the kettle has the potential to be brought to a boil at 100 degrees Celsius in standard pressure, but it lacks any potential for boiling at 70 degrees Celsius in standard pressure. This way of approaching the matter parallels what Aristotle has to say about potentiality. A.E. Taylor introduces Aristotle's antithesis between potentiality and actuality in these words:

> What this antithesis means we can best see from
> the case of the growth of a living organism. . . .
> [W]e may say of a given germ, "though this is not
> yet actually an oak, it is potentially an oak", mean-
> ing not merely that, if uninterfered with, it will in
> time be an oak, but also that by no interference can
> it be made to grow into an elm or a beech.[62]

A complete discussion of the concept of potentiality – mine or Aristotle's – would also take account of what may become of things if they *are* interfered with. A lamb is a potential sheep and also a potential dinner.

It is noteworthy that in explaining Aristotle's meaning, Taylor automatically brings in the idea of 'interference', which strongly suggest agency – and not necessarily human agency, either. We are brought back once again to the insight, expressed by von Wright, that to see the world as an arena of causes and effects is to see it under the aspect of possible agency.[63]

Causes and laws

In concluding this chapter, I would like to allude to the issue of whether a particular statement of causal connection entails or presupposes laws of causation relating events or states of affairs similar to the cause to events or states of affairs that are similar to the effect.

From the account I gave of the idea of causal efficacy – making something happen – it will be plain that I do not regard singular attributions of efficacy as having any implications whatever as to the existence of covering laws. Basic judgments, made on the strength of sense perception or reflection, about what has made something happen, are all particular. Their entailments of general statements are confined to the platitudinous ones such as "Combustion of natural gas in the furnace heated up the house; therefore, something heated up the house".

From another point of view, however, there is an important distinction to be made between the occasions when I attribute efficacy to myself ("I made that sound", "I am holding the nail in place") and the occasions when I make attributions of efficacy to other agents, animate or inanimate ("The dog made that noise", "The load-bearing walls are holding up the building"). I ascribe efficacy to myself on the basis of immediate experience; but to ascribe efficacy to another agent is always to adopt some hypothesis which, if we are to be thorough in defending our beliefs, must be supported by indirect evidence. Since we do not observe the efficacy of other agents, as it were, from the inside, the only way to procure evidence of it is to observe the behavior of agents like them. Then we need to construct inferences involving laws of nature in order to use the evidence of that behavior for the purpose of verifying our hypotheses about the efficacy of the particular agents before us.

Thus when we see a potato being peeled, we don't, as J.L. Mackie points out, *see* the knife *making* the peel come up.[64] I have been claiming that we do *judge* – i.e., come to believe the hypothesis – that the knife-edge is making the peel come up. I agree with Mackie, furthermore, that we do make the counterfactual judgment that each bit of peel would not have come up if the knife had not moved in there. Why make such a judgment? Because we believe there is a law of nature which entails that the movement of the knife was causally necessary, in the circumstances, for the lifting of the peel. That is to say, it would have been impossible for any natural agent to bring about the lifting of the peel in those circumstances unless the knife had moved in. There is plenty of evidence out there, in the experience of many human beings, for the existence of such a law – and of course its existence is itself a hypothesis, one of the many strands in the interconnected web of hypotheses that makes up our view of the world. The law plays an indispensable role in relating this wealth of experience to the hypothesis that the knife-edge is making the peel come up. The plain judgment that the moving knife is making the peel come up does not, then, entail or presuppose the law; rather, it requires the law for its empirical justification.

---

1   J.L. Austin 1956, in Austin 1961, p. 178.

2   Don Locke 1976.

3   Cf. P.H. Nowell-Smith 1960.

4   See Nicholas Freeling 1977, pp. 238 and 242-243. I humbly apologize to any mystery buffs who have not yet read the book and would have preferred not to know how the story ends.

5   I have played with such a device at the science museum of the St. Paul Ramsey Arts and Science Center, Saint Paul, Minnesota.

6   St. Thomas Aquinas 1952, q. 2, art. 12 (p. 117).

7   See Pierre Laplace 1951, pp. 3-6.

8   John Thorp 1980, p. 18.

9   Aristotle, *Rhetoric*, III, 17; 1418a 3-5.

10 Aristotle, *De Interpretatione*, 19a 23-25.

11   Aristotle, *Nichomachean Ethics*, VI, 2; 1139b 7-9.

12   Thorp 1980, p. 144, n. 14. I am indebted to this particular note in Thorp's book for the three quotations from Aristotle just cited.

13   See Michael J. Loux's introduction to Michael J. Loux 1979, p. 28, and G.E. Hughes and M.J. Creswell 1968, pp. 75-80.

14   See Loux 1979, p. 23, and Hughes and Cresswell 1968, *loc. cit.*

15   Hughes and Cresswell 1968, pp. 4, 8, and 17-21.

16   Cf. Hughes' and Cresswell's formulation of System T, in Hughes and Creswell 1968, p. 31, to which I am indebted for this element of System TA.

17   See Loux 1979, p. 16, and Hughes and Cresswell 1968, p. 31.

18   Thorp 1980, p. 29.

19   Austin 1956, in Austin 1961, p. 166.

20   Winston Nesbitt and Stewart Candlish 1978, p. 419.

21   Locke, *Essay*, Book II, ch. i, para. 4; Vol. I, p. 124.

22   See G.E. Moore 1965, p. 88.

23   Cf. Donald Brown 1968. Brown, however, uses the term 'natural agent' in a sense that excludes human beings.

24   I have used the subscript 'c' to distinguish the causal modalities, which are defined by means of the idea of a natural agent, from the modal terms referring to agency in general.

25   See esp. Karl Popper, "Science: Conjectures and Refutations" (1953) and "Three Views concerning Human Knowledge" (1956), in Popper 1963, pp. 33-65 and 97-119.

26   Antony Flew 1975, p. 4.

27   Wesley Salmon 1975b, p. 131.

28   For a clinical study of some of the complex and surprising phenomena which are relevant here, see Jean Piaget 1930.

29   Flew 1961, p. 132.

30   Douglas Gasking, "Causation and Recipes", *Mind*, N.S., 64 (1955), p. 485.

31   Georg Henrik von Wright 1973, p. 307; pp. 306-307. See also von Wright 1971, pp. 69-82.

32   Stephen Toulmin 1953, pp. 120-121.

33   Mackie 1980, p. ix.

34   Hume, *Treatise*, Book I, Part III, Section XIV, p. 165.

35   See Robert C. Stalnaker 1976.

36   Stalnaker 1976, p. 75.

37   *Ibid.*

38 For the first version, see Hans Reichenbach 1947. The second is found in Reichenbach 1954.

39 Reichenbach 1947, pp. 393, 371, 369, 368.

40 Reichenbach 1947, pp. 361-368. Cf. Reichenbach 1954, pp. 29-32.

41 Reichenbach 1954, esp. ch. vi.

42 Reichenbach 1954, p. 85.

43 Reichenbach 1954, p. 87.

44 See Reichenbach 1956, Kenneth M. Sayre 1977, and Salmon 1975.

45 Mackie 1974, p. 54. The theory examined here is found in the Preface and in chapters 2, 3 and 8 of Mackie 1974, and partly in Mackie 1973, ch. 3.

46 Mackie 1974, pp. 229-230.

47 Mackie 1974, p. 60.

48 Mackie 1974, p. 115. Cf. Mackie 1973, pp. 199-202.

49 Popper 1959, New Appendix x, p. 433. Quoted by Mackie in Mackie 1974, p. 209.

50 Mackie 1974, p. 211.

51 Mackie 1974, p. 229.

52 The image of a continuous "rope of causation" is to be contrasted with the traditional metaphor of a "chain of causation" whose "links" are discrete events. For what I believe to be the earliest use of the notion of a "rope of causation", see John Venn 1866, p. 320.

53 Mackie 1974, pp. 228-229.

54 Mackie 1980, pp. x, 228, ix.

55 Mackie 1973, pp. 114, 106, 92.

56 J.A. Foster 1975.

57 Mackie, 1979, p. 22.

58 Mackie 1980 p. ix.

59 Popper 1959, p. 438.

60 Moore 1965, pp. 88-89.

61 Mackie 1973, p. 90.

62 A.E. Taylor 1955, p. 48.

63 See von Wright 1974, pp. 48-54.

64 Mackie 1974, p. 133; quoted above, ch. 2, pp. 61-62.

CHAPTER 4
Cause and Effect

We have considered two subdivisions of the family of concepts having to do with causation: the basic notion of efficacy – making something happen – and the modal family – necessity, possibility, and so on. In both cases, we examined how some key member of the group of concepts could be related to experience in a way that would satisfy the demand posed by an empiricist theory of knowledge that ideas be based on or derived from experience. I have intimated that I take the desired relationship to be one of unequivocal instantiation, rather than a relation of copy to original. And I have sought to offer a concept or idea that could plausibly be supposed to have figured in the mental life of a pre-verbal child. (In view of this, it might be better to speak of a "proto-concept" rather than a concept *simpliciter.*) Then, in each case, we saw how the basic idea could be taken as a logically primitive item in our conceptual apparatus. In the case of the modal family, this opened the way to defining causal necessity and the notion of a law of nature.

It is time now to tackle the other element in our thinking about causation: the asymmetrical relation that obtains between a cause and its effect. The conclusion that results will be found to have a direct bearing upon the related issue of the asymmetries of explanation – the fact that when a state of affairs is success-fully explained by a set of particular and general facts, there is an asymmetrical relation between the state of affairs to be explained – the explanandum – and the facts which do the explaining – the explanans.

Many philosophers have chosen to settle the question of causal priority – the sense in which a cause is *prior to* its effect – in a sum-mary fashion, by declaring that causal priority is simply temporal priority: a cause is, by definition, an event or state of affairs that occurs earlier in time than the effect. Hume is the outstanding representative of this philosophical position. In the *Treatise* he sets down contiguity and succession as two essential elements in the re-lation of cause and effect.[1] In the *Enquiry* he drops the requirement of contiguity, tacitly acknowledging that action at a distance can-not be ruled out *a priori,* but retains the requirement of temporal succession in both of his two celebrated definitions of 'cause'. Both begin by defining a cause as "an object, followed by another ..."[2]

But this approach, which makes it a matter of definition that causes occur earlier than their effects, runs into problems. First there is the problem of effects that appear to be simultaneous with their causes. Stand outdoors on a sunny day and wave your arms around. The shadows of your waving arms appear on the ground without any observable delay. Yet no one would have any hesita-tion in saying that the waving arms are the cause and the moving shadow is the effect. Thanks to having proved that the speed of light is finite, we now know that the effect does in fact occur a tiny fraction of a second later than the cause. But there was a time when the velocity of light was not known, and scientists took seriously the possibility that it might turn out to be infinite. Still no one would have had any doubt that the waving arms cause the moving shadow on the ground, not vice versa. (Or consider the shadow of a falling leaf, if you feel like having an example that does not involve human agency.) This makes it plain that at the common-sense level, we possess some concept of causal priority that does not include or entail temporal succession.

Secondly, and more radically, philosophers need to take seriously the possibility of causes that work backward in time. I am not about to argue that there are in fact examples of backward causation; but I do consider it an error to rule them out *a priori*.

Prophetic dreams and other putative instances of precognition provide telling examples of phenomena which tempt us, if only a little, to conclude that effects can, perhaps, sometimes occur earlier than their causes. The prophetic cognition occurs; later comes the event that renders it true, verifying the prediction that may or may not have been explicitly made on the basis of the prophetic cognition. Are we to (1) dismiss this sequence of events as nothing more than a coincidence; (2) insist that there *must* be an explanation involving only causes that work forward in time; or (3) entertain the hypothesis that the later truth-making event was the cause of the prophetic cognition? If we are even to give a coherent meaning to the third option – let alone examine what evidence might be used to support such a hypothesis – we need a concept of causal priority that is independent of temporal succession.

Once again I intend to take a logically primitive idea that is derived from experience, in the sense that experience will provide unequivocal instantiations of it, and use it to define a key concept relating to causality – in this case, causal priority. Once again the logically primitive item will be an idea or proto-concept that can reasonably be supposed to have been acquired very early in life – indeed, to be part of the mental furniture of pre-verbal children.

The idea I propose to take as logically primitive in this context is the idea of doing one thing *by* doing another, or making one thing happen by making some other thing happen. The idea, even in its logically primitive form, needs to be tied or relativized to a set of relevant background conditions. Thus, to take an example from very early experience, a baby might come to realize, "By waving my arm back and forth while holding my rattle in my hand, I produce this entertaining noise". Needless to say, whatever form the baby's cognizance of this fact might take, it would not involve any verbalization, least of all the use of the first-person singular pronoun. What we need to attribute to the child – or to a grownup user of the concept – is, first, the basic experience of making something happen; secondly, the awareness of making the arm movement and producing the noise as two distinguishable actions; and lastly, the awareness that the background condition (holding the rattle in one's hand) makes a difference to the outcome. Holding a spoon, or holding nothing at all, will not have a similar result. It also goes without saying that a considerable amount of experience of waving one's arms back and forth, with and without a rattle in one's hand, is needed in order to engender the awareness of doing Y by doing X in the presence of background condition B. Nevertheless it is the single experienced situation, not the requisite *prior* experience, that instantiates the idea.

Having the concept of doing Y by doing X enables us to define the notion of a basic action – an action that an agent performs, but not *by* doing anything else.[3]

Causal priority

Using the core concept of efficacy and also the concept of causal possibility developed in the last chapter, I now define causal priority as follows:

> (D1) A condition C is causally prior to an event or condition E relative to a set of background conditions B if and only if

(i) it is possible to bring about C in B relatively directly, *and*

(ii) it is not possible to bring about C in B without thereby tending to bring about E,

whereas the converse relation does not hold – i.e., *either*

(iii) it is not possible to bring about E in B relatively directly,

or

(iv) it is possible to bring about E in B without thereby tending to bring about C.

Typically, this relation between C, B, and E will hold in virtue of a set of covering laws {L}. Also, it is necessary to specify that C and E are distinct events or conditions. That is because it is frequently correct to say 'Agent A, by doing X, did Y' when 'X' and 'Y' are simply different descriptions of the same action or event. By posting a sign, the management of a store warns its customers that shoplifters will be prosecuted; but in the circumstances, to post the sign *is* to issue the warning. By giving birth to her first child, my daughter-in-law made me a grandfather; but my becoming a grandfather was not a distinct event over and above the birth of the baby. No event or condition can be causally prior to itself.

In the above definition, 'possible' means causally possible; and causal possibility is to be identified with what is possible, in the agency sense, for some *logically* possible natural agent. We are not, therefore, confining ourselves to what is humanly possible, and I am happy to count many subhuman beings as natural agents.

When I speak of bringing about the condition C "relatively directly", I mean directly relative to E: to bring about C relatively directly is to bring about C but not *by* bringing about E. We do not alter the length of a pendulum *by* altering its period; altering the length is something we do relatively directly. On the other hand, if it is not possible to bring about E directly, relative to C, this means that neither we nor any other natural agent could bring about E *except* by bringing about C.

One can show that it is possible to bring about a condition C relatively directly, by showing that this can be done by means which make no use of the law-like relationship between C and E expressed in the set of covering laws {L}. Thus we can alter the length of a pendulum without giving a hoot about whether we are altering the period with which it will swing. The techniques we use will be the techniques we employ for altering the length of any object made of that kind of material – wood, metal, string, or whatever – regardless of whether it will ever do duty as a pendulum. But barring changes in the gravitational force acting on the bob, neither we nor any other natural agent could alter the period of a pendulum except by means of altering its length – thus making use of the law-like relationship between length and period. We may say, then, that given the gravitational force acting on the bob, a change in the period can be brought about only relatively indirectly.

You could, of course, grab hold of the pendulum bob and move it back and forth with any rhythm you pleased; but then, by definition, you would no longer have a free-swinging pendulum covered by the law relating period to length.

These considerations bring out the relevant asymmetry between cause and effect, between the explaining condition and the phenomenon to be explained. We thus have a solution to the difficulty noted by Carl Hempel,[4] and since dubbed "the problem of the asymmetries of explanation": the explaining condition must be causally prior to the explanandum. I will have more to say on this topic in the next chapter.

A contrasting example

The example of the free-swinging pendulum, whose length is causally prior to, and therefore explains, its period, has the following structural feature: given the background conditions B, the explanatory factor C is causally necessary and sufficient for the explanandum event E. In instances such as this, clauses (i), (ii) and (iii) of the above definition apply: it is possible to bring about C in B relatively directly, it is not possible to bring about C in B without thereby tending to bring about E, and it is not possible to bring about E in B relatively directly.

If, given B, C is causally sufficient, but not necessary, for E, we will have a situation in which clauses (i), (ii) and (iv) apply: it is possible to bring about C in B relatively directly, it is not possible to bring about C in B without thereby tending to bring about E, and it is possible to bring about E in B without thereby tending to bring about C.

Consider a toy train moving along its track at a constant velocity. C is the force exerted by the locomotive, E is the motion of the boxcars; B includes the fact that the train is securely coupled together, and the fact that the locomotive contains a motor whereas none of the boxcars does. We can bring about C relatively directly, by engaging the motor of the locomotive and supplying power; these means of bringing about C make no use of the law-like connection between C and E. But we could not bring about C in B, the laws of nature being as they are, without thereby bringing about E. We could, however, bring about E relatively directly – by grasping the first boxcar and pulling the train by hand, or alternatively by pushing it from behind with a second locomotive. This would have no tendency to bring about C, which is the force exerted on the first boxcar by the locomotive. C is thus causally prior to E in the sense we have defined.

It should be noted that if C were specified to mean, not the *force* exerted by the locomotive, but rather the *motion* of the locomotive, then it would turn out that C is not causally prior to E. This is because we could not, in B, bring about E (the motion of the boxcars) without also bringing about C (motion of the locomotive). B includes the circumstance that the locomotive is coupled to the first boxcar, and couplings transmit forces both ways. So the structure of the example has been significantly altered by letting C stand for the motion of the locomotive, rather than for the force it exerts. We now have a situation in which the causal biconditional 'C if and only if E' holds, yet neither clause (iii) nor clause (iv) of the definition of causal priority is satisfied. We *can* bring about E in B relatively directly, and we *cannot* do so without tending to bring about C. The structure of the example is thus different from that of the pendulum example.

This consequence of the definition may appear at first sight to be a weakness. In fact, I will contend, it is not a weakness at all; it is just what we want. The *motion* of the locomotive, as such, does *not* cause the motion of the boxcars. Equally, it does not *explain* the motion of the boxcars. If the train were on a frictionless track and not subject to air resistance, locomotive and boxcars would move together, and the motion of each would be explained by Newton's first law without reference to the motion of any of the others. (In that situation, the locomotive would not be exerting any force on the first boxcar; if it did, the train would start to accelerate.) The everyday sense in which the locomotive *pulls* the train includes the idea of exerting a mechanical force; to think that one could analyze this everyday sense in terms of motion alone would be sheer carelessness.

Before we leave the toy train example, one further observation is in order. Because of the friction between the track and the wheels of the boxcars, the cars exert a retrograde force on the locomotive which explains why, despite the torque being applied to *its* wheels, the locomotive does not accelerate. If the force exerted by the locomotive is causally prior to the motion of the boxcars, the retrograde force exerted by the boxcars through the same coupling is causally prior to, and is the cause of, the non-acceleration of the locomotive.[5]

Probabilistic causes: Nancy Cartwright's poison oak, and a tale of two poisons

We have considered examples in which the antecedent condition C is necessary and sufficient for E, and an example in which it is sufficient but not necessary. I spoke of the bringing about of one state of affairs *tending* to bring about another, rather than simply "bringing about another", in order to allow for the type of case in which C, in B, is neither necessary nor sufficient for E, but is sufficient for there being a non-zero probability of E's occurring. Nancy Cartwright has produced an example that is well on the way to being the philosophers' classic illustration of the sort of thing I have in mind:

> I consider eradicating the poison oak at the bottom of my garden by spraying it with defoliant. The can of defoliant claims that the spray is 90 per cent effective; that is, the probability of a plant's dying given that it is sprayed is .9, and the probability of its surviving is .1.[6]

Here we may say that the spraying of a poison oak plant is causally prior to the plant's dying, because one could not spray the plant without tending to bring about its death. I would wish to say the same thing even if the defoliant were, say, 30 per cent effective, or even if it were no more than 0.01 per cent effective, so long as it had some tendency to bring about the death of the plant.

We need not suppose that the spraying is causally necessary for the death of the plant: the background conditions might be such that there is a very slight probability of the plant's dying even if it were not sprayed.

This aspect of the definition of causal priority calls for a number of comments.

(1) Its intent is to bring within the scope of our account of causality those causes which operate by way of laws of a probabilistic kind. It does, I believe, require us to presuppose some notion of lawful, objective physical probabilities. Without such a notion, it would be difficult to give any sense at all to the idea of bringing it about that a particular concrete event, when it was about to occur, had a certain definite probability of occurring. The propensity theory of objective single-case probabilities will serve the purposes of the present theory of causality very well.[7]

(2) In order for C to be causally prior to E relative to the background conditions B, it is not necessary that C *raise* the probability of E from what it would otherwise have been in B. It may indeed happen that C will lower the probability of E; in other cases, it will leave it unchanged.

Consider this example.[8] At a remote campsite a young child poisons himself by drinking a quantity of powerful acid. The probability of the child's dying, if he goes untreated, is .8. The only available antidote is a strong alkali which is also poisonous. A physician who is present calculates that if she were to administer a large enough dose of the alkali to swamp the effect of the acid, there would be a probability of .1 that the child would be fatally poisoned by the alkali. She decides to risk it. The child dies, and a subsequent autopsy shows that death was due to alkali poisoning.

In this case we have no hesitation in saying that the administering of the alkali caused the death of the child, so our theory had *better* count it as causally prior, despite the fact that in the circumstances, the doctor's action lowered the probability of the child's dying from .8 to .1.

But what if the child had lived? The doctor would surely be credited with saving his life, and rightly so, since her action raised the probability of his surviving from .2 to .9.

The noteworthy thing about this example is that whichever outcome occurs, our instinctive judgment is that that outcome was caused by the action of the physician. The reason, it seems, is that

(a) in either case there was a causal process leading from the physician's action to the outcome;

(b) if the child lives, the physician's action may be seen as having raised the probability of the outcome which actually came to pass;

(c) if the child dies, her action will be seen to have initiated a process that pre-empted another causal process which might otherwise have led to the child's death. As this example has shown, one process can pre-empt another process that was tending toward the same result, while actually lowering the probability of the result.

As a first approximation, I suggest that to say the physician's action was causally prior to the outcome is equivalent to saying that (a) holds – i.e., causal priority, as I have defined it, corresponds to the presence of a causal process or mechanism connecting two events or conditions. A refinement of this first approximation will be introduced later.

But apparently our common-sense concept of causation is such that a cause, properly so called, must either increase the probability of its effect, or else pre-empt another potential cause of that same effect. So there is more to causing than being causally prior. This conclusion is corroborated by the following variations on the tale of two poisons.

First variation: Rather than administer a dose of the dangerous alkali which would be enough to cancel the entire effect of the acid, the physician acts more cautiously. She administers only enough to reduce the probability of fatal acid poisoning to .1. The child dies, and autopsy reveals that death was due to acid poisoning. Here we feel no temptation to say that the doctor's action caused the death of the child; her action, we say, was *merely* an unsuccessful attempt to avert his death. (Unlike the unsuccessful attempt described in the original version of the story, which unfortunately caused the very thing it was intended to avert.) This, I am suggesting, is because her action neither increased the probability of the child's dying nor pre-empted another potential cause of death. However, had the child lived, we would have credited her with saving his life, just as in the original story, since her action raised the probability of his surviving from .2 to .9.

Second variation: The doctor at first acts cautiously, as in the first variation, administering a dose of alkali which reduces the probability of death by acid poisoning to .1. She is then informed that the child suffers from a rare congenital condition, as a result of which the acid (but not the alkali) would very likely cause him to go blind even if he survived. Thus it is especially important to counteract all the effect of the acid. She thereupon gives the child a second dose of the alkali, enough to erase the entire effect of the acid and to raise the probability of fatal alkali poisoning to .1. Now if the child dies and the autopsy reveals that death was due to alkali poisoning, we would say that the second dose of alkali, coming as it did on top of the first, had caused his death. This would be an instance of a cause which pre-empts another potential cause but does not alter the probability of the effect at all: the probability that the child would die was .1 both before and after the second dose was given.

But what would we say, in this case, if the child lived? My own intuition would be to say that giving the *first* dose of alkali had prevented his death. The giving of the second dose did nothing to prevent his death, but merely brought about a change in the manner of its prevention – though of course it might be said to have prevented a probable case of blindness.

Not surprisingly, this intuition of mine is in line with the general position I have taken concerning the use of the term 'cause'. But I feel less certain of this particular intuition than of other linguistic intuitions I have appealed to. This, I suppose, is to be expected, since we are dealing with cases at the very borderline of what we would intuitively term causes.

In what follows I will adhere to ordinary usage as we have discovered it to be, and reserve the term 'cause' for a causally prior condition which either raises the probability of the effect, or pre-empts another potential cause.

(3) Thus a condition C may be causally prior to an occurrence E, yet not be acknowledged by common sense as having caused E. In the first variation on the story of the two poisons, the relatively modest dose of the alkali administered to the child in a vain attempt to save his life would count as causally prior to his death, since it was sufficient for there being a probability of .1 that he would die. Yet, as we saw, we would not say that it had caused his death. Similarly, in the second variation on the story, the giving of the second dose of alkali is causally prior to the child's survival, in the event that he does survive, since it is sufficient for there being a probability of .9 that he will survive.

I think it is appropriate to keep the name *'causal* priority' for the relation to which I have applied the term, despite the fact that the events which are its relata form a somewhat larger class than the class of events we recognize as causes and effects. In the first place, what distinguishes the cause from the effect, in full-blooded cases of causation, is that the cause is causally prior to the effect. Secondly, the causal history of an occurrence may reasonably be taken to be made up of the conditions that are causally prior to it, rather than by the slightly smaller class which we would call its causes. If a child has died by poisoning, and we are investigating the causal history of this unhappy event, we will be interested in knowing that the probability of his death, when it occurred, was .1, and we will certainly be interested in the measures taken by the doctor which reduced the probability of death from .8 to .1, whether or not these measures also caused his death. Likewise if the child had lived, and certain of the doctor's actions, while not altering the probability of death, had made a difference to the mechanism by which it came about that the probability of the child's survival was .9.

(4) Why this interest? The conclusion seems inescapable. Because causally prior factors, and not only causes in the narrower sense, are *explanatory*. I think this is true whenever we are dealing with explanations that appeal to causal laws to account for particular phenomena. So I find it appropriate to use the expression 'causal explanation' to mean explanation in terms of causally prior factors, rather than explanation in terms of causes proper.

This conclusion runs counter to what has been claimed in some recent discussions of the subject. I suspect this is because those discussions have been undertaken without the benefit of a clear conception of causal priority, or anything else that would make sense of the asymmetries of explanation.

Thus Nancy Cartwright, discussing her poison oak example, writes:

> Here . . . only the probable outcome, and not the
> improbable, is explained by the spraying. One can

> explain why some plants died by remarking that
> they were sprayed with a powerful defoliant; but
> this will not explain why some survive.[9]

It is evident that this point is connected in her mind with the
thought that only causes, in the narrower sense, can explain; for a
few lines further on we read:

> It is true that spraying with defoliant causes death
> in plants, but it is not true that spraying also causes
> survival. Holding fixed other causes of death,
> spraying with my defoliant will increase the prob-
> ability of a plant's dying; but holding fixed other
> causes of survival, spraying with that defoliant
> will decrease, not increase the chances of a plant's
> surviving.[10]

I think it is plain that although in this case it is the probable outcome which, for Cartwright, is explained by the spraying, in other
circumstances the improbable outcome, and not the probable one,
would be explained. If she had sprayed the poison oak with a defoliant that was 30 per cent effective, this would still, on her view,
explain why some plants died, but not why some survive.

But though spraying plants with a defoliant that is 90 per cent
effective does not cause them to survive, it *does* sometimes explain
their survival. If one of Nancy Cartwright's neighbors were to in-
quire 'How come some of your poison oaks are still surviving – you
sprayed them all with defoliant, didn't you?' the reply 'That defoliant was only 90 per cent effective' would provide exactly the piece
of explanatory information that was required. Being 90 per cent
effective, after all, entails being no more as well as no less than 90
per cent effective.

(Naturally, if another acquaintance, who knew nothing of the spraying, were to ask 'Why are those poison oak thriving so well at the bottom of your garden?' the appropriate response would be 'You don't know the half of it – they are thriving like that even after being sprayed with defoliant.' The search for an explanation of their remarkable vigor could then begin.)

An account very close to the one I would favor has been proposed by Peter Railton, who uses an example which is a variant of Cartwright's.

> Suppose that we are applying a herbicide to a patch of healthy milkweed, and suppose that a dose of this herbicide alters the biochemical state of milkweeds from a normal, healthy state S, in which plants have probability .9999 of surviving 24 hours, to a state S', in which there is but probability of .05 of lasting that long. When we return to the milkweed patch 24 hours after spraying and find to our consternation that a particular plant which received a full dose of herbicide is still standing, how are we to explain this? Presumably, we should point out that the plant was in state S' after the spraying, that in this state it had probability .05 of surviving 24 hours, and that, by chance, it did. The spraying, then, is part of the explanation of survival even though it *lowered* the probability of survival for this plant from what it would otherwise have been. We may not wish to speak of the spraying as a *probabilistic cause* of survival, since we may want to reserve the expression 'probabilistic cause' for factors that *do* raise the probability of an event in the circumstances. Thus, for those plants

failing to survive, we could speak of the spraying as a probabilistic cause of their deaths, while for the plant that survived, it would be strained at best to speak of the spraying as a probabilistic cause of its survival. This suggests that probabilistic explanation is not a mere subspecies of causal explanation.

(Footnote: I have borrowed this example of a plant surviving herbicide spraying from Nancy Cartwright (in conversation), who used it to make a different point. I am, of course, assuming that the effect of the herbicide is genuinely probabilistic – perhaps owing its indeterminism to the chance factors (such as electron location) that influence chemical bonding.)[11]

As I have indicated, I would go along with reserving the term 'probabilistic cause' for factors which either raise the probability of the effect or pre-empt another potential cause. And I would claim that probabilistic explanation *is* a subspecies of causal explanation, in the wider sense of the term I have proposed: explanation by reference to causally prior factors.

Effects with zero probability

What, finally, of the type of case in which C is causally necessary for E in conditions B, but does not suffice to confer a non-zero probability upon E in B? Let us try to construct an example. Betty McPhee was alive and in good health for the past hour. One of the reasons for her survival was an uninterrupted supply of air sufficiently rich in oxygen that she was able to breathe without difficulty. (Another was that the ambient temperature was neither too high nor too low for human life.) Oxygen is, in general, causally necessary, but not sufficient, for survival, and is surely causally prior to the effect, continued life. We know enough to establish an explanatory asymmetry, because clauses (i) and (iii) of the definition of causal priority apply: we can bring about C, the oxygen supply, relatively directly, but no natural agent could create or sustain life except by means that made use of the law-like connection between life and a supply of oxygen. So far, so good. What about clause (ii): could one supply oxygen without tending to produce or sustain life? Not, of course, in the circumstances actually imagined. If, as supposed, the prevailing set of conditions B includes Betty's being in good health and not in any life-threatening situation – why, in those circumstances, C is causally sufficient for E. In other circumstances – e.g., if Betty were gravely ill – supplying oxygen would do no more than raise the probability of her survival from zero to a value less than 1. Given that the probability of a human being's surviving for an hour in the absence of oxygen is zero, the only case in which supplying oxygen fails to raise the probability of survival is the case in which some other factor is present which causes the probability to remain at zero – e.g., if another factor which is causally necessary for life is lacking. If the temperature of the air adjacent to Betty's skin were minus 150 degrees Celsius, supplying oxygen would not raise the probability of her staying alive for an hour. In such a case, there would be no effect E, Betty's survival, to be explained. It is next to impossible, therefore, that there should actually be a pair of events or conditions C and E such that C is causally necessary for E and yet C does not, in the prevailing conditions, confer a non-zero probability on E.

The only conceivable type of counterexample would be a case in which E occurred despite having a probability of zero. Consider, for instance, what happens when you throw a dart at a dartboard. The number of geometrical points on the surface of the board is nothing less than a non-denumerable infinity. Hence for any one point, the probability that it will be the point of impact of the exact center of the pointy end of the dart is zero. Yet some one point will in fact be the point of impact.

I see three possible ways of responding to this type of example.

(1) One may flatly refuse to describe events in the real world in this sort of way. Any real dartboard can, after all, be divided into sub-regions, each of which will have a non-zero probability of being the region in which the dart makes its impact. We can make the sub-regions small as we please; when we outrun the capabilities of our actual measuring instruments, we can imagine we have finer and more accurate ones. Thus we can approach asymptotically to the description of the situation in terms of geometrical points, while insisting that being able, strictly and soberly, to apply such a description, is a terminus that can never be reached even in theory.

(2) One may adopt a non-standard measure theory – one which allows probability measures to take infinitesimal values. It then becomes possible to say that for each point on the surface of the dartboard, the probability that it will be the point of impact of the center of the dart is infinitesimally small, but nevertheless not zero.[12] This leaves us free to deny that events with a physical probability of zero ever occur, and to affirm that the throwing of the dart is causally prior to its striking a particular geometrical point on the dartboard.

(3) Lastly, one may concede that E, the impact of the center of the dart at a particular geometrical point, did occur, despite having a physical probability of zero, and that therefore C, the throwing of the dart, is not causally prior to E. In such a case, we could say that C made E possible, and that C is antecedent to E in the weakened sense that clauses (i) and (iii) of the definition of causal priority apply. But we could not say that C was causally prior to E in the sense of satisfying the definition as a whole.

Absolute causal priority

The relative concept of causal priority defined above, which makes the priority of C to E relative to a set {B} of background conditions, will be the one most frequently used. It is possible, nevertheless, to specify a relation of absolute causal priority, which is defined along the lines of the definition already given, but without being relativized to a set of background conditions. I present, first, an overall condition for the priority of one event or circumstance over another, and then a trio of formulae akin to the "reduction sentences" of Rudolf Carnap.[13] Taken together, the four formulae specify conditions that are necessary and sufficient for C's being causally prior to E absolutely:

(D2) C is causally prior to E only if either N_c (~C ⊃ ~E) or N_c (C ⊃ E) or N_c (C ⊃ Prob(E) > 0).[14]

(D2.1) If N_c (~C ⊃ ~E), then C is causally prior to E if and only if

(i) it is possible to bring about C relatively directly, but

(ii) it is not possible to bring about E relatively directly.

(D2.2) If ~N_c (~C ⊃ ~E), but N_c (C ⊃ E), then C is causally prior to E if and only if

(i) it is not possible to bring about C without thereby bringing about E, but

(ii) it is possible to bring about E without thereby bringing about C.

(D2.3) If $\sim N_c (\sim C \supset \sim E)$ and $\sim N_c (C \supset E)$, but $N_c (C \supset Prob(E) > 0)$, then C is causally prior to E if and only if

(i) it is not possible to bring about C without thereby bringing it about that $Prob(E) > 0$, but

(ii) it is possible to bring about E without thereby bringing it about that $Prob(C) > 0$.

The definitions just given may be used to define asymmetrical relationships of causal necessity and sufficiency, thus:

(D2.4) C is causally necessary for E $=_{df} N_c (\sim C \supset \sim E)$ and C is causally prior to E.

(D2.5) C is causally sufficient for E $=_{df} N_c (C \supset E)$ and C is causally prior to E.

It is a consequence of (D2.4) and (D2.5) that there will be pairs of occurrences {A,B} which are causally connected in the sense that the causal biconditional $N_c (A \equiv B)$ holds, but of which we will be unable to say that either is necessary or sufficient for the other, in the stronger sense we have just introduced. A clear example would be if a single cause C has two effects, E_1 and E_2, such that C is necessary and sufficient both for E_1 and for E_2, yet E_1 and E_2 are connected only by their common cause C.

In what has gone before, I have refrained from calling into question the idea that 'C is causally necessary for E' could be equated simply to the conditional N_c ($\sim$C $\supset$ $\sim$E), and 'C is causally sufficient for E' to N_c (C $\supset$ E). But I have only *used* the expressions 'causally necessary' and 'causally sufficient' in cases where the strengthened definitions (D2.4) and (D2.5) would apply. I believe that (D2.4) and (D2.5) accurately capture what is ordinarily meant by 'causally necessary' and 'causally sufficient', although some philosophers have expressly adopted the weaker definitions that make no mention of causal priority.[15]

Consequences of these definitions

I have portrayed causal priority as the relation that obtains between a cause and its effect, and between stages of a causal process. In the recent discussion, some philosophers have approached the topic by way of inquiring into the nature of cause and effect, and others have approached it by way of asking what constitutes a causal explanation. That causal priority is the same thing as explanatory antecedence tends to be either overlooked or taken for granted. J.L. Mackie notes that "causes explain their effects and not vice versa".[16] He takes this as a datum to be explained, not as a theoretical position in its own right which would need to be argued for. Carl Hempel and Paul Oppenheim state that the antecedent conditions which figure in a deductive-nomological explanation of an explanandum event E may be said to cause E.[17] N.R. Hanson writes, "The primary reason for referring to the cause of x is to explain x. There are as many causes of x as there are explanations of x".[18] I have yet to see the identity argued for – not that I think that an argument is required: all that is needed is the recognition that we do regard causal priority as explanatory.

It would seem that the only argument *against* the identification of causal priority with explanatory antecedence would stem from an "actualist" or "extensionalist" view of causation. Some philosophers have maintained that causation needs to be treated separately from explanation, on the grounds that causation, unlike explanation, is a relation between concrete occurrences that are describable in an extensional language referring only to the actual world.[19] Now the analysis I have given of causal priority, in terms of modalities derived from the language of agency, will certainly rule out the possibility of giving a complete description of causal relations in extensional terms, *unless* the modal terms themselves can be construed in an extensionalist fashion. There has indeed been a noteworthy assault on the problem of causality which employs the modal term 'causally necessary' but offers a non-intensional analysis of its meaning: I refer to Hans Reichenbach's philosophy of causality, which has already been examined in some detail.[20] But I know of no actualist account of causal priority, as such, other than that of J.L. Mackie – an account which its own author has admitted is unsuccessful.[21] What follows from this is not that extensionalists need shrink from identifying causal priority with explanatory antecedence, but simply that they will need to develop an alternative analysis of causal priority. But this they will need to do in any case. When and if they were to succeed in producing an actualist or extensionalist analysis of causal priority, we could proceed to ask ourselves whether it would also serve as a criterion of explanatory antecedence.

I deliberately defined causal priority in such a way that it would be an asymmetrical relation. It follows immediately that the relation is also irreflexive: no occurrence can be causally prior to itself. What is not immediately obvious is whether causal priority is transitive or non-transitive.

There is a strong case for declaring it to be transitive: I cannot think of a clear example of a trio of occurrences C, D, E, which might turn up in the normal course of events, such that relative to the same set of background conditions, C is causally prior to

D, and D to E, but not C to E. Yet as metaphysicians, it behoves us to allow, whenever we can, for the logical possibility of wildly abnormal trains of events, as well as for the normal. And it turns out that, if we were to commit ourselves to the idea that causal priority must be a transitive relation, one class of conceivable though highly abnormal sequences of events would thereby be ruled out, viz., closed causal loops. This follows from the fact that causal priority is asymmetrical and irreflexive. But to say *a priori* that closed causal loops are impossible seems foolish; it should be a matter for empirical investigation whether or not the universe contains causal processes or mechanisms which form closed loops. Professional caution therefore suggests that we should take causal priority to be non-transitive.

Moreover, this approach still leaves us the possibility of defining a transitive relation of *causal ancestry* which may be applied to causal processes and mechanisms. Let a, b, c, ... be a finite sequence of events or circumstances such that, in the prevailing conditions, a is causally prior to b, b is causally prior to c, and so forth. Such a sequence may be called a causal process. One occurrence may then be said to be the causal ancestor of another if and only if there is a causal process leading from the one to the other.[22] Causal ancestry, thus defined, is non-symmetrical and non-reflexive. If there are such things as closed causal loops, then there will be some events which are their own causal ancestors. (Similarly, if there were such a thing as time travel, a man might be his own grandfather.) In the normal run of things, however, the causal ancestors of any occurrence are all causally prior to it.

We have managed to define causal priority without reference to the temporal relation between cause and effect. This leaves open the logical possibility of backward causation – sequences of events in which the effect occurs earlier than the cause. Whether or not backward causation ever occurs in nature, or is indeed *causally* possible, is a matter which, along with the business of closed causal loops, we leave to the empirical sciences to investigate. That, I think, is as it should be.

Our analysis has this consequence, however: *if* there is such a thing as backward causation, then some conceivable natural agent will have the power to bring about the past, i.e., to act so as to bring about a state of affairs C at t_2 which causes an event E to occur at an earlier time t_1. This is not to say, of course, that any human agent would then have such powers, much less the ability to exercise them in a controlled fashion. It is conceivable that some subatomic particles might be discovered occasionally to travel backwards in time, yet humans find they lack the power to *make* a particle do this.

Lastly, it should be noted that bringing about the past is not the same thing as altering the past. The latter notion *is* self-contradictory. It involves the idea of acting to bring about C at t_2, which causes E at t_1, when in fact ~E was the case at t_1. But E and ~E cannot both be the case. If there is backward causation, some things which have already happened may turn out to be caused by things which have yet to happen. But what has already happened cannot – logically cannot – be made not to have happened. Even if the past can be brought about, it cannot be altered or prevented.[23]

I have said that it is typically in virtue of a set of covering laws that one occurrence is causally prior to another, relative to a given set of background conditions. This entails a dual role for laws: they must say, not only what states of affairs and sequences of events are causally possible, but also which kinds of occurrences are causally prior to which other kinds. If we recall our analysis of basic causal notions in terms of natural agency, it becomes clearer just what this amounts to. Laws of nature express, in general terms, systematic constraints that limit the activities of natural agents. These constraints impose limitations, both upon the results it is possible to achieve, and upon the means by which it is possible to bring them about. In particular, laws will tell us that in conditions of kind B, it is possible to bring about C without having to do so by bringing about E, but it is not possible in such conditions to bring about E except by bringing about C, and so forth.

Levels of causal analysis

In conclusion, we need to note that the analysis of a causal process, in terms of natural agents and the possibility of bringing about one event or state of affairs by bringing about another, may be carried out on different levels. There can be a "broad-brush" account and a more detailed, fine-grained account of one and the same process. In most everyday accounts of human behavior, raising one's forearm is treated as a basic action, not one that is accomplished *by* doing something else. For instance, by raising your forearm while holding the handle of your coffee cup, you lift the cup to your lips.

But in fact, raising your forearm is the end stage of a complex causal process that begins in the brain: you raised your forearm by contracting your biceps, and you contracted your biceps by sending certain impulses through the efferent nerves, and so on. The smaller details of the process of raising your forearm will be irretrievably far beneath the level of consciousness. If the process of unearthing tiny details is carried far enough, we will get to the point where individual molecules are being treated as natural agents, making things happen. What is more, it will be reasonable to say that the act of raising your forearm begins with the transmission of impulses from the brain; yet it will not be reasonable to insist on naming a precise moment when the act begins.

It is necessary to emphasize this point in order to forestall a certain confusion. A physiologist who was investigating the workings of the efferent nervous system, and wished the laboratory subject who was under study to send those impulses that would result in a contraction of the biceps, would give the order, "Raise your forearm". By *beginning* to raise her forearm, the subject would produce the nerve impulses that were of interest to the physiologist. The act of raising her arm begins well before the arm is fully raised – even before impulses travel along the efferent nerves. So we have here no grounds for concluding that "by raising her forearm, the subject sends impulses through her efferent nerves", in any sense that would imply the presence of backward causation or even a misleading appearance thereof.

---

1   Hume, *Treatise*, Book I, Part III, Section II, pp. 75-76.

2   Hume, *Enquiry*, Section VII, Part II, pp. 76-77.

3   I take this way of defining 'basic action' from Georg Henrik von Wright 1971, p. 68. Von Wright in turn got it from F. Stoutland 1968. See von Wright, *loc. cit.*, and n. 39, for the reasons for preferring this definition to the original one used by Arthur Danto.

4   See Carl G. Hempel 1962, esp. pp. 108-110. The pendulum example was first introduced into the discussion by Hempel in this paper.

5   Examples of this type are discussed by David H. Sanford in Sanford 1976, and by J.L. Mackie in Mackie 1979.

6   Nancy Cartwright 1979, pp. 429-431.

7   See Popper 1957, p. 69; Peter Railton 1978, p. 222; also R.N. Giere 1973, pp. 467-483, which Railton mentions in his article.

8   See Cartwright 1979, p. 428, for the simple illustration which was the starting point for the development of my more elaborate one.

9   Cartwright 1979, p. 425.

10 Cartwright 1979, pp. 425-426.

11 Railton 1981, p. 238.

12 I owe this suggestion to Peter Railton, in conversation.

13 See Rudolf Carnap 1936.

14 As in Chapter 3, I have used the subscript 'c' to distinguish causal modalities, which are defined by means of the idea of a natural agent, from the modal terms referring to agency in general.

15 Notably Richard Taylor. See Taylor 1966, pp. 28-29, and Taylor 1974, p. 99. J.L. Mackie distinguishes the two possible ways of defining 'causally necessary' and 'causally sufficient' – i.e., with, and without, a mention of causal priority – in Mackie 1974, p. 53.

16 Mackie 1974, p. 185.

17 Carl G. Hempel and Paul Oppenheim 1948, in Hempel 1965, p. 250.

18 N.R. Hanson 1958, p. 54.

19 See, e.g., Donald Davidson 1967, pp. 691-703.

20 See above, ch. 3, pp. 108-116.

21 See above, ch. 3, p. 124.

22 The stratagem used here is based upon the one used by David Lewis in Lewis 1973, p. 563. Lewis there calls it the "usual way" of constructing the definition of a transitive relation when one has the definition of a corresponding non-transitive relation already in hand.

23 For references to the literature on backward causation, see Mackie 1974, p. 162, n. 2, and Bob Brier 1974, pp. 102-103.

CHAPTER 5
Laws and Explanations

Causes produce their effects – make them happen. That has been the basic, unsurprising message of this essay so far; but there are complications concerning such matters as possibility and necessity, laws of nature, and the direction of causation. Had it not been for those complications, there would have been no excuse for this essay.

Likewise, causes explain their effects. This is another side – the epistemological side – of the same issue. But again there are complications; so we need to examine the concept, and the practice, of explanation.

In the very simplest cases of experiencing our own agency, and perceiving our efficacy in making things happen, the explanation of the effect by the cause is immediately apparent. You raise your arm: this is something you did; your arm goes up *because* you raised it, and the 'because' expresses both the causation and the explanation of what happened. Nothing more is called for, at this very primitive level of enquiry. But as soon as enquiring minds get busy asking more searching questions about why things happen as they do, more elaborate patterns of explanation come into play; and these now need to be examined.

The varieties of explanation

Put very generally, we consider a phenomenon to be explained when we are able to see it in an appropriate context. To give an explanation is to assemble the required elements and arrange them in a pattern which is an instance of some accepted type of configuration – what I shall call, hereafter, a "schema of explanation". When one sees this to have been successfully done, one's reaction is, "Now I understand why this phenomenon occurred. But for perceiving it in this context, I would have known *that* it occurred, but not *why*". The concept of explanation is normative in the same kind of way as other epistemological concepts, such as 'knowledge', 'evidence', 'justified belief', and so forth.

It will be my contention that we in this culture have, and use, at least four different schemata of explanation. Quite possibly we have more than that; but for our purposes we need discuss only four. As I shall define them, none of the four is reducible to any of its fellows, and I do not believe it would help matters to redefine them so that reductions of this sort would be possible. The gain in systematization would, I think, be purchased at too high a cost in analytical power.

I define an explanation as a set of true statements, one of which describes the phenomenon to be explained. This latter statement will be termed, following Hempel and Oppenheim, the *explanandum*; the other statements in the set, which are adduced to account for or explain the phenomenon described in the explanandum, will be called, collectively, the *explanans*.[1]

Of the four schemata of explanation I propose to distinguish and discuss, three will be examined in this chapter: the deductive-nomological (D-N) schema, the statistical relevance (S-R) schema; and lastly, the deductive-nomological-probabilistic (D-N-P) schema. The fourth one, which I will call the rational agency (R-A) schema, will be discussed in the following chapter in the context of the causation of rational behavior.

THE DEDUCTIVE-NOMOLOGICAL (D-N) SCHEMA

(a) The Hempel-Oppenheim account

Of the four schemata, the D-N schema is the most familiar to students of philosophy. Spelled out as early as 1843 by John Stuart Mill, and in 1935 by Karl Popper, it received its classic formulation in the 1948 paper by Carl Hempel and Paul Oppenheim.[2] Their formulation of the D-N schema, which they designate form (2.1), is as follows:[3]

$$
\text{Logical deduction} \left[\begin{array}{l} \left\{ \begin{array}{ll} C_1, C_2, \ldots, C_k & \text{Statements of antecedent conditions} \\ L_1, L_2, \ldots, L_r & \text{General Laws} \end{array} \right\} \text{Explanans} \\ \overline{} \\ \quad\;\; E \qquad\quad \left. \begin{array}{l} \text{Description of the empirical phenomenon to be explained} \end{array} \right\} \text{Explanandum} \end{array} \right.
$$

An adequate explanation, they remark, must consist entirely of true statements; this is the empirical condition of adequacy. In addition, it must satisfy three logical conditions of adequacy.

(R1) The explanandum must be a logical consequence of the explanans; in other words, the explanandum must be logically deducible from the information contained in the explanans, for otherwise, the explanans would not constitute adequate grounds for the explanandum.

(R2) The explanans must contain general laws, and these must actually be required for the derivation of the explanandum. We shall not make it a necessary condition for a sound explanation, however, that the explanans must contain at least one statement which is not a law; for, to mention just one reason, we would surely want to consider as an explanation the derivation of the general regularities governing the motion of double stars from the laws of celestial mechanics, even though all the statements in the explanans are general laws.

(R3) The explanans must have empirical content; i.e., it must be capable, at least in principle, of test by experiment or observation. This condition is implicit in (R1); for since the explanandum is assumed to describe some empirical phenomenon, it follows from (R1) that the explanans entails at least one consequence of empirical character, and this fact confers upon it testability and empirical content.[4]

An important concern, for our purposes, will be the status of the general laws that figure in explanations of the D-N type. Hempel and Oppenheim make it plain that they intend to refer to causal laws such as those of chemistry and celestial mechanics, and these must be exceptionless regularities:

The type of explanation which has been considered here so far is often referred to as causal explanation. If E describes a particular event, then the antecedent circumstances described in the sentences $C_1, C_2, \ldots, C_k$ may be said jointly to "cause" that event, in the sense that there are certain empirical regularities, expressed by the laws $L_1, L_2, \ldots, L_r$, which imply that whenever conditions of the kind indicated by $C_1, C_2, \ldots, C_k$ occur, an event of the kind described in E will take place. Statements such as $L_1, L_2, \ldots, L_r$ which assert general and unexceptional connections between specified characteristics of events, are customarily called causal, or deterministic laws. They are to be distinguished from the so-called statistical laws which assert that in the long run, an explicitly stated percentage of all cases satisfying a given set of conditions are accompanied by an event of a certain specified kind. Certain cases of scientific explanation involve "subsumption" of the explanandum under a set of laws of which at least some are statistical in character. ... The present essay will be restricted to an examination of the deductive type of explanation.[5]

Later on in the essay, they give an exact explication of the notion of a causal law in terms of a formal language L, whose syntactical structure is that of the first-order functional calculus.

However, there are problems with this account of the nature of causal laws, springing from the fact that the artificial language L is an extensional language, containing no modal terms of any kind. In particular, the terms 'causally necessary' and 'causally possible' are missing from the vocabulary of L. Hempel came to be very much aware of these now familiar problems, and wrote in 1966:

We saw that the laws invoked in deductive-nomological explanations have the basic form: 'In all cases when conditions of kind F are realized, conditions of kind G are realized as well'. But, interestingly, not all statements of this universal form, even if true, can qualify as laws of nature. ...

[C]onsider the statement: 'All bodies consisting of pure gold have a mass of less than 100,000 kilograms'. No doubt all bodies of gold ever examined by man conform to it; thus, there is considerable confirmatory evidence for it and no disconfirming instances are known. Indeed, it is quite possible that never in the history of the universe has there been or will there be a body of pure gold with a mass of 100,000 kilograms or more. In this case, the proposed generalization would not only be well confirmed, but true. And yet, we would presumably regard its truth as accidental, on the ground that nothing in the basic laws of nature as conceived in contemporary science precludes the possibility of there being – or even the possibility of our producing – a solid gold object with a mass exceeding 100,000 kilograms.

Thus, a scientific law cannot be adequately defined as a true statement of universal form: this characterization expresses a necessary, but not a sufficient, condition for laws of the kind here under discussion.

What distinguishes genuine laws from accidental generalizations? . . .

One telling and suggestive difference . . . is this: a law can, whereas an accidental generalization cannot, serve to support *counterfactual conditionals*, i.e., statements of the form 'If *A* were (had been) the case, then *B* would be (would have been) the case', where in fact *A* is not (has not been) the case. . . . Similarly, a law, in contrast to an accidentally true generalization, can support *subjunctive conditionals,* i.e., sentences of the type 'If *A* should come to pass, then so would *B'*, where it is left open whether or not *A* will in fact come to pass. ...

Closely related to this difference is another one, which is of special interest to us: a law can, whereas an accidental generalization cannot, serve as a basis for an explanation.[6]

Now if we were to add to Hempel and Oppenheim's language L a modal operator, "causally necessary", and with it a set of syntactical rules and axioms which would turn L into a modal or intensional language, the problem of marking off causal statements from other statements would be solved at a stroke. Causal laws would simply be those universal generalizations to which the operator "causally necessary" was attached; they could be classified as fundamental or derivative according as they were, or were not, free of ineliminable references to particular entities, events, or spatio-temporal regions. Causal conditionals would be those derivable from causal laws, and would be similarly flagged by the modal operator "causally necessary".

(Alternatively, a notion of causal entailment might be introduced, and treated as a dyadic modality along the lines suggested by some contemporary logicians for coping with logical entailment. This approach has the virtue of avoiding the "paradoxes of causal implication", parallel to Lewis's paradoxes of strict implication, which would inevitably result from writing causal conditionals in the form $N_c[p \supset q]$.[7])

Taken by itself, such a move represents, at best, a linguistic advance. It does nothing to resolve the dispute between supporters of a "regularity" or "actualist" theory of causation and those who believe that "a complete account of causality is ineluctably modal".[8] That dispute will concern the *semantics* of the operator "causally necessary", or of whatever other symbol is employed to mark the distinction between causal laws and causal conditionals, on the one hand, and accidentally true generalizations and material conditionals, on the other. Likewise, the question of how we know causal propositions to be true may be regarded as a question about the pragmatics of the term "causally necessary".

But in the light of the results reached in Chapter 3, we may take "causally necessary" to connote what holds in all possible worlds in which the laws of nature are the same as in the actual world, and understand a law of nature to be a systematic constraint on the abilities of whatever natural agents there happen to be. As for how we acquire knowledge of such constraints on the abilities of natural agents, it is above all by actively manipulating experimental situations and doing our utmost to bring about exceptions to the laws that we have guessed might obtain in the universe. Failure to bring about an exception will signal success in confirming our conjecture.

The way is thus cleared for viewing causal necessity, as defined in chapter 3, as the feature that distinguishes laws of nature from accidentally true generalizations, and causal conditionals from material conditionals.

The second change we may proceed to make in the "classical" account of the D-N schema, as formulated by Hempel and Oppenheim and quoted above, has to do with the statements of antecedent conditions which form part of the explanans. It appears that at the time of writing their 1948 paper, Hempel and Oppenheim took "antecedent conditions" to mean, simply, conditions which occurred earlier in time than the event to be explained. They did not stop to consider the possibility that the conditions which explain a given state of affairs might be, not antecedent, but simultaneous to it. More remote still from their thinking would have been the suggestion that the explanatory conditions might, as a matter of logical possibility, occur *later* than the event or state of affairs that they explain. But once we are equipped with the concept of causal priority developed in Chapter 4, it is possible to say simply that events and conditions mentioned in the explanans of a D-N explanation must be causally prior to the event or state of affairs mentioned in the explanandum. As we have seen, such an approach will provide a solution to the problem of the asymmetries of explanation – a problem which began to plague Hempel once he returned to the topic and perceived that this was a major difficulty with the version of the D-N schema he and Oppenheim had set out in the 1948 paper.[9]

Writing in 1962, Hempel presented the problem by considering two examples that subsequently were widely discussed in the literature. The first of these concerned how the period of a free-swinging pendulum throughout a given interval of time is explained by the length of the pendulum, together with the gravitational force acting on the bob. The length of the pendulum explains the period, but not *vice versa* – and neither can be said to be antecedent to the other, as the same interval of time is involved. The second example, which Hempel credited to his colleague Sylvain Bromberger, concerned a flagpole that subtends an angle of 45 degrees when viewed from ground level at a distance of 80 feet. From these facts, together with some elementary geometry, one can deduce that the flagpole is 80 feet high; but this is no explanation of the height of the pole, despite the fact that the *argument* fits the pattern of a D-N explanation. If anything, it is the height of the pole that explains the subtended angle.[10]

It would not be profitable to trace the whole history of the debate concerning the asymmetries of explanation. For our purposes, it is sufficient to note that we may now complete the characterization of the D-N schema of explanation thus. In a complete D-N explanation, the explanatory conditions C_1, C_2, . . ., C_k must be antecedent to the explanandum E in the sense that the conjunction $C_1 \bullet C_2 \bullet \ldots \bullet C_k$ is causally prior to E absolutely. It then follows that each C_i is causally prior to E relative to the remaining members of the set $C_1, C_2, \ldots, C_k$ as background conditions.

(b) Explanations of laws

One type of scientific explanation that is not covered by the D-N model as outlined above is the type in which a law or regularity is explained by being deduced from a more profound or comprehensive scientific law. One of Hempel's favorite examples was the deduction of Kepler's laws of planetary motion from Newton's laws of motion and gravitation.[11] Beyond all doubt we find such derivations explanatory and intellectually satisfying. We have no hesitation in making the judgment, *"That's* why a planet in orbit around a star sweeps out equal areas in equal times: Newton's laws entail that any body orbiting around another body would do so". But since no particular circumstances or conditions have been mentioned, we do not have an instance of the D-N schema of explanation. Nor can one physical law be said to be causally prior to another; the relation between the more comprehensive law and the derived law is simply one of logical entailment.

What caused Hempel and Oppenheim to set aside this class of explanations, while acknowledging that they had not been covered by their D-N model, was the difficulty of finding a satisfactory criterion of comprehensiveness. Plainly Newton's laws are more comprehensive than Kepler's; however, Kepler's laws (K) could also be deduced from the simple conjunction of K with Boyle's law, B. But the deduction of K from K•B "would not be considered as an explanation of the regularities stated in Kepler's laws; rather, it would be viewed as representing, in effect, a pointless 'explanation' of Kepler's laws by themselves".[12]

Michael Friedman and others have pursued this problem of the criterion of comprehensiveness; but since there is nothing I wish to add to what they have said, I will not pursue it further myself.[13]

(c) D-N explanation, necessity, and determinism

An important feature of D-N explanation, as we have characterized it, is that the explanandum E is causally necessitated by the conjunction of explanatory conditions $C_1 \bullet C_2 \bullet \ldots \bullet C_k$. Put another way, the truth of the explanans entails that E had to occur; given the antecedent conditions, there was no causally possible alternative to its occurring. In virtue of the covering laws $L_1, L_2, \ldots, L_r$, the conjoint state of affairs $C_1 \bullet C_2 \bullet \ldots \bullet C_k \bullet {\sim}E$ would be causally impossible.

It will be my contention that this is not a feature of the other schemata of explanation; hence, not a requirement for explanation in general.

Determinism may now be defined as the thesis that there is a D-N explanation for every occurrence and every state of affairs. It will be seen that from the thesis of determinism, thus defined, it does not follow that anyone will ever *know* the explanation of every (or any) state of affairs. For all determinism asserts to the contrary, there might be happenings whose explanation remained forever unknown. This is due to the fact that we defined an explanation as a set of statements that are true – not as a set of statements that are known to be true.

THE PRAGMATICS OF EXPLANATION

(a) Two senses of "complete explanation"

In the light of what has been said, a further question now arises: what is meant by a *complete* D-N explanation? We may distinguish two senses of "complete explanation"; I will call them the ambitious sense and the modest sense. The modest sense is the one that will prove to be the more useful of the two.

An explanation that was complete in the ambitious sense would relate the *whole* causal history of the explanandum, starting with the Big Bang and omitting not the tiniest twitch of the lowliest subatomic particle. Not only that; each twist and turn of the story would be traced back to previous phases by means of theoretical principles so luminous and comprehensive as to satisfy the most strenuous intellectual curiosity. It would be nothing less than what Peter Railton calls an "ideal explanatory text".

> [A]n ideal text for the explanation of the outcome of a causal process would look something like this: an inter-connected series of law-based accounts of all the nodes and links in the causal network culminating in the explanandum, complete with a fully detailed description of the causal mechanism involved and theoretical derivations of all the covering laws involved. ... It would be the whole story concerning why the explanandum occurred, relative to a correct theory of the lawful dependencies of the world. Such an ideal causal D-N text would be infinite if time were without beginning or infinitely divisible, and plainly there is no question of ever setting such an ideal text down on paper. (Indeed, if time is continuous, an ideal causal text might have to be non-denumerably infinite – and thus "ideal" in a very strong sense.) ...
>
> Is it preposterous to suggest that any such ideal could exist for scientific explanation and understanding? Has anyone ever attempted or even wanted to construct an ideal causal or probabilistic

> text? It is not preposterous if we recognize that the
> actual ideal is not to *produce* such texts, but to have
> the ability (in principle) to produce arbitrary parts
> of them.[14]

Now when we do succeed in producing an arbitrary part of some ideal explanatory text, what we produce may or may not be a complete explanation in the modest sense. By the latter I mean simply a set of statements that conforms to one of the accepted schemata of explanation, such as the D-N schema, with all of the required elements present. A complete explanation (in the modest sense) is to be contrasted with a truncated explanation, as a fully articulated argument is contrasted with an enthymeme.

Seldom do we humans ever give expression to a complete explanation, even in the modest sense. Most often we give truncated versions, taking for granted a substantial amount of background information.

Let me make very clear what is being claimed here. When I say that a speaker takes a certain fact for granted, I do not mean that he knows it to be a fact, consciously assumes it to be a fact, would be able to cite it if questioned, or even would understand what the question meant.

"Why is the grass so much greener today?" "Because it rained yesterday".

The gardener who produced this explanation, and more or less knew it to be correct, might have not the slightest idea of the other factors that must be present in order for a rainfall to cause the greening of the grass. Nor need he know any biochemistry. Nor need he even have at his command any statement of the regularities concerning the conditions under which rainfall is followed by greening of the grass. (It isn't always, and he might very well know that.)

He takes background conditions and covering laws for granted only in the following sense. The explanation he gives, 'Because it rained yesterday', mentions one causally relevant factor. It invites the further question, 'What has rain got to do with it?' A brief answer to this question would invite yet more questions requesting clarification of the connection between the explanans, as so far given, and the explanandum. The correct answers to *these* questions could be assembled into a complete D-N explanation, or else into a complete explanation exemplifying some other schema. When we have a complete D-N explanation, it does not invite further questions in the same way. If an inquirer is stimulated to ask further why-questions, those questions will be requests either for an explanation of one of the C_i or for a set of laws more comprehensive or intellectually satisfying than $L_1, L_2, \ldots, L_r$. Analogously for the other schemata of explanation.

To say that a given situation "invites" certain questions is not to say that anyone will in fact ask those questions. But it is to imply that the pragmatics of the language or conceptual scheme being employed rule those questions in order. By the same token, to say that the D-N pattern is one of the schemata of explanation we employ is to make a claim about the pragmatics of our language; it is to say that once a complete D-N explanation is offered, a further question of the form, 'What has that explanans got to do with the explanandum?' is out of order.

Which schemata of explanation we employ is thus a matter to be settled by examining the pragmatics of our language. At the same time, I think it will be possible to characterize each of those schemata in logico-semantic terms. That is to say, I think it will be possible to formulate, for each schema, a criterion that reads, "A set of statements is an explanation of this type if and only if the following conditions are met . . ." and then mentions conditions having to do with the truth-values of the statements, and with their relationships to one another, but *not* with the context in which they are uttered or in which it would be appropriate to utter them.

This means that I think of explanation as essentially a logico-semantic concept (though of course there are rules belonging to the pragmatics of our language which tell us when and how to apply it). Contrasted with a logico-semantic concept is what may be called a purely pragmatic concept. A purely pragmatic concept is one that cannot be characterized in logico-semantic terms, but can only be explicated by going to the level of pragmatics. For instance, there have been those who contended that 'law of nature' is a purely pragmatic concept. What they have meant by this is that it is impossible to say correctly 'A statement is a law of nature if and only if...', filling in the blank with conditions having to do with the syntax and semantics of the statement. Rather, they say, one must look at how a statement is used by a particular speaker on a particular occasion. If he takes a universal statement 'All F are G' and uses it to back up the counterfactual assertion 'If a had been F, it would have been G', this is an indication that he is employing 'All F are G' as a law of nature on this occasion. But there is nothing more to *being* a law of nature than *being used as* a law of nature.[15] On such a view

> [l]aws are to universal truths what shims are to slivers of wood and metal; the latter *become* the former by being used in a certain way. There is a functional difference, nothing else.[16]

It will, I think, be evident that I do not concur with this "functionalist" view, which portrays 'law of nature' as a purely pragmatic concept. But for the present, our business is with the concept, and practice, of explanation.

(b) Bas van Fraassen and the pragmatics of explanation

In his discussion of the pragmatics of explanation, Bas van Fraassen notes two features of the linguistic situation that obtains when a speaker asks 'Why E?' and intends his question as a request for an explanation of E.[17]

First, it is normal for the speaker to have in mind a set of alternative possible events or conditions, any one of which might have occurred in place of E. Van Fraassen calls this the *contrast-class* X. E itself may or may not be taken to be a member of X. The question 'Why E?' is then construed by van Fraassen to mean 'Why E and *not* any (other) member of X?' The height of the flagpole, for example, explains why the subtended angle is 45 degrees and not any other angle. It follows that the same form of words 'Why E?' may be used to form different explanation requests.

Consider the question

3. Why did Adam eat the apple?

This same question can be construed in various ways, as is shown by the variants:

3a. Why was it Adam who ate the apple?
3b. Why was it the apple Adam ate?
3c. Why did Adam *eat* the apple? . . .

The difference between these various requests is that they point to different contrasting alternatives. For example, 3b may ask why Adam ate *the apple* rather than some other fruit in the garden, while 3c asks perhaps why Adam *ate* the apple rather than give it back to Eve untouched. So to 3b, 'because he was hungry' is not a good answer, whereas to 3c it is.[18]

Van Fraassen's second point is that what a person will accept as a good answer to the question 'Why E?' will depend upon his background and interests. Suppose E is the death of a motorist in a highway accident. To the pathologist, the cause of death – the explanatory factor – is multiple hemorrhage; to the insurance adjuster, it is negligence on the part of the driver; to a mechanic it is defective brakes; to a civic planner it is the presence of tall shrubbery at the corner.

> It is important to notice that in a certain sense these different answers cannot be combined. The civic planner 'keeps fixed' the mechanical constitution of the car, and gives his answer in the conviction that regardless of the mechanical defects, which made a fast stop impossible, the accident need not have happened. The mechanic 'keeps fixed' the physical environment; despite the shrubbery obscuring vision, the accident need not have happened if the brakes had been better. What one varies, the other keeps fixed, and you cannot do both at once. In other words, the selection of the salient causal factor is not simply a matter of pointing to the most interesting one, not like the selection of a tourist attraction; it is a matter of *competing* counterfactuals.[19]

Having made these valid and illuminating points concerning the pragmatics of explanation, van Fraassen draws a conclusion that does not in fact follow from his observations. He would apparently have us believe that explanation is a purely pragmatic notion; that there is no such thing as a *semantics* of explanation. If this were so, it would be impossible to explicate the statement 'S explains E' (where 'S' stands for the conjunction of all the statements in the explanans) in terms of the content and truth of the statements in S and their logico-semantic relations to one another and to E. One could only ever characterize S as an explanation of E relative to certain features of the context in which the question 'Why E?' had been asked. Van Fraassen writes:

> The description of some account as an explanation
> of a given fact or event, is incomplete. It can only be
> an explanation with respect to a certain *relevance*
> *relation* and a certain *contrast-class*. These are con-
> textual factors, in that they are determined neither
> by the totality of accepted scientific theories, nor
> by the event or fact for which an explanation is re-
> quested. .... [I]nformation is, in and by itself, not an
> explanation; just as a person cannot be said to be
> older, or a neighbour, except in relation to others.[20]

If van Fraassen's conclusions were correct, the project I have undertaken in these pages would be utterly futile; for I have set out to characterize the D-N schema, and the other schemata of explanation, in such a way that any set of true statements bearing the appropriate logico-semantic relations to one another and to E would count as an explanation of E.

In drawing the conclusion he does draw from the observations that have gone before, van Fraassen has apparently been tricked into a fatal equivocation by the slipperiness of the indefinite article. It is not the status of S as *an* explanation of E which is relative to contextual factors; it is only its status as *the* explanation of E, in the sense of being the answer which will uniquely satisfy the individual who has posed the question 'Why E?'. Nothing more is implied, or even remotely suggested, by the data which van Fraassen takes as premises of his argument.

There is no obstacle, therefore, to seeking necessary and sufficient conditions of a logico-semantic, non-context-dependent kind, for S's being an explanation of E; but we must not assume that there is one and only one explanation of any happening.

A parallel remark may be made about causation. It is only so long as the doctor, the adjuster, the mechanic and the city planner are each taken to be seeking the cause of the motorist's death that we need to view them as having differing, context-dependent criteria of success. All of them will surely agree that the victim's death was caused by hemorrhaging, and by the driver's negligence, and by the defective brakes, and by the improperly placed shrubbery.

What is more, all of them may be expected to agree that the union of sperm and egg which produces a human being neither explains nor causes his or her death, despite the fact that, in view of the mortality of humans, and their mode of coming into existence, conception is both necessary and sufficient for death. It seems that whenever anyone asks for an explanation of the death of an organism, it is assumed that a causal history can be given which will explain why the organism died at the particular time it did, rather than surviving until a later date. Thus a story which shows only why the organism was bound to die at some time or other will not be an adequate explanation. What this shows is that a certain amount of information about the contrast-class should be considered to be part of the explanandum. But what is part of the explanandum does not vary with context.

Van Fraassen remarks:

> It might be thought that when we request a *scientific*
> explanation, the relevance of possible hypotheses,

and also the contrast-class are automatically determined. But this is not so, for both the physician and the motor mechanic are asked for a scientific explanation. The physician explains the fatality *qua* death of a human organism, and the mechanic explains it *qua* automobile crash fatality. To ask that their explanations be scientific is only to demand that they rely on scientific theories and experimentation, not on old wives' tales.[21]

This shows that he is in agreement with one of the points I have been insisting upon, namely, that there can be more than one explanation – indeed, more than one *scientific* explanation – of a single phenomenon.

Someone might respond to the car crash example by noting that the physician and the mechanic are interested in different parts of the story leading up to the victim's death. Well then, are they not simply seeking, and finding, different parts of the one, exhaustive scientific account which would be a *complete* explanation of the fatal crash in the ambitious sense discussed earlier? I believe that this is indeed so; and I accept what it entails, namely, that for any given phenomenon, there can be but one explanation which is a complete explanation in the ambitious sense. Once one has told the whole story, there is nothing more to tell.

But this view has a consequence which may come as a surprise: it is more than possible, it is probable, that in many cases the one explanatory story which is complete in the ambitious sense will contain mutually irreducible strands or sub-plots, each of which is complete in the modest sense. As Jerry Fodor has noted, the predicates of natural languages cross-classify the natural kinds of physics, and it is likely that the kind predicates of the special sciences will forever do so as well:

Physics develops the taxonomy of its subject matter which best suits its purposes. . . . But this is not the only taxonomy which may be required if the purposes of science in general are to be served: e.g., if we are to state such true, counterfactual supporting generalizations as there are to state. So there are special sciences, with their special-ized taxonomies, in the business of stating some of these generalizations. If science is to be unified, then all such taxonomies must apply *to the same things.* If physics is to be basic science, then each of these things had better be a physical thing. But it is not further required that the taxonomies which the special sciences employ must themselves reduce to the taxonomy of physics. It is not required, and it is probably not true.[22]

Probably, then, there will always be cases in which we have two or more explanations of a single event, derived from different sciences – mutually irreducible, and each one complete in the modest sense. The insurance adjuster's story about negligence and the city planner's story about dangerously placed shrubbery will be conjoined, but not merged, in the exhaustive causal history of the accident.

(c) Van Fraassen on the asymmetries of explanation

As an argument in favor of his view that explanation is a purely pragmatic affair, van Fraassen points to the ability of his theory to account for the asymmetries of explanation. He writes:

[I]f the asymmetries of explanation result from a contextually determined relation of relevance, then it must be the case that these asymmetries can at least sometimes be reversed by a change in context. In addition, it should then also be possible to account for specific asymmetries in terms of the interests of questioner and audience that determine this relevance. These considerations provide a crucial test for the account of explanation which I propose.[23]

Soon afterwards comes the tale entitled "The Tower and the Shadow". In this little romance, we are presented with two competing answers to the question 'Why must that tower have such a long shadow?' The Chevalier's explanation is that the tower was built 175 feet high because Queen Marie Antoinette would have been 175 years old in the year of its construction, 1930. A side effect of the height of the tower is the long shadow that falls upon the terrace with every setting sun. But the servants, it is said, have a different explanation. They believe that, for reasons having to do with love, betrayal and dark deeds in his own past, the Chevalier had the tower built 175 feet high *in order* to cast a shadow upon the terrace with each setting sun.

Since van Fraassen's intention is to provide a pair of explanatory stories in which the explanandum and some crucial explanatory factor change places, the romance of the Tower and the Shadow does not serve his purpose at all well. In the Chevalier's story, the length of the shadow, which is the explanandum, is explained as a side effect of the height of the tower. It would be correct to say that in the servants' story, the length of the shadow is explained as the *intended* effect of the height of the tower. But now it is evident that the servants' story will not do the job van Fraassen wishes it to do: the shadow is still the explanandum. If we attempt to draw from the servants' story an explanation in which the height of the tower is the explanandum (which is what van Fraassen says he wishes to do), then we find the explanatory factor must be, not the present-day shadow that falls upon the terrace, but the Chevalier's *plan*, formed prior to the tower's construction, to have a shadow fall upon the terrace. But by no stretch of the imagination can it be maintained that this was the explanandum in the Chevalier's story: he would have denied having had such a plan.

Does this show that explanatory antecedence can never be reversed by a change in context, and that van Fraassen's theory has therefore failed what he said would be a crucial test? No: it merely shows that the example is unsatisfactory. Here is a better one.

All through a frigid January day the air temperature in my living room remains at a cozy 21 degrees Celsius, plus or minus 0.2 degrees. The laws of thermodynamics operate with the marvelous constancy we have come to expect, and as a result, the objects in the room assume, and then remain at, the ambient air temperature. (That this is somewhat higher near the hot air inlet and lower near the cold air duct need not detain us.) For any object in the room, its having a temperature of 21 degrees C ± 0.2 degrees throughout the day is explained by the fact that that is the temperature of the surrounding air. That is all there is to it, for all of the objects in the room save one: the thermostat. Of the thermostat, it is also true to say that *its* having a temperature of 21 degrees ± 0.2 degrees *explains* the fact that that is the temperature of the surrounding air. (Whereas if someone had come along and parked a hot potato on the thermostat, thus raising the temperature of the thermostat above that of the room, the room temperature would have dropped.) The second explanatory story, in which the temperature of the thermostat is depicted as causally prior to that of the room, involved a more complicated set of laws and background conditions – notably the fact that the thermostat is set at 21 degrees and the fact that the heating system is in working order. This second story must also be thought of as *omitting* to mention that the thermostat is in fact located in the living room, so that the air in the living room is in contact with it. But for this omission, the asymmetrical relation of causal priority between explanatory factor and explanandum would fail to obtain.

Any physical system that incorporates a negative feedback loop will furnish a pair of explanatory stories analogous to the pair I have just told about my thermostat. Unlike van Fraassen's two stories about the tower and the shadow, the members of such a pair will be mutually compatible, and in the standard case, both true.

We have a situation, then, in which there are two phenomena, A (the air temperature) and T (the temperature of the thermostat), such that relative to one subset B_1 of the prevailing background conditions, A is causally prior to T, yet relative to another subset B_2 of those same conditions, T is causally prior to A. Immediately the question springs to mind: which is prior to which relative to the whole set $\{B_1 \cup B_2\}$ of background conditions? The answer must be: neither. This result is unavoidable, just because we took such care to define causal priority in such a way that it could not fail to be an asymmetrical relation.

But what *does* explain the fact that the room temperature stays constant all day? The nerve of any serious answer to the question would be, '*Whenever* the air temperature starts to fall and cools the thermostat to 20.9 deg., the thermostat cuts in, and then as soon as the thermostat is warmed to 21.1 deg., it cuts out again'. This answer calls attention to the fact that our phenomenon A, "the air temperature's remaining at 21 deg. C ± 0.2 deg. all day", is a composite of subordinate phenomena such as the temperature's being 20.9 deg. at 10:00 a.m., 21.1 deg. at 10:15 a.m., and so on. Each of these subordinate phenomena will have an explanation in which the temperature of the thermostat at some earlier time will figure as a causally prior condition. Similarly, the temperature of the thermostat at any particular time will have an explanation in which the temperature of the air at some prior time is mentioned. But it is only by a kind of semantic gerrymandering of the subordinate phenomena that we are able to define a pair of larger phenomena, such as A and T, which can switch places in a pair of explanatory stories.

I cannot think of a pair of explanatory stories in which the asymmetry of explanation is reversed, which does not depend upon the sort of semantic gerrymandering exhibited in the thermostat example. Not that I believe it would be fatal to the theory of explanation here advanced, if someone did produce a satisfactory example.[24]

But now what of van Fraassen's theory? We cannot conclude that it has failed the crucial test: that would have been our conclusion only if we had found that explanatory antecedence can never be reversed by a change in context. But neither should we conclude that van Fraassen's theory ought to be accepted. The competing theory proposed in these pages, employing the concept of causal priority, accounts equally well for the reversibility of explanatory antecedence in every instance in which it is found to obtain.

In a sense I very nearly agree with van Fraassen that "the asymmetries of explanation result from a contextually determined relation of relevance". I have said that for most purposes, the sense of causal priority we will need is the sense in which C is prior to E relative to a set {B} of background conditions. In all such cases, causal priority, and hence explanatory antecedence, will be relative to the explanatory story being told. Only when one factor is absolutely, and in general, prior to another, as the presence of oxygen is prior to combustion, will we have an instance in which causal priority is not relative to a particular explanatory story. Even in cases of absolute causal priority, the relationship holds in virtue of a set of covering laws; and the universe does contain some pairs of general phenomena {A,B}, such that $N_c(A \equiv B)$, A is absolutely prior to B in virtue of one set of covering laws L_1, and B is absolutely prior to A in virtue of another set of covering laws L_2. In such cases neither

A nor B is prior to the other in virtue of the combined set of covering laws $\{L_1 \cup L_2\}$. But once again, all the examples I can think of exhibit the same sort of semantic gerrymandering that went into the construction of the thermostat example.

It is worth our while, I think, to take note of at least one clear, if gerrymandered, example of this type of thing. In an earlier age, probably, everyone would have accepted the existence of chickens and the existence of eggs as a pair of general phenomena exhibiting the relationship of reversible absolute causal priority discussed in the last paragraph. But that was before we learned that chickens could be brought into existence by cloning as well as by hatching eggs. Advancing scientific knowledge forces us to look for more subtle examples; but it is the same advancing science that finds them. Let A stand for the existence of a certain species of nudibranch found in the Bay of Naples, and B for the existence of a certain species of medusa. The relationship between these creatures is described by Lewis Thomas:

> When first observed, the nudibranch, a common sea slug, was found to have a tiny vestigial parasite, in the form of a jellyfish, permanently affixed to the ventral surface near the mouth. In curiosity to learn how the medusa got there, some marine biologists began searching the local waters for earlier developmental forms, and discovered something amazing. The attached parasite, although apparently so specialized as to have given up living for itself, can still produce offspring, for they are found in abundance at certain seasons of the year. They drift through the upper waters, grow up nicely and astonishingly, and finally become full-grown, handsome, normal jellyfish. Meanwhile,

the snail produces snail larvae, and these too begin to grow normally, but not for long. While still
extremely small, they become entrapped in the
tentacles of the medusa and then engulfed within
the umbrella-shaped body. At first glance, you'd
believe the medusae are now the predators, paying back for earlier humiliations, and the snails
the prey. But no. Soon the snails, undigested and
insatiable, begin to eat, browsing away first at the
radial canals, then the borders of the rim, finally
the tentacles, until the jellyfish becomes reduced
in substance by being eaten while the snail grows
correspondingly in size. At the end, the arrangement is back to the first scene, with a full-grown
nudibranch basking, and nothing left of the jellyfish except the round, successfully edited parasite,
safely affixed to the skin near the mouth.

It is a confusing tale to sort out, and even more
confusing to think about. Both creatures are designed for this encounter, marked as selves so that
they can find each other in the waters of the Bay
of Naples. The collaboration, if you want to call
it that, is entirely specific; it is only this species
of medusa and only this kind of nudibranch that
can come together and live this way. And, more
surprising, they cannot live in any other way; they
depend for their survival on each other.[25]

It is conceivable that the universe should contain a
non-gerrymandered pair of general phenomena exhibiting a pri-
mordial medusa-and-snail relationship that could not be broken
down (as can the relationship between the medusa and the snail, or

between chickens and eggs) into a series of relationships involving particular individuals. If that should be so, it would prove that the relation of absolute causal priority defined earlier need not be as absolute as all that.

Again, I very nearly agree with van Fraassen that "it should ... be possible to account for specific asymmetries in terms of the interests of questioner and audience that determine this relevance". I grant that explanatory antecedence is relative to the explanatory story being told. It is obvious enough that the interests of a questioner and an audience determine which (true) story will satisfy the specific desire for enlightenment expressed in the question 'Why E?' Thus their interests will account for the appearance of a specific asymmetry in the story they accept as "*the* explanation of E". This is not the same thing, however, as accounting for the asymmetry itself.

It is possible I have mistaken van Fraassen's intentions, because, from the text of his book, it is not quite plain what he thinks he has proved. But I *think* he thinks he has demonstrated that explanation is a purely pragmatic concept, and that a set of statements S can only be said to explain E relative to a specific construal of the question 'Why E?' He has not.

PROBABILISTIC EXPLANATION: FROM HEMPEL TO SALMON

It is beyond controversy that there are certain phenomena for which we are unable to construct D-N explanations, given the information available to us, but which we nevertheless take to be at least partly explained on the basis of statistical generalizations.

Susan Small just died. We explain this by noting that she developed inoperable lung cancer eighteen months ago, and "malignant tumors of the lung, if they cannot be removed surgically, lead to an average survival of less than one year".[26] The roulette wheel halted on a red stop three times in the course of five trials: that the stops are half red and half black helps to explain this. Mary Cavendish is putting in longer hours at her job, now that she is being paid on the basis of fee-for-service, than she did when she earned a salary, although she does not really need the additional money. The theory of operant conditioning helps explain her behavior: the repetition of an operant is more probable under ratio reinforcement than under interval reinforcement.[27] A man's developing paresis is explained by the fact that he has untreated latent syphilis; "72 out of 100 untreated persons [with latent syphilis] go through life without the symptoms of late [tertiary] syphilis, but 28 out of 100 untreated persons were known to have developed serious outcomes [paresis and others] and there is no way to predict what will happen to an untreated infected person".[28]

For further examples, of special significance, we may look at radioactive decay and other phenomena exhibiting quantum indeterminacy.

> The uranium atom, for example, may decay by emitting an alpha-particle from its nucleus. The nucleus constitutes a strong enclosure, and the alpha-particle races frantically back and forth, bumping into the wall of the nucleus about 10^{21} . . . times per second, and on the average an alpha-particle makes it out in about a billion years. In other words, it has about one chance in 10^{38} of getting out any time it bombards the barrier of its nuclear prison. When we ask why a particular uranium atom decayed in this manner at this particular time, the answer is that an alpha-particle "tunnelled out" of its nucleus. When we ask why the alpha-particle escaped on that trial, having

failed on countless other occasions, the answer is simply that there is a probability of about 10^{-38} of such an outcome on any given bombardment of the wall. That is all there is to it.[29]

Wesley Salmon has made the last two examples well known to philosophers. Here is another of Salmon's examples, the Stern-Gerlach experiment:

[I]t is a consequence of quantum mechanics that atoms of silver, when shot between the poles of a magnet, will be deflected either up or down, but there is no way, even in principle, of determining beforehand which way a particular atom will go. Each one has a 50-50 chance of going either way, and that is all there is to it.[30]

(a) Hempel's inductive-statistical (I-S) schema

Carl Hempel responded to examples such as these by proposing the Inductive-Statistical (I-S) schema of explanation; he thought of D-N and I-S as being two varieties of covering-law explanation. Letting "$P(G/F) = r$" abbreviate "the statistical probability of G, given F, is r", where $0 < r < 1$, Hempel described I-S explanation as

. . . a . . . kind of probabilistic explanation, which invokes quantitatively definite statistical laws and which may be schematized as follows:

$P(G/F) = r$

Fi

========[r]

Gi

An explanatory argument of this form would serve to account for the fact that a given individual case i exhibits the characteristic G by pointing out that i is a case of F; that the statistical probability for an F to exhibit characteristic G is r; and that ... this explanatory information confers the logical probability r upon the explanandum statement. I will refer to r also as the probability *associated with* the explanation. Of course, an argument of this kind will count as explanatory only if the number r is fairly close to 1. But it seems impossible, without being arbitrary, to designate any particular number, say .8, as the minimum value of the probability r permissible in an explanation.[31]

In this account, logical probability, or the degree of credibility or support conferred upon one statement by another, is thought of as a semantical relation between statements, knowable *a priori*. The logical probability of a hypothesis h is always relative to some set e of statements which are functioning as an evidential base. Logical probability is sometimes termed epistemic or inductive probability. Statistical probability, on the other hand, is a factual matter. On the frequency interpretation, statistical probability is a relation between classes or series of phenomena: the statistical probability of G, given F – $P(G/F)$ – is the proportion of F's which, in a long series of trials, turn out to be G's. That is a vague statement: different versions of the frequency theory represent different ways of making it precise.[32] On any of the standard versions of frequency theory, however, a statistical probability is a pattern displayed by a class or sequence of phenomena in the actual world. The distinction between logical and statistical probability was made by Carnap, with a clarity which has made Carnap's treatment a classic.[33]

In the essay cited, Hempel does not adopt a frequency theory of statistical probability, but instead defines statistical probability as a disposition of an experimental setup that is F to produce a certain proportion of G-type outcomes over the long run. The difference between a theory that represents a statistical probability as an attribute of a series of results, and one that represents it as an attribute of the apparatus which generates the series of results, is more important than may appear at first sight.

Hempel acknowledges his view of statistical probability to be in close accord with the "propensity" interpretation advocated by Karl Popper.[34] Popper himself claims that the propensity view "differs from the purely statistical or frequency interpretation *only* in this – that it considers the probability as a characteristic property of the experimental arrangement rather than as a property of the sequence".[35] But Hempel notices a second, very significant difference, which Popper apparently overlooked, but could hardly have denied. The propensity interpretation allows us to infer subjunctive and counterfactual conditionals from probability statements.

> [W]e might say that a law of the form 'P(G/F) = r' refers not only to all actual instances of F, but, so to speak, to the class of all its potential instances. Suppose, for example, that we are given a homogeneous regular tetrahedron whose faces are marked 'I', 'II', 'III', 'IV'. We might then assert that the probability of obtaining a III, i.e., of the tetrahedron's coming to rest on that face upon being tossed out of a dice box, is 1/4. But, while this assertion says something about the frequency with which a III is obtained as a result of rolling the tetrahedron, it cannot be construed as simply specifying that frequency for the class of all tosses which are, in

fact, ever performed with the tetrahedron. For we might well maintain our hypothesis even if we were informed that the tetrahedron would actually be tossed only a few times throughout its existence, and in this case, our probability statement would surely not be meant to assert that exactly, or even nearly, one-fourth of those tosses would yield the result III. Moreover, our statement would be perfectly meaningful and might, indeed, be well supported (e.g., by results obtained with similar solids) even if the given tetrahedron happened to be destroyed without ever having been tossed at all. What the probability statement attributes to the tetrahedron is, therefore, not the frequency with which the result III is obtained in actual past or future rolling, but a certain *disposition*, namely, the disposition to yield the result III in about one out of four cases, in the long run. This disposition might be characterized by means of a subjunctive conditional phrase: if the tetrahedron were to be tossed a large number of times, it would yield the result III in about one-fourth of the cases. Implications in the form of counterfactual and subjunctive conditionals are thus hallmarks of lawlike statements both of strictly universal and of statistical form.[36]

In keeping with this view of probability statements, Hempel says that an argument conforming to the I-S schema will be acceptable as an explanation only if the probability statement in the explanans, $P(G/F) = r$, is a law-like statement which mentions a potentially infinite class F. "Lawlike sentences, whether true or false, are not just conveniently telescoped summaries of finite sets of data concerning particular instances".[37] It follows that last year's mortality tables for the U.S.A., while they might serve to assign a definite probability to the prediction that an arbitrarily chosen 49-year-old American female will live for another year, would not serve to explain the fact that she has survived for the last twelve months. The class of arguments which will serve for purposes of explanation is but a subset of those which will serve for prediction – a point to which we shall shortly return.

Hempel's account of D-N explanation was seminal, but ran into difficulties over the issue of explanatory antecedence. The I-S schema he proposed as a model for probabilistic explanation was equally seminal; but it, likewise, ran into difficulties, and that for two reasons. First, it is a consequence of Hempel's view that events that occur despite having a middling or low probability are inexplicable. This is counterintuitive: we would wish to say that having untreated syphilis *does* explain why a man develops paresis, despite the fact that the explanandum has a logical probability of only .28 relative to this explanans. Peter Railton has a further, very telling example:

> [W]hy should it be explicable that a ... wheel of fortune with 99 red stops and 1 black stop came to a halt on red, but inexplicable that it halted on black? Worse, on Hempel's view, halting at any *particular* stop would be inexplicable, even though the wheel must halt at some particular stop in order to yield the explicable outcome *red*. [38]

The second difficulty, like the first, flows from Hempel's view that a probabilistic explanation is a statistical inference that confers a certain inductive probability on the explanandum. The probability of Henry's surviving for a year may be very high relative to all the facts about his age, physical health, occupation, and safe driving habits, yet very low relative to the fact that he has just jumped off the Golden Gate Bridge. This illustrates what became known as the problem of the reference class. An event has differing probabilities, relative to the many different classes of events to which it belongs – or, if you will, relative to different properties of the experimental setup by which it is generated. This presents a problem for Hempel's theory which would not be removed even by relaxing the requirement that the explanans confer a *high* inductive probability upon the explanandum. Hempel was well aware of this problem; but it is beyond the scope of this study to examine the various ways in which he refined his theory in the attempt to solve it.[39]

(b) Explanation versus inference

Richard Jeffrey provided the liberating insight: statistical explanation is not the same thing as statistical inference. The function of an explanation is not to show that the explanandum was probable, or predictable; it is, rather, to provide an understanding of the process by which it came about.

> [T]he explanation is basically the same no matter what the outcome: it consists of a statement that the process was a stochastic one, following such-and-such a law. (One may gloss this statement by pointing out that the actual outcome had such-and-such a probability, given the law of the process; but this gloss is not the heart of the explanation.) ...
>
> Nor is the situation changed when (as usual) the probable happens. Because such cases are usual, we can usually give a statistical *inference* of

strength 1/2 or more when we can give a statistical explanation; and this, I take it, is why it is easy to mistake the inference for an explanation. That the inference is *not* an explanation is shown, I think, by the fact that even when the improbable chances to happen, we give the same sort of account: the happening was the product of a *stochastic* process following such-and-such a probabilistic law. And we gloss this by pointing out that in this case the unexpected happened. My point is that it is no less a gloss, and no more essentially a part of the explanation, when we point out in the more usual cases that the *expected* happened.[40]

Jeffrey might well have generalized this point. Not only are statistical explanations not the same thing as statistical inferences; other types of explanation are not inferences either. Inferring and explaining are both activities carried on by thinkers employing statements. Inferring is the process of drawing a conclusion from a set of premises: when we start the process we are in possession of the premises, and when it is over we are also in possession of the conclusion. Explaining is the other way round: when the process starts we have only the explanandum, and when it is over we are also in possession of a set of statements which constitutes an explanans.

Now it is true that a set of statements that constitutes a completed D-N explanation also constitutes a deductively valid argument which could be employed to infer the explanandum from the explanans. The end product of the explaining process is thus identical, in this instance, to the end product of a certain process of inference. We should not let this blind us to the very different nature of the two processes.

We should note, furthermore, that while every completed D-N explanation is a valid argument with the explanandum as conclusion, not every valid argument with covering laws of universal form and non-redundant singular statements as premises, and another singular statement as conclusion, is a D-N explanation. Some such arguments have premises that mention conditions which are not causally prior to the phenomenon described by the conclusion. But no such causal priority is required for correct inference; only deductive validity. It is perfectly all right to *infer* the length of a pendulum from the period of its swing and the strength of the gravitational field, as everyone has been aware all along.

This is the place for a brief digression on prediction and retrodiction. Prediction, when it is not simply the making of a blind and arbitrary guess, is a process of inference: a statement about the future is inferred from data already in hand. Retrodiction is a similar process in which a statement about the past is inferred; it is thus different from remembering, which I take to be non-inferential. Because causes regularly precede their effects in time, we regularly use arguments for the purpose of prediction which would also serve as explanations. (We also use some which emphatically would not: barometer readings are fine for predicting the weather, but not for explaining it.)[41] This, I believe, must have been a major source of the illusion that explanation and prediction are the same type of activity, and necessarily employ all and only the same arguments. Had there been causes which were known to precede their effects in time, it would have been obvious from the first that explanation and prediction are not the same thing, even in the D-N case.[42]

Since explanation is not the same thing as inference, there is no reason to suppose that the sets of statements which result from sound inferences will, in general, be exactly the same sets which result from sound explanations. In the case of rational-agency explanation (to be examined in the next chapter), it so happens that

201 Laws and Explanations

there *is* a correspondence between the set of statements which constitutes an explanans and the set of statements which would have figured in the agent's own practical reasoning, provided he had been honest, self-aware, and articulate about the real reasons for his action. In the case of probabilistic explanation, there is, as Jeffrey perceived, no analogous correspondence.

The publication of Jeffrey's article touched off a fresh examination of probabilistic explanation, resulting in two new proposals for the formulation of the underlying schema: the Statistical Relevance (S-R) schema proposed by Wesley Salmon, and the Deductive-Nomological-Probabilistic (D-N-P) schema due to Peter Railton.

(c) Salmon's statistical relevance (S-R) schema

Salmon's approach is to think of the explanans, not as a set of statements from which the explanandum could plausibly be inferred, but as a set of statements mentioning factors that are statistically relevant to the explanandum:

> Suppose we are dealing with some particular object or event x, and we seek to determine the probability (weight) that it has attribute B. Let x be assigned to a reference class A, of which it is a member. $P(B/A)$ is the probability of this attribute within this reference class. A set of mutually exclusive and exhaustive subclasses of a class is a *partition* of that class. We shall often be concerned with partitions of reference classes into two subclasses; such partitions can be effected by a property C which divides the class A into two subclasses, A.C and A.C̃. A property C is said to be *statistically*

relevant to B within A if and only if $P(B/A.C) \neq P(B/A)$. This notion of statistical relevance is the fundamental concept upon which I hope to build an explication of inductive explanation.[43]

Salmon next constructs safeguards against specious statistical relevancies that might crop up and deceive us if our statistics happened to be biased. He begins with the notion of a place selection, derived from Richard von Mises. A place selection is the selection of a subset of the reference class A made without employing the attribute B in a way that would bias the sample. In the example being considered, the reference class is "an unending sequence of draws of balls from an urn", and the attribute class is "the class of red things".[44]

A place selection effects a partition of the reference class into two subclasses, elements of the place selection and elements not included in the place selection. In the reference class of draws from our urn, every third draw starting with the second, every *kth* draw where *k* is prime, every draw following a red result, every draw made with the left hand, and every draw made while the sky is cloudy would all be place selections. "Every draw of a red ball" and "every draw of a ball whose color is at the opposite end of the spectrum from violet" do not define place selections, for membership in these classes cannot be determined without reference to the attribute in question [red].[45]

The notion of statistical relevance and the notion of a place selection are now used to define the notion of a homogeneous reference class:

> If every property that determines a place selection is statistically irrelevant to B in A, I shall say that A is a *homogeneous reference class* for B. A reference class is homogeneous if there is no way, even in principle, to effect a statistically relevant partition without already knowing which elements have the attribute in question and which do not. Roughly speaking, each member of a homogeneous reference class is a random member.[46]

Salmon, unlike Hempel, is not regarding a statistical explanation as an inference. The specific probability mentioned in the explanatory generalization is, for him, no more than a gloss on the explanation; it is not a vital element. Hence he views the problem of the reference class as an incidental problem in *applied* statistics. For him, it lacks the central importance it had for Hempel. However, he does comment on the matter.

> The aim in selecting a reference class to which to assign a single case is not to select the narrowest, but the widest, available class. However, the reference class should be homogeneous, and achieving homogeneity requires making the reference class narrower if it was not already homogeneous. I would reformulate Reichenbach's method of selection of a reference class as follows: choose the broadest homogeneous reference class to which

the single event belongs. I shall call this the *reference class rule.*

Let us make it clear immediately that, although I regard the above formulation as an improvement over Reichenbach's, I do not suppose that it removes all ambiguities about the selection of reference classes either in principle or in practice.[47]

A homogeneous partition of the reference class A with respect to B is a partition of A into a number of subclasses, each of which would be a homogeneous reference class for B. Salmon's schema for S-R explanation can now be stated:

[A]n explanation of the fact that x, a member of A, is a member of B would go as follows:
$$P(B/A.C_1) = P_1$$
$$P(B/A.C_2) = P_2$$
.

.

.
$$P(B/A.C_n) = P_n$$
where
A.C_1, A.C_2, ..., A.C_n is a homogeneous partition of A with respect to B,
$p_i = p_j$ only if $i = j$, and
$x \, \varepsilon A.C_k$.[48]

In every case, I think, the question takes the form, "Why is this x which is A also B?" The answer then takes the form, "Because this x is also C". C must be an attribute that is statistically relevant to B within the reference class A.[49]

An important feature of Salmon's treatment is his use of the so-called screening-off relation, a concept due to Reichenbach. As an approach to this, consider the well-known barometer example. There is an observable, repeatable correlation between a sudden drop in the barometer reading and the onset of a storm. On the S-R model as so far described, we would have to say that the drop in the barometer reading explains the storm. Salmon writes:

> I am willing to admit that symptomatic explanations seem to have genuine explanatory value in the absence of knowledge of causal relations, that is, as long as we do not know that we are dealing only with symptoms. Causal explanations supersede symptomatic ones when they can be given, and when we suspect we are dealing with symptoms, we look hard for a causal explanation. The reason is that a causal explanation provides a more homogeneous reference class than does a symptomatic explanation. Causal proximity increases homogeneity.[50]

In commonsensical terms, we discover that the drop in the barometer reading is caused by a drop in the atmospheric pressure, and that this and the stormy weather are two effects of a common cause, a low-pressure system. Once we know that, we no longer take the drop in the barometer reading to be an explanation of the storm. Salmon's way of reproducing this bit of common sense, in terms of his fundamental notion of statistical relevance, is to note that since barometers occasionally malfunction, the probability of a storm given a drop in atmospheric pressure is not the same as the probability of a storm given a drop in the barometer reading. But the probability of a storm given a drop in atmospheric pressure is the same as the probability of a storm given a drop in atmospheric pressure *and* a drop in the barometer reading. The drop in atmospheric pressure *screens off* the drop in the barometer reading from the occurrence of the storm. "Screening off" refers simply to the relations of equality and inequality between the three conditional probabilities.

> More formally, we may say that D screens off C from B in reference class A iff (if and only if)
> $$P(B/A.C.D) = P(B/A.D) \neq P(B/A.C)\ ^{51}$$

To put this in terms of the example we have been using, let 'Days' be the reference class of days on which observations are taken, 'Storm' be the class of days on which a storm occurs, 'Bar' be the class of days on which there is a sudden drop in the barometer reading, and 'Pres' be the class of days on which there is a sudden drop in the atmospheric pressure. Then

> P(Storm/Days.Bar.Pres) = P(Storm/Days.Pres) ≠ P(Storm/Days.Bar).

> By means of this formal definition, we see that D screens off C from B, but C does not screen off D from B. The screening-off relation is, therefore, not symmetrical, although the relation of statistical relevance is symmetrical.
>
> When one property in terms of which a statistically relevant partition in a reference class can be effected screens off another property in terms of which another statistically relevant partition of that same reference class can be effected, then the screened-off property must give way to the property

which screens it off. This is the *screening-off rule*. The screened-off property then becomes irrelevant and no longer has explanatory value. ... The unwanted "symptomatic explanations" can be blocked by use of the screening-off concept, which is defined in terms of statistical irrelevance alone. We have not found it necessary to introduce an independent concept of causal relation in order to handle this problem. Reichenbach believed it was possible to define causal relatedness in terms of screening-off relations; but whether his program can be carried through or not, it seems that many causal relations exhibit the desired screening-off relations.[52]

Salmon did not regard the S-R schema as the sole model for all scientific explanation; he acknowledged that explanation by means of scientific theories in the "fullest sense" of the term 'theories' might have a different logical structure.[53] But he did regard it as the model for all explanation by means of empirical laws, and thought of D-N explanation as a special case of S-R explanation.[54]

He was acutely aware that the success of his project – explicating nomological explanation by means of the S-R schema – was very much tied up with the eventual success of Reichenbach's project of giving a statistical account of causality.

I should be inclined to harbor serious misgivings about the adequacy of my view of statistical explanation if the statistical analysis of causation cannot be carried through successfully, for the relation between causation and explanation seems extremely intimate.[55]

Since the publication of "Statistical Explanation" in 1970, Salmon has been directing his efforts to the development of a statistical or probabilistic account of causality.[56] The salient feature of his approach has been to postpone consideration of causal relations between events, and concentrate first on continuous causal processes and their interactions. Processes, rather than events, are treated as logically primitive. Fine; but sooner or later one must be prepared to say something about causal relations between events, whether events are pictured as links in a causal chain or as slices carved from a causal sausage.

(d) Problems for Salmon's theory

This is not the place to indulge in a detailed examination of Salmon's later work, though in a subsequent section I will comment in a general way on its prospects of success. What we should take note of is the fact that *unless* someone succeeds in giving a probabilistic analysis of causation, Salmon's theory of explanation is in deep trouble on a number of counts.

(1) Conformity to Salmon's S-R schema is not a sufficient condition for a set of statements to be an explanation, as the following example illustrates:

> [I]n England and Wales between the years 1924 and 1937 a high correlation could be found between the numbers of wireless licences issued and the number of notified mental defectives. The correlation coefficient is 0.998; this may be a 'nonsense correlation' and it may not.[57]

If it did prove to be a 'nonsense correlation', it would be a clear instance of statistical relevance without explanatory force. The problem would be solved, of course, if we had a way of explicating, in statistical terms, the statement that the issuing of radio licences was not causally connected to the registering of mental defectives.

(2) Salmon's schema, unless supplemented with an account of causality, will not provide a necessary criterion for an explanation either. Bas van Fraassen has provided the example to prove this point:

> Suppose, as a medical fiction, that paresis can result from either syphilis or epilepsy, and from nothing else, and that the probability of paresis given either syphilis or epilepsy equals 0.1. Suppose in addition that Jones is known to belong to a family of which every member has either syphilis or epilepsy (but, fortunately, not both), and that he has paresis. Why did *he* develop this illness? Surely the best answer *either* is 'Because he had syphilis' *or* is 'Because he had epilepsy', depending on which of these is true. Yet, with all the other information we have, the probability that Jones would get paresis is already established as 0.1, and this probability is not changed if we are told in addition, say, that he has a history of syphilis.[58]

(3) According to Salmon's account, a "symptomatic" explanation must be accepted as explanatory, until a better one is found which supersedes it. So it is a relative matter whether or not a particular set S of true statements explains another true statement E: it depends on whether we know S to be true, and what other truths we know. This is an unfortunate result. Far better to be able to say that a phenomenon is explained by the conditions which, in point

of fact, cause it, regardless of how much we language users happen to know at the time.

(4) The first symptom of bubonic plague is a characteristic rash in the shape of a ring of roses, which appears on the patient's chest. The second symptom to manifest itself is a high fever. Both symptoms are caused by the presence of the plague bacillus *Pasteurella pestis* in the bloodstream; it is not the rash that causes the fever. But the rash occurs if and only if *Pasteurella pestis* is present. Hence the presence of the bacillus fails to screen off the rash from the fever, since

$$P(\text{Fever/Bacillus.Rash}) = P(\text{Fever/Bacillus}) = P(\text{Fever/Rash}).[59]$$

Likewise, if barometers never malfunctioned, the drop in atmospheric pressure would not screen off the drop in the barometer reading from the storm. Yet surely we would still wish to say, in both these cases, that the common cause explains each of its several effects, but it is not the case that one effect explains another. So it is not necessary for some factor C to screen off E_1 from E_2 within a reference class A in order for C to explain both E_1 and E_2 while E_1 and E_2 lack explanatory force with respect to each other.

(5) But neither is it sufficient. Suppose that on a mythical island, the natives had learned from experience that eating the local oysters frequently, but not always, caused food poisoning. Along come some researchers from a developed country; they discover that some 70 per cent of the oysters are infected with tiny parasites, and that ingesting the parasites *always* causes food poisoning. Letting 'Pois' stand for 'being afflicted with food poisoning', 'Oys' for 'ingesting oysters', and 'Par' for 'ingesting parasites', we have, for the reference class of humans,

$$P(Pois/Oys.Par) = P(Pois/Par) \neq P(Pois/Oys).$$

The ingesting of parasites thus screens off the eating of oysters from food poisoning. Yet the natives' belief that some cases of food poisoning were explained by the eating of oysters has not been superseded. Their knowledge has been refined and added to, and the researchers might well say to them, "It isn't the oysters as such that cause food poisoning; it's the parasites". Yet the eating of oysters still has explanatory value with respect to food poisoning, for the eating of oysters is the mechanism through which the parasites are ingested, and is thus a causally prior factor.

(6) So long as the relation between explanans and explanandum is explicated solely as a relation of statistical relevance, no foundation has been provided for an account of the asymmetries of explanation. The relation of statistical relevance is symmetrical, as Salmon notes.[60] But, he says, "Reichenbach's principle of the common cause . . . helps us to establish the temporal asymmetry of explanation".[61] Now this evades the main problem even before the investigation has been fairly begun. It was not a temporal asymmetry that had to be established or explicated in the first place, but rather an asymmetry that is independent of any temporal relations. The period of the swinging pendulum during a given interval of time is explained by its length during that same interval, but not *vice versa*; the height of the flagpole explains the angle subtended when it is viewed from ground level, and the laws involved are laws of physical geometry which make no reference to time.

Adolf Grünbaum changed the flagpole example, taking the length of the flagpole's *shadow* as the explanandum, rather than the angle subtended by the pole when viewed from ground level. This has the consequence that the covering laws must now be laws of physics, rather than geometry; however, Grünbaum, in the text in question, considers geometrical examples as well. He views both the latter examples and the flagpole example as cases in which the cause (explanans) is simultaneous with the effect (explanandum).[62]

Salmon then picks up the altered flagpole example, ignores the possibility of examples from physical geometry, and notes that since there is a very short time lapse between the moment a photon passes the top of the flagpole and the moment it strikes the ground, the shadow is not, after all, simultaneous with its cause.[63] This would not be much of an argument in the best of circumstances: people were well aware of the asymmetries of causation long before they knew that the velocity of light is finite. Considering that the good examples of effects that are simultaneous with their causes have not been discussed at all, Salmon's argument cannot begin to make a case for saying that the asymmetry of explanation is, or always coincides with, a temporal asymmetry. The whole matter, therefore, will hinge on someone's being able to give an account of causal priority in terms of statistical probabilities.

One could, without inconsistency, add on to Salmon's S-R schema a requirement that the explanans be causally prior to the explanandum, in the sense outlined earlier.[64] But this would introduce modal notions that Salmon apparently wishes to eschew.

(7) Lastly, Salmon's claim to have provided the schema of all nomological explanation will be impossible to maintain, unless a satisfactory probabilistic account of causality is forthcoming. Salmon writes:

> From the standpoint of the present theory, deductive-nomological explanations are just a special case of statistical explanations. If one takes the frequency theory of probability as literally dealing with infinite classes of events, there is a difference between the universal generalization, "All A are B", and the statistical generalization "$P(B/A) = 1$", for

the former admits no As that are not Bs, whereas the latter admits of infinitely many As that are not Bs. For this reason, if the universal generalization holds, the reference class A is homogeneous with respect to B, whereas the statistical generalization may be true even if A is not homogeneous. Once this important difference is noted, it does not seem necessary to offer a special account of deductive-nomological explanations.[65]

That a philosopher as eminent as Salmon should have committed a howler of this magnitude is amazing. It may be a matter of opinion how much, or how little, one needs to offer by way of a special account of D-N explanation. But Salmon has invited us to regard D-N explanations as simply a special case of S-R explanation, while perceiving clearly that D-N explanations have logical features which are *incompatible* with their being S-R explanations, however special.

Even after we have recovered from our amazement, there is more to be said. Two pages further on, Salmon notes:

[I]n remarking above that statistical explanation is nomological, I was tacitly admitting that the statistical or universal generalizations invoked in explanation should be lawlike. I have made no attempt to analyze lawlikeness . . .[66]

In earlier chapters I have attempted an analysis of the key notions of causal necessity and causal priority in terms of primitive concepts related to natural agency. Now it seems to me that the probabilistic account of causality Salmon will need in order to save his theory of explanation must embody both of these essential elements. If the need to cope with the asymmetries of explanation makes it particularly obvious that an account of causal priority is needed, this final difficulty makes it very plain that Salmon requires an analysis of lawlikeness as well.

Suppose that Salmon were to remedy his howler about D-N explanation, and allow that it and S-R explanation are two distinct species of explanation by covering laws. He would still owe the world an account of law-like generalizations, be they universal or statistical, which would solve the old problem about subjunctive and counterfactual conditionals.

Salmon is apparently committed to the project of carrying out this analysis along actualist lines, following in the footsteps of Reichenbach. I gather he wishes to have no part of any theory of causality that employs an "other-worldly" semantics – i.e., a semantics which countenances talk about possible worlds other than the actual world. Hence his enthusiastic study of Reichenbach's attempt to give an actualist explication of the causal modalities.[67] Hence, too, his loyalty to the frequency theory of probability – the theory that the statistical probability of an event of type A simply *is* the proportion of As in some (possibly infinite) reference class R in the actual world, or alternatively, the limit to which that proportion tends as the membership of R increases without limit.

QUANTA, RANDOMNESS, AND EXPLANATION

(a) Superficial versus fundamental randomness

Recalling Jeffrey's point that a statistical explanation exhibits its explanandum as the outcome of a stochastic process that follows a certain probabilistic law, we must now distinguish between two types of stochastic process. I will call them superficially random, or superficially indeterministic processes; and fundamentally random, or fundamentally indeterministic processes. Alpha-decay of uranium atoms, and the deflection, up or down, of atoms of silver in the Stern-Gerlach experiment, are, to the best of our knowledge, fundamentally random processes. According to quantum mechanics, they follow laws which are irreducibly probabilistic, so that in explaining an event that is the outcome of one of these processes, one must say, as Salmon does, that in virtue of the law of the process, the event had such-and-such a probability of occurring, and "that is all there is to it".[68] On the other hand, the process by which a victim of inoperable lung cancer comes to die, and which follows the probabilistic law which we express by saying that the average period of survival is less than one year, must be viewed as a superficially random process. That is because it normally is supposed that there are in fact precise initial conditions and deterministic laws, unknown to us, which entail that if the disease takes its course, the victim will die at some precise time, no sooner and no later. The process by which a roulette wheel comes to rest at a particular stop is likewise regarded as a superficially random process, because it may be that if we had a sufficiently exact description of the initial conditions, known laws of physics would suffice to construct a D-N explanation of the outcome. A superficially random process, then, is one which *may* be deterministic at some underlying level. (On the other hand it may not: Peter Railton gives an example of a superficially random biological process that should be thought of as fundamentally random also.)[69]

Now according to the quantum theory, *all* physical processes, save for some of the most elementary ones, are fundamentally random processes. The only fundamentally deterministic processes will be those which are wholly governed by basic laws of deterministic form, such as the law of conservation of mass/energy. When quantum theory was first proposed, the reaction of

conservative-minded physicists was to say that the indeterministic character of quantum phenomena must surely be superficial: nature *had* to be *fundamentally* deterministic. This was the
point of Albert Einstein's celebrated remark, "I cannot believe that
God would choose to play dice with the world".[70] But John von
Neumann demonstrated that to posit any underlying mechanism
of a deterministic kind would contradict the quantum-mechanical
description of microphenomena; and for the latter we have extremely strong empirical evidence.[71] I cannot go into details of an
issue that is, in any case, still the subject of disagreement amongst
physicists. I shall content myself with citing the remarks of three
philosophers. First, J.R. Lucas:

> Quantum mechanics, as we have it, cannot be a
> partial expression of a more complete system, in-
> volving further parameters, which is, when com-
> plete, deterministic. Any attempt to add such
> parameters to the present theory, would result
> in inconsistency. Unless we jettison the whole of
> quantum mechanics (which we can be as sure as
> we can be of anything that we will not ever do), we
> are faced with some indeterminism.[72]

Here is Wesley Salmon's summary of the position:

> [T]he present quantum mechanics could be re-
> placed – not merely supplemented – by a thor-
> oughly deterministic theory. . . . Some first-rate
> physicists are presently working to find a determin-
> istic theory to replace the current quantum me-
> chanics, one by which it will be possible to explain
> what now seems irreducibly statistical by means of

"hidden variables" that cannot occur in the present theory. No one can say for sure whether they will succeed; any new theory, deterministic or indeterministic, has to stand the test of experiment. The current quantum theory does show, however, that the world *may* be fundamentally and irremediably indeterministic, for according to the best currently available knowledge, it is.[73]

Peter Railton comments:

[T]he successes of the quantum-mechanical formalism, and the existence of "no hidden variable" results for it, place the burden of proof on those who would insist that physical chance is an illusion.[74]

This has significant consequences, in principle, for all explanation, as Railton perceives:

Once restrictions have been lifted from the value a chance may have in probabilistic explanation, virtually all explanations of particular facts must become probabilistic. All but the most basic regularities of the universe stand forever in peril of being interrupted or upset by intrusion of the effects of random processes. It might seem a fine explanation for a light's going out that we opened the only circuit connecting it with an electrical power source, but an element of chance was involved: had enough atoms in the vicinity of the light undergone spontaneous beta-decay at the right moment, the electrons emitted could have kept it glowing. The success of a social revolution might appear to be explained by its overwhelming popular support, but this is to overlook the revolutionaries' luck: if all the naturally unstable nuclides on earth had commenced spontaneous nuclear fission in rapid succession, the triumph of the people would never have come to pass.

No doubt this proliferation of probabilistic explanations is counterintuitive, but contemporary science will not let us get away with any other sort of explanation in these cases – it simply cannot supply the requisite non-probabilistic laws. Because they figure in the way things *work*, tiny probabilities appropriately figure in explanations of the way things *are*, even though they scarcely ever show up in the way things turn out.[75]

Nevertheless, most of the familiar deterministic laws are correct to within a very high (though not uniform) degree of approximation. Far from undermining the whole of classical physics, quantum mechanics *entails* that most of classical physics is very nearly correct. So most of the time we can safely get away with using the well-known classical laws, not only for practical purposes, but also for the theoretical purpose of understanding and explaining physical phenomena.

There is a certain analogy between the relation of classical mechanics to quantum mechanics, and its relation to relativity theory. It would be irrational to employ anything other than Newtonian mechanics either to understand or to control the acceleration of a steel ball on an inclined plane. This despite the fact that Newton's theory is known to incorporate falsehoods – e.g., that simultaneity is a transitive relation. The reason is that the corrections one would have to make if one were to apply the more accurate, but more complicated, theory of relativity, would be so small as to be negligible (and would be far less than the margin of error in any actual measurement). One simply notes that Newton's laws are approximately correct but not strictly true, and lets it go at that.

If we accept quantum mechanics in its current form, we shall adopt a similar attitude towards many of the deterministic laws of physics and the other sciences. Strictly speaking, they are false; and they are particularly misleading in their suggestion that certain occurrences are *impossible* which, in point of fact, are no more than highly improbable. For all that, it would be foolish to abandon them, even for the purpose of explanation: they are a very close approximation to the truth. And it is not cheating, it is *quite* correct, to say that the processes they describe are *superficially deterministic* processes. Moreover, each of them will be deterministic to within a specifiable degree of approximation – i.e., we can specify, in each case, the probability of an "impossible" thing's happening.

What of the processes that are superficially random? The great majority of them, like the great majority of physical processes generally, will be fundamentally random processes. On the surface, also, they are random processes; yet some of them are deterministic at an *intermediate* level, to within a certain degree of approximation. These processes – and there are many of them – will have to be pictured as, so to speak, three-tiered ontological layer cakes. This may seem to be an overly elaborate way to conceive of such common, everyday goings-on as the spinning of a roulette wheel; but I do not see how anything simpler can do justice to the facts, as we now understand them to be.

I have defined the three "layers" of physical processes in strictly ontological terms – viz., in terms of what is, not in terms of what any inquirer knows or believes. It follows that we may sometimes encounter a superficially random process in the world, unfolding in accordance with a probabilistic pattern, and *not know* whether we are dealing with something that is *just* a fundamentally random process, or with a process which is deterministic, at some level or other, to within one or another degree of approximation. That 28 per cent of untreated syphilitics develop paresis, or other serious outcomes, may be the result of a fundamentally indeterministic mechanism which gives each untreated syphilitic a physical probability of .28 of developing a serious outcome. Alternatively, it may be the result of an initial condition that works in a deterministic fashion, and is present in 28 per cent of the population. We just don't know.

(b) Peter Railton's deductive-nomological-probabilistic (D-N-P) schema

Railton's D-N-P schema of explanation is tailor-made for events that result from fundamentally random processes. Indeed, he takes these to be the only proper object for any type of probabilistic explanation. The kind of process I have termed "superficially random", Railton calls "pseudo-random". He writes:

> For Hempel, a statistical [i.e., probabilistic] expla-
> nation . . . is one that "makes essential use of at
> least one law or theoretical principle of statistical
> form" ("Aspects", p. 380). Since Hempel distin-
> guishes between statistical laws and mere statis-
> tical generalizations, and asserts that the former
> apply only where "peculiar, namely probabilistic,
> modes of connection" exist among the phenomena
> ("Aspects", p. 377), his characterization permits
> statistical explanation only of genuinely indeter-
> ministic processes. Were some process to have
> the appearance of indeterminism owing to arcane

workings or uncontrolled initial conditions, then no "peculiar . . . probabilistic" modes of connection would figure essentially in explaining this "pseudo-random" process's outcomes. Not only would statistical explanation be unnecessary for such a process, it would be impossible: no probabilistic *laws* would govern it.[76]

We shall have occasion to return to this point.

Railton considers the decay of a particular nucleus u of Uranium-238, and offers the following as the explanation of such an event:

(2) (a) All nuclei of U^{238} have probability $(1 - \exp(-\lambda_{238}.\theta))$ to emit an alpha-particle during any interval of length θ, unless subjected to environmental radiation.

   (b) u was a nucleus of U^{238} at time t_0, and was subjected to no environmental radiation before or during the interval $t_0 - (t_0 + \theta)$.

   (c) u had probability $(1 - \exp(-l_{238}.\theta))$ to emit an alpha-particle during the interval $t_0 - (t_0 + \theta)$.

(2), it appears, gives a D-N explanation only of the fact that u had such-and-such a probability to decay during the interval in question, but we should look a bit closer. I submit that (2), when supplemented as follows, is the probabilistic explanation of u's decay:

(3) A derivation of (2a) from our theoretical account of the mechanism at work in alpha-decay.

The D-N inference (2).

A parenthetic addendum to the effect that u did alpha-decay during the interval $t_0 - (t_0 + \theta)$.[77]

We may note that the theoretical derivation of (2a), though of great interest to a scientific investigator, is not *needed* for a complete explanation of u's decay unless 'complete explanation' is taken in the ambitious sense. The D-N argument (2) – please let's not say "inference" – and the parenthetic addendum, together form a D-N-P explanation which is complete in the modest sense. The pragmatic test is met: the question 'What has this got to do with the explanandum?' cannot arise.

When it comes to setting out the schema of D-N-P explanation in general terms, Railton notes that it will include, first, a law:

(4a) $\forall t \, \forall x \, [F_{x,t} \rightarrow \text{Prob } (G)_{x,t} = p]$
    "At any time, anything that is F has probability p to be G".

Next, we adduce the relevant fact(s) about the case at hand, e:
(4b) F_{e,t_0}",
    "e is F at time t_0",

and draw the obvious conclusion:
(4c) $\text{Prob } (G)_{e,t_0} = p$
    "e has probability p to be G at time t_0".

To which we add parenthetically, and according to
how things turn out:
(4d) $(G_{e,t_0} / \sim G_{e,t_0})$
   "(e did/did not become G at t_0)".

   Whether a D-N-P explanation is true will depend solely upon the truth-values of its premises
and addendum, and the validity of its logic. ...
   The law premise (4a) will be true if all things
at all times satisfy the conditional 'F<x,t> $\rightarrow$ Prob
(G)<x,t> = p', using whatever reading of '$\rightarrow$' we
decide upon for the analysis of natural laws in general. It will be false if there exists a partition of the
Fs into those with *physical* probability r to be G and
those with *physical* probability s to be G, where s $\neq$ r
$\neq$ p. Such a partition might exist according to some
other interpretation of probability, but this would
not affect the truth of (4a).[78]

We must next take note of how Railton understands physical
probabilities. His view is a development of Popper's "propensity"
view, and he draws out its consequences with a rigor which makes
it very evident how far this view departs from the frequentist view
of Reichenbach, von Mises and Salmon:

   Physical probabilities of the sort being considered
   here are ... to be contrasted with *statistical* probabilities; the former express the strength of a certain
   physical possibility for a given system, while the
   latter reduce to claims about the (limiting) relative
   frequencies of traits in sample populations. Much
   well-founded doubt has been expressed about the

applicability of statistical probabilities to single cases, but physical probabilities are *located* in the features of the single case. ...

(2a) thus neither reports a summary of past observations nor expresses a mere statistical uniformity that scattered initial conditions would lead us to anticipate. Instead, it is a law of irreducibly probabilistic form, assigning definite, physically-determined probabilities to individual systems.

It follows that the derivation of conclusions from (2a) by universal instantiation and *modus ponens* is unexceptionable. Were (2a) but a statistical generalization, properly understood as meaning "$(1 - \exp(-\lambda<238>. \theta))N$ of U-238 nuclei in samples of sufficiently large size N, on average, decay during the interval $t_0 - (t_0 + \theta)$", it could not undergo universal instantiation, and would not permit detachment of a conclusion about the probability obtaining in a single case.[79]

Railton agrees that the D-N-P model of explanation will not be viable unless we can make sense of "propensities, or of objective, physical, lawful, single-case probabilities by any other name". He would, one expects, be glad to echo Popper's words: "[P]ropensities are not only as objective as the experimental arrangements but also *physically real* – in the sense in which forces, and fields of forces, are *physically real*".[80] Nothing less will suffice for this style of explanation.

Another feature of D-N-P explanation is that what is explained is not an event in all its concrete particularity, but a fact about it – which may be concrete and particular enough, but is not the whole congeries of features occupying a given chunk of space-time. This will come as a disappointment to those philosophers who strove to avoid any opaque contexts in statements of the form "S explains E". Railton writes:

> Let us return to explanation (3), and admit that it is not the whole story: 23% of the alpha-particles emitted by U-238 have kinetic energy 4.13 MeV, while the remaining 77% have 4.18 MeV. Therefore there are two different decay constants, $\lambda<4.13, 238>$ and $\lambda<4.18, 238>$; both are distinct from $\lambda<238>$, used in (3). Hence we must be quite careful in stating what exactly (3) explains. It does *not* explain the particular *event* observed, for this was either a 4.13 or a 4.18 MeV decay, neither of which has probability $\lambda<238>$ in unit time. Instead, (3) explains the particular *fact about* the event observed that we set out to explain, namely, that an alpha-decay with unspecified energy (or direction, or angular momentum, etc.) took place at nucleus u during the time interval in question. This fact *does* have probability $\lambda<238>$ of obtaining in unit time, representing the sum of the two energy-correlated probabilities with which such a decay might occur. ...
>
> Nor is law (2a) falsified by the discovery of a 23:77 proportional distribution of decay energies, and the associated difference in decay rates. For according to our nuclear theory, there is no difference in initial condition between a nucleus about to emit a 4.13 MeV alpha-particle and one about to emit a 4.18 MeV alpha-particle. It remains true

that *all* U-238 nuclei have probability $\lambda<238>$ to decay in unit time, but it is further true that all have probability $\lambda<4.13, 238>$ to decay one way, and probability $\lambda<4.18, 238>$ to decay another.[81]

(c) The uses of S-R and D-N-P explanation

With the qualifications already noted, I accept Railton's D-N-P schema as an account of how events resulting from fundamentally indeterministic processes are explained by reference to probabilistic laws governing those processes. As with Hempel's schema for D-N explanation, I would add that the explanatory conditions must be causally prior to the explanandum event, in the sense specified earlier.

But if we were to take the Railtonian D-N-P schema as the sole model for probabilistic explanation, we would have to reject explanations that are commonly offered and accepted in other contexts – i.e., when we are dealing with superficially random processes. Railton saw this implication of his theory, and valiantly attempted to make a virtue of necessity:

It is widely believed that the probabilities associated with standard gambling devices, classical thermodynamics, actuarial tables, weather forecasting, etc., arise not from any underlying physical indeterminism, but from an unknown or uncontrolled scatter of initial conditions. If this is right, then D-N-P explanation would be inapplicable to these phenomena even though they are among the most familiar objects of probabilistic explanation. I do not, however, find this troublesome: if something does not happen by chance, it cannot be explained

by chance. The use of epistemic or statistical probabilities in connection with such phenomena un-
questionably has instrumental value, and should
not be given up. What must be given up is the idea
that *explanations* can be based on probabilities that
have no role in bringing the world's explananda
about, but serve only to describe deterministic
phenomena.[82]

Now this was indeed a heroic position to take. One cannot but ad-
mire the courage of a man who is prepared to stand up and tell me-
teorologists, thermodynamics experts, economists, demographers,
and B.F. Skinner, that all their sciences fail to explain anything.
But before accepting so drastic a conclusion, we should look again
at the theory of explanation which generated it, and ask ourselves
whether there is an acceptable alternative.

There is: we do not need to take Railton's D-N-P schema as the
model for all kinds of statistical or probabilistic explanation. And
we do need to appreciate what a difference it makes whether the
statistical laws that figure in our explanations are describing fundamentally random, or perhaps only superficially random processes.

When we believe ourselves to be dealing with a superficially
random process, and describe its pattern of working by means of
statistical probabilities, then, as Railton says, we believe that those
probabilities "arise, not from any underlying physical indeterminism, but from an unknown or uncontrolled scatter of initial conditions". In such a case, those statistical probabilities "have no role
in bringing about" the events which result from the process, and
therefore need not be mentioned in a full explanatory account of
those events. The full account – that is, the ideal text, the complete
explanation in the ambitious sense – would include a D-N explanation giving a precise, detailed description of the initial conditions,

given which the events in question could not but have happened, in view of the deterministic laws governing the process. Well, almost could not; and almost deterministic. For in most cases, the fragment of the ideal text which we are able to formulate, now that we know about quantum mechanics, would go further: it would exhibit those "deterministic" laws as the result (correct to within a certain degree of approximation) of more fundamental laws of a probabilistic character. The probabilities mentioned in *those* laws are the ones which genuinely have a role in bringing about the events we have been talking about.

Nevertheless, the statistical probabilities with which we began do give information about the process, *qua* member of a certain reference class of processes. To be sure, when we say that the roulette wheel has a fifty-fifty chance of stopping on red when half the stops are red, or that there is a 40 per cent chance of rain today, we gloss over many details of the causally relevant conditions that are beyond our knowledge or beyond our control. Analogously – but the analogy must not be pressed too far – when we say that there are five people in the room, we gloss over great quantities of detail about the identity and the characteristics of those persons. For all that, the statement expressing the statistical probability is objective, informative, and if we are lucky, correct, as is the indefinite statement that there are five people in the room.

So long as the distinction between superficially random processes and fundamentally random processes is observed, I see nothing objectionable in a "propensity" interpretation of the statistical probabilities by which superficially random processes are characterized. Such an interpretation would enable us to say, with Hempel, that a regular tetrahedron which was in point of fact destroyed, without ever being tossed, *would* have had a statistical probability of 1/4 of yielding the result 'III' *if* it had been tossed. All the while maintaining that tetrahedron tossing is a deterministic process at what we have been calling the intermediate level.

Statistical probabilities, then, give information about superficially random processes, although this information is admittedly less detailed and precise than it could, in principle, be, and probability numbers do not play the indispensable role in this context that they play in the explanation of fundamentally random processes. Since we have some honest-to-goodness information about the world expressed in the form of statistical probabilities, it would be silly not to use it, when we profitably can, to construct explanations; and use it we do.

We use it when we know, or assume, that there is a complicated deterministic process underlying the relatively simple and accessible random process we are describing – as when we explain the behavior of the roulette wheel or apply classical thermodynamics. We use it when we know, or assume, that we are dealing with a class of explananda which will each have a particular explanation of the rational-agency kind – as when we correlate marriage and divorce rates with the state of the economy. We use it when we simply do not know whether the underlying processes are deterministic or not, as with the syphilis/paresis case. Lastly, we might perfectly well use it if we had reason to suspect we were dealing with a fundamentally random process, but had not yet uncovered the precise, fundamental laws governing the process and/or the precise initial conditions which would enable us to construct D-N-P explanations of its workings. This, I shall argue later, is the category in which explanations of behavior by the laws of operant conditioning should be placed.

When we use this statistical information for explanatory purposes, the schema of explanation we employ is, I think, Salmon's S-R schema, or something very like it. What then of Railton's claim that we must give up the idea that explanations can be based on probabilities which have no role in bringing the world's explananda about?

In a more recent article, Railton has qualified his earlier heroism, and adopted a view not unlike the one I have been defending.[83] He recognizes that it would be foolish to dismiss as worthless all those explanations which portray the explanandum as the outcome of a superficially random process. Such explanations he regards as conveying partial information about ideal texts. But he does not take up the question of the form or pattern exhibited by the less-than-ideal texts we are actually able to formulate in certain other contexts. I have in mind such contexts as economics or weather forecasting, in which the partial information available to us is articulated in a precise quantitative fashion in the form of statistical probabilities. For such cases as these, it is well that we have Salmon's S-R schema to fall back on.

(d) Explanatory antecedence

To these remarks I must now add an important qualification. Explanatory information is always, but always, taken to be antecedent to the explanandum. Any theory of explanation must assert this, on pain of being refuted at a stroke by the acknowledged asymmetries of explanation. Our criterion of explanatory antecedence is that the set of explaining conditions must be causally prior to the explanandum, in the manner specified in connection with the D-N schema of explanation.[84] But since causal priority was defined in a way that does not demand or presuppose a deterministic connection between explanans and explanandum, the same criterion of explanatory antecedence may be applied to D-N-P and S-R explanations.

To look ahead now to what will be more fully explored in the next chapter, I will note that the same criterion of explanatory antecedence will be applicable to rational-agency (R-A) explanations, in which the explanans cites facts in the light of which the explanandum is a rational thing to do (or choose, or desire), and which gives the real and efficacious reason for the occurrence of the explanandum. The definition of causal priority refers to one condition tending to bring about another: this embraces tight deterministic causation, law-like probabilistic connections, and the common-sense platitude that motives and reasons have a tendency to produce the appropriate behavior (or choices, or reasoned desires).

Now in order to give S-R explanation its place in the sun alongside the other kinds, I am prepared simply to add to Salmon's S-R schema the requirement that the explanatory conditions in an S-R explanation be antecedent to the explanandum event, that is, causally prior to it in the way I have specified. But I suspect that Salmon himself would resist this suggestion.

What alternatives might Salmon, or his defenders, see fit to propose? I look forward with genuine interest to discovering the answer to this question. But whether one chooses to explicate explanatory antecedence my way or some other way, there is one implication of the way I have done it which I take to be indispensable. The asymmetrical relationship of antecedence between an explanatory condition C and an explanandum event E holds in virtue of either a lawful or a rational connection between C-type conditions and E-type events. (I shall argue later that it is correct to call either of these a *causal* connection, provided the differences between the two types of causes are duly recognized.) No lawful or rational connection, no explanatory antecedence; no antecedence, no explanatory force. When we accept a factor C, which we observe to be statistically relevant to E, as explaining E, it is because we know or presume that there is a causal connection underlying the observed statistical correlation. And not any old causal connection, either:

not, for instance, a connection in virtue of which E is the cause of C, or one in virtue of which C and E are effects of a common cause A.

If the presumed connection is a lawful rather than a rational one, we may have little or no idea what the underlying law may be. As is now apparent, we may not know whether it is likely to be a deterministic or a probabilistic law; for we may be unable to guess whether the process connecting C with E is a fundamentally random, or merely a superficially random process. But without the belief in a lawful connection of one or the other kind, all temptation to accept C as an explanation of E simply evaporates. If someone claimed to have discovered a close correlation between the level of sunspot activity and the average speed of traffic on the Champs-Elysées, we might be amused, but we would not be inclined to regard either one as the cause, or the explanation, of the other. We would not even feel the urge, mentioned by Salmon, to look for an explanation of the two as effects or symptoms of a common cause. Our background knowledge, and the theories about the world which we accept, rule out the possibility of a lawful connection of either kind between the two.

When a lawful connection – known, or presumed, to be under-lying the statistical correlation between C and E – is what gives C its explanatory force with respect to E, it is this same supposed law-ful connection which gives the statement of statistical probability $P(E/C) = r$ its somewhat law-like character. We confidently assert the counterfactual to the effect that Hempel's regular tetrahedron would have had a statistical probability of yielding the result 'III' if it had been tossed, because of our belief in a set of laws underlying this statistical probability. But a statistical generalization presumed to result from mere coincidence – such as the imagined correlation between sunspots and Paris traffic – is not employed to support counterfactuals in this way.

In closing this account of probabilistic explanation, I will observe that it resembles R-A explanation, and differs from D-N explanation, in that we are sometimes obliged to rule inexplicable certain complex facts consisting of a certain phenomenon E together with the non-occurrence of other members of a certain contrast-class. We can explain why John Jones developed paresis, but none of his brothers did: he was the only brother with untreated latent syphilis. But to the question why John was stricken with paresis, while the other untreated syphilitics in his country club escaped unscathed, we have no reply. If the process by which some untreated syphilitics develop paresis turns out to be a fundamentally random process, that will mean that there is, as a matter of objective fact, no reply to the latter question. We would thus be misrepresenting reality if we were to suggest that the question admits of an answer.

As with R-A explanation, this feature of probabilistic explanation – that certain requests for explanations must be rejected – springs from the fact that the explanans does not rule out all possible alternatives to the explanandum; it does not show that the effect *had to* occur.

Railton is clear, and emphatic, on this point. Referring to the D-N-P explanation (3) of the alpha-decay of uranium atom u, he writes:

> Still, does (3) explain why the decay took place? It does not explain why the decay *had to* take place, nor does it explain why the decay *could be expected to* take place. And a good thing, too: there is no *had to* or *could be expected to* about the decay to explain – it is not only a chance event, but a very improbable one. (3) does explain why the decay *improbably* took place, which is how it did. . . . If alpha-decays are chance phenomena of the sort

described, then once our theory has achieved all that (3) involves, it has explained them to the hilt, however unsettling this may be to *a priori* intuitions. To insist upon stricter subsumption of the explanandum is not merely to demand what (alas) cannot be, but what decidedly should not be: sufficient reason that one probability rather than another be realized, that is, chances without chance.[85]

(e) Teleological explanation

We have now completed the characterization of three of the four schemata of explanation. R-A explanation will be taken up in more detail in the next chapter. I do not claim that this classification of patterns of explanation is exhaustive; there may well be others in use. I have, however, consciously *not* included teleological explanations as a distinct type, because I take it to be the prevailing view in our culture that such explanations are always truncated specimens of explanations conforming to one or another of the four schemata we have already discussed.

"Why do cars have headlights? So that the drivers can see where they are going at night". This I take to be an abbreviated version of the R-A explanation, "Car makers *build* cars with headlights so that the drivers can see where they are going at night".

"Why do animals have eyes? So that they can see". In a theological context, this might likewise be taken as an abbreviated version of the R-A explanation, "God created animals with eyes so that they would be able to see". But most adult members of this culture, if they were to offer or to hear this explanation in a non-theological context, would take it as an abbreviated version of an explanatory story, either D-N or probabilistic, which would run roughly thus: "Eyes are part of the biological mechanism which serves the function of seeing. Seeing has adaptive value. Therefore animals which possess this mechanism tend to survive and reproduce, while animals which lack such a mechanism tend, other things equal, to die out. That is why the earth is now populated with many species of animals which have eyesight".

When it is said that Aristotle saw nature as a system of processes which act with purpose, yet without conscious design, to bring about certain ends, this is because he accepted teleological explanations of natural phenomena without attempting to reduce them to explanations of other types.[86] Young children, I have observed, tend to be Aristotelians: they will offer, and accept, teleological explanations of things in nature without seeing any need to expand them into R-A, D-N, or probabilistic explanations.

---

1   See Hempel and Oppenheim 1948, in Hempel 1965, p. 247.
2   John Stuart Mill 1843, Book III, ch. xii, sec. i; Popper 1935, sec. 12. For further references, see Hempel and Oppenheim 1948, in Hempel 1965, p. 251, n. 7.
3   Hempel and Oppenheim 1948, in Hempel 1965, p. 249.
4   *Ibid.,* pp. 247-248.
5   *Ibid.,* pp. 250-251.
6   Hempel 1966, pp. 55-56.
7   See Clarence Irving Lewis and Cooper Harold Langford 1932, p. 17 ff. and p. 248 ff.; D. Paul Snyder 1971, ch. vii; and Alan Ross Anderson and Nuel D. Belnap Jr. 1975.
8   The phrase is from G.J. Reid's review of Mackie 1974, *Australasian Journal of Philosophy* 54 (1976), p. 79.
9   See Hempel 1962, esp. pp. 108-110.
10   Hempel 1962, pp. 109-110.
11   See Hempel and Oppenheim 1948, in Hempel 1965, p. 273, n. 33.
12   *Ibid.*
13   See Michael Friedman 1974 and Philip Kitcher 1976.
14   Railton 1981, p. 247. A typographical error has been corrected.
15   See esp. Nelson Goodman 1965, pp. 20-21.

16 Fred I. Dretske 1977, p. 251. See Dretske 1977, *loc. cit.*, n. 6, for references to other statements of the functionalist position regarding laws of nature.

17 Bas C. van Fraassen 1980, ch. v.

18 Van Fraassen 1980, p. 127.

19 Van Fraassen 1980, p. 126. The example is due to N.R. Hanson; see Hanson 1958, p. 54.

20 Van Fraassen 1980, p. 130.

21 Van Fraassen 1980, p. 129.

22 Jerry A. Fodor 1975, p. 25.

23 Van Fraassen 1980, pp. 130-131.

24 I am indebted to Prof. David Lewis for helpful comments he made on an earlier formulation of these arguments, during discussion of a paper I read to the Western Canadian Philosophical Association at the University of Calgary, October 1981.

25 From the title essay in Lewis Thomas 1979, pp. 4-5.

26 *Encyclopedia Americana* 1980, vol. V., p. 531.

27 B.F. Skinner 1953, ch. vi.

28 Salmon 1971, p. 86, n. 56. Salmon is quoting Edwin Gurney Clark, M.D., and William D. Morimer Harris, M.D., "Venereal Diseases", *Encyclopaedia Britannica* 1961, vol. XXIII, p. 44.

29 Salmon 1975a, pp. 361-362. Salmon refers to George Gamow 1961, pp. 111-115, in connection with this example.

30 Salmon 1975a, p. 355. This experiment, known as the Stern-Gerlach experiment, is discussed in A. d'Abro 1951, pp. 599-601, to which Salmon refers.

31 Hempel, "Aspects of Scientific Explanation", in Hempel 1965, p. 390.

32 See, for example, Hans Reichenbach 1949, and Richard von Mises 1957.

33 Rudolf Carnap 1945.

34 Popper 1957. Quoted in Hempel 1965, p. 378, n. 1.

35 Popper 1957, pp. 67-68; emphasis added.

36 Hempel 1965, pp. 377-378.

37 Hempel 1965, p. 377.

38 Railton 1978, p. 212.

39 See Hempel 1965 and Hempel 1968.

40 Richard C. Jeffrey 1970, in Salmon *et al.* 1971, pp. 24-25.

41 Michael Scriven was probably the one responsible for introducing this now celebrated example into the philosophical discussion of explanation. See Scriven 1959, esp. p. 480.

42 See, e.g., Hempel and Oppenheim 1948, in Hempel 1965, p. 249, and Reichenbach 1944, p. 13.
43 Salmon 1970, in Salmon 1971, p. 42. Salmon's notation for conditional probability, 'P(A,B)', has been altered to 'P(B/A)' to conform with that of Hempel used earlier.
44 Salmon 1971, p. 40.
45 Salmon 1971, p. 43.
46 Ibid.
47 Ibid.; also Reichenbach 1949, sec. 72.
48 Salmon 1971, pp. 76-77.
49 Salmon 1971, p. 51.
50 Salmon 1971, p. 54.
51 Salmon 1971, p. 55.
52 Ibid.
53 Salmon 1971, p. 81.
54 Salmon 1971, p. 79.
55 Salmon 1971, p. 81.
56 See Salmon 1975b, 1977, 1978 and 1980.
57 Ardon Lyon 1967, p. 4. The example is taken from G. Udny Yule and M.G. Kendall 1950, pp. 315-316.
58 Van Fraassen 1980, p. 108.
59 See John Blackburn 1968, p. 53 and p. 59.
60 Salmon 1971, p. 55.
61 Salmon 1971, p. 71.
62 Adolf Grünbaum 1963, pp. 307-308; Grünbaum 1973, pp. 309-311.
63 Salmon 1971, pp. 71-72.
64 Above, ch. 4, pp. 139-142.
65 Salmon 1971, p. 79.
66 Salmon 1971, p. 81.
67 See especially his foreword to Reichenbach 1976.
68 Salmon 1975a, p. 362.
69 Railton 1981, p. 238, n. 9.
70 Albert Einstein, in a letter to Max Born. Quoted in George Seldes 1960, p. 226.
71 John von Neumann 1955. For this summary view of von Neumann's result I am indebted to Michael Scriven 1957, pp. 734-735.
72 J.R. Lucas 1970, p. 113.

73 Salmon 1975a, p. 356.

74 Railton 1978, p. 223.

75 Railton 1978, pp. 223-224.

76 Railton 1978, p. 209.

77 Railton 1978, p. 214.

78 Railton 1978, p. 218.

79 Railton 1978, pp. 214, 216.

80 Popper 1957, p. 69; Railton 1978, p. 222. See also R.N. Giere 1973, which Railton mentions in this context.

81 Railton 1978, pp. 219-220. On the attempt to avoid opaque contexts in explanations, see Israel Scheffler 1963, pp. 57-76.

82 Railton 1978, p. 223.

83 Railton 1981, esp. pp. 249-255.

84 Above, pp. 171-172.

85 Railton 1978, p. 216.

86 See, e.g., A.E. Taylor 1955, p. 52.

CHAPTER 6
The Causation of Rational Actions

When R.G. Collingwood set out to investigate the different meanings of the word 'cause', he discovered that the oldest sense of the word in English, and of its counterparts in classical Latin and Greek, is the sense in which the intentional actions of a rational agent are caused by that person's desires, beliefs and priorities. He therefore listed this as sense I of the three senses he ultimately distinguished:

> In sense I of the word 'cause' that which is caused is the free and deliberate act of a conscious and responsible agent, and 'causing' him to do it means affording him a motive for doing it. For 'causing' we may substitute 'making', 'inducing', 'persuading', 'urging', 'forcing', 'compelling', according to differences in the kind of motive in question.
>
> This is a current and familiar sense of the word (together with its cognates, correlatives, and equivalents) in English, and of the corresponding words

in other modern languages. A headline in the *Morning Post* in 1936 ran, 'Mr. Baldwin's speech causes adjournment of House'. This did not mean that Mr. Baldwin's speech compelled the Speaker to adjourn the House whether or no that event conformed with his own ideas and intentions; it meant that on hearing Mr. Baldwin's speech the Speaker freely made up his mind to adjourn. In the same sense we say that a solicitor's letter causes a man to pay a debt or that bad weather causes him to return from an expedition.[1]

We need to observe, first, that it is not the bad weather *per se* but the explorer's belief that the weather was turning bad, which is causally related to his action; and secondly, that even this belief would fail to bring about his action of turning back if it were not for his desire to return home safely. Collingwood himself makes both of these points.

By consulting historical dictionaries, Collingwood ascertained that his sense I is the oldest sense of 'cause' in Western civilization. The English word 'cause' was used this way in the Middle Ages; in Latin it is the oldest sense of '*causa*'; in Greek the term '*aitia*' meant originally 'guilt', 'blame', or 'accusation', but then was used to mean 'cause' (sense I) in certain literature of the fifth century B.C.E.[2] This sense of 'cause' cannot, therefore, have been derived from some other sense; if anything, other senses have been derived from this one.

A cause in this sense is a sufficient reason for an action, in the normative sense of 'sufficient', which is also the real reason for the action. Depending on the precise content of the rationale, a cause in this sense may or may not entail that the agent was unable to do otherwise. Again, it may, or may not, entail that he *was* able to do otherwise. Hence the action may or may not have been a free action. I cannot agree with Collingwood that what is caused in this sense is necessarily a *"free* and deliberate act", since, as we have seen, some unfree actions may be said to be caused, in Collingwood's sense I, by the desires and beliefs of the agent.[3] Also, as we shall shortly see, it is not only actions, but choices, decisions, and motivated desires, which are commonly said to be caused (sense I) by the motivating factors.

This chapter will be devoted to an examination of the rational-agency sense of 'cause', and the *phenomenon* of rational-agency causation. These call for a somewhat different treatment than nomic causation, the type that has been the focus of our attention in the preceding chapters. Collingwood's senses II and III of 'cause' will not be examined here: they relate to what I have called nomic causation, but in a way that I did not find helpful as a springboard for further discussion.

Rational-agency (R-A) explanation

A great deal of the philosophical debate that has had a bearing upon rational-agency causation has been carried on by philosophers who took themselves to be debating the epistemological issue of explanation rather than the ontological issue of causation. In fact these are two faces of the same mountain, and it has struck me as nothing less than astonishing that for a number of years, distinct groups of philosophers carried on the discussion of the two problems in the journals in mutual isolation. That artificial separation of the two issues no longer continues; yet I find it helpful to introduce what I have to say about rational-agency causation by alluding to some of the discussion that was focused on explanation.

(a) William Dray and J.R. Lucas

It has long been held by some philosophers that when the action of a human being, or an attempt or decision to act, is explained by reference to the desires, beliefs, and abilities of the agent, a distinctive type of explanation is involved. William Dray calls it "rational explanation":

> [T]his use of the expression 'rational explanation' is a narrower one than is often found in philosophical and semi-philosophical literature. It is sometimes said, for instance, that all science, all systematic inquiry, seeks a rational explanation for what is observed, where all that is meant is an explanation which takes account of all the facts considered puzzling, and which does not violate, say, the canons of coherence and induction. I intend something much more restricted than this: an explanation which displays the *rationale* of what was done.
>
> The goal of such explanation is to show that what was done was the thing to have done for the reasons given, rather than merely the thing that is done on such occasions, perhaps in accordance with certain laws (loose or otherwise). The phrase 'thing to have done' betrays a crucially important feature of explanations in terms of agent calculations[.] . . . For the infinitive 'to do' here functions as a value term. I wish to claim therefore that there is an element of *appraisal* of what was done in such explanations; that what we want to know when we ask to have the action explained is in what way it was *appropriate*.[4]

J.R. Lucas picks up Dray's point, and adds:

> Rational explanations are two-faced. They give the reasons why *I did* the action in question, but also

reasons why *one should*. The latter need not be, although they may be, moral reasons. Any reasons, moral, prudential, intellectual, aesthetic, or any other, may be given, provided only that they make my action *intelligible* to the questioner. He needs to be brought to understand how I came to act as I did. The reasons I give must be *my* reasons – else I am rationalizing, not giving my real reasons –, but they must be *reasons* which could be reasons for him – else my action will remain opaque and unexplained. In accepting my reasons as reasons which could be reasons for him, the questioner does not have to accept them as morally cogent or as the only relevant reasons. He may understand, and still condemn. To explain my action may not be, in the ordinary sense, to justify it. But it must begin to justify. If I give as a reason for my action something which could never lead the questioner to think of doing it in any circumstances, under any description, then my reason will not explain to him at all why I acted as I did. It is only because my actual reasons are ones which he could conceive as being, under some conditions, reasons why he should have acted similarly, that my stating them helps him to understand why I acted on them.[5]

It is beyond dispute that explanations of this type are employed by all of us in accounting for our own behavior and that of our fellow humans. Rational explanations, and the inventing and confirming of hypotheses which are explanatory in this sense, are the stuff of history, legal argument, detective work, and pre-scientific psychology. I am inclined to think that a good deal of such "folk psychology", incorporating rational explanations, is in turn presupposed by scientific psychology. That is *not* beyond dispute; but it a dispute I shall leave to one side.

(b) Paul Churchland's formulation

It is one thing to note the pervasiveness of rational explanation. It is another thing to work out the general schema of rational-agency (R-A) explanation, as Hempel and Oppenheim did for deductive-nomological explanation. And yet another to determine whether or not R-A explanations form a subspecies of D-N explanation. I believe they do not; but it so happens that the philosopher who, in my opinion, has achieved the greatest success in formulating the principles of the R-A schema of explanation did so in the context of arguing that R-A explanations can be viewed as a subclass of D-N explanations. The philosopher in question is Paul M. Churchland, and this is his formulation of the R-A schema:

If one says, "X A-ed because he wanted ϕ", one has made a true statement if (apparently) and only if:

(1) X wanted ϕ, and

(2) X believed (judged, saw) that A-ing was a way for him to achieve ϕ under those circumstances, and

(3) there was no action believed by X to be a way for him to bring about ϕ, under those circumstances, which X judged to be as preferable to him as, or more preferable to him than, A-ing, and

(4) X had no other want (or set of them) which, under the circumstances, overrode his want ϕ, and

(5) X knew how to A, and

(6) X was able to A.

All this is, in a sense, common knowledge. Few of us could produce this list on demand, but we all know how to criticize statements of the form "X A-ed because he wanted ϕ", and we would not offer such a statement if we knew that any one of (1) through (6) were false.[6]

Having noted that the R-A schema of explanation, as just spelled out, is in everyday use, Churchland attempts to account for this fact by suggesting that we language users all take a certain law-like statement L_1 to be true. (More accurately, L_1 is a law sketch that roughly defines a whole class of law-like statements which, according to Churchland, we take to be true.) L_1 contains the six clauses of the R-A schema, with the verbs changed from the past tense to the present.

L_1: (X) (ϕ) (A) If (1) - (6), then X A's[7]

Churchland makes it plain that he is not defending the idea that L_1 will never be shown to be untrue, for one cannot be certain that "the collective wisdom of the human race is sufficiently great that no *false* proposition could ever come to underlie our common explanatory practices".[8] He maintains only that L_1 is not obviously false, and that its truth is in fact presupposed by our everyday explanatory procedures.

Before commenting on what I take to be the shortcomings of this approach, I would like to note some of its strengths.

The variable 'X' in L_1 need not be expressly restricted to agents, much less to rational agents, because the antecedent of L_1 will only be true of entities to whom beliefs, wants and abilities can sensibly be ascribed. It has been cogently argued by Jeffrey Foss that if we are to attribute beliefs to an entity at all, we must presuppose that it possesses a certain minimal rationality.[9] Otherwise we will not be able, after attributing a particular belief to a particular creature, to draw the normal inferences about the other states of the creature, such as its wants and abilities, or its probable behavior. It is a merit of Churchland's approach that it brings out the connection between our readiness to ascribe wants, beliefs and abilities to a thing and our readiness to explain its behavior in accordance with the R-A schema.

The variable 'A' in L_1 is a surrogate for verb phrases in the active voice. The door has been opened for the argument that action in a "full-blooded" sense is behavior which is appropriate or reasonable in the light of the desires and beliefs of the agent. We can say (if we wish) that a bit of behavior is an action in the full-blooded sense if and only if we can successfully explain it in accordance with the R-A schema. At the same time, we have the means for avoiding an unduly narrow and rationalistic conception of action.

The deliberate, well considered, non-routine behavior of a mature, wide-awake, sane human being is, I suppose, our paradigm of action in the full-blooded sense. Such behavior is also, to us, the most obvious candidate for R-A explanation. Other candidates may be located at various distances, in various directions, from the paradigm case. Impulsive, habitual, or unthinking conduct of humans may be treated as action in something weaker than the full-blooded sense, so long as we are dealing with behavior that is voluntary rather than involuntary, with operants as opposed to reflexes.[10] Similarly for some at least of the operant behavior of animals of other species, and of infant members of our own species. The operations of computers and other "intelligent" machines are removed in a different direction from the central paradigm case.

As 'rationality', 'appropriateness in the light of the agent's desires and beliefs' and 'explanatory success' are concepts admitting of degrees, so is 'approximation to the paradigm of action'. We do in fact feel less unease in attributing rationality to things, and we do in fact regard their behavior as something more closely approximating action in the full-blooded sense, the more successful we are in explaining their doings by accounts conforming to the R-A schema. Churchland's approach to the subject sheds considerable light on these features of our conceptual scheme.

Next, there is 'ϕ', the other variable appearing in L_1. Churchland writes:

> I shall understand it as a running surrogate for the completely general "that P (be the case)". In one indirect way or another, wants, like beliefs, are all identified by references to some specific proposition.[11]

Placing 'X wanted ϕ' as the first clause of the R-A schema, and of L_1, makes it clear that, on the one hand, it is an essential part of our conception of 'wanting' that wants play a role in the explanation of action,[12] and that, at the same time, wants can sometimes be identified independently of the actions they motivate. Sometimes, then, when we know that X A's and that (2) - (6) hold, we conclude that he must have wanted ϕ, because that makes his A-ing understandable in the circumstances. At other times, we know *ab initio* that X wants ϕ – because he tells us, or because it is a motivated desire and we know what is motivating it, or because we *are* X and experience the desire.

It is worth taking note of the distinction between motivated and unmotivated desires, as this removes a source of confusion surrounding the application of the R-A schema. I take the distinction from Tom Nagel, who explains it as follows:

> It has been pointed out before that many desires, like many beliefs, are *arrived at* by decision and after deliberation. They need not simply assail us, though there are certain desires that do, like the appetites and in certain cases the emotions. The same is true of beliefs, for often, as when we simply perceive something, we acquire a belief without arriving at it by decision. The desires which simply come to us are unmotivated though they can be explained. Hunger is produced by lack of food, but is not motivated thereby. A desire to shop for groceries, after discovering nothing appetizing in the refrigerator, is on the other hand motivated by hunger. Rational or motivational explanation is just as much in order for that desire as for the action itself.
>
> The claim that a desire underlies every act is true only if desires are taken to include motivated as well as unmotivated desires, and it is true only in the sense that *whatever* may be the motivation for someone's intentional pursuit of a goal, it becomes in virtue of his pursuit *ipso facto* appropriate to ascribe to him a desire for that goal.[13]

Finally, Churchland makes it crystal clear that the normative connection which obtains between explanans and explanandum in the R-A schema – the fact that the explanandum is reasonable or appropriate in the light of the explanans – is not sufficient to show that R-A explanation is a distinct species from D-N explanation. For all the normative overtones of the judgment 'X A'd because he wanted f', this might still prove to be nothing but a special type of D-N explanation.

To say "The numeral '100' appears on the display of my pocket calculator because I pressed the buttons 'Clear', '5', '0', 'x', '2', '=', in that order" is to give an explanation with undeniable normative overtones: the explanandum is the *correct* answer to a certain arithmetical problem. The story related by the explanans is that I gave the calculator that very problem to solve. Yet it does not follow that the operations of pocket calculators demand a unique type of explanation that cannot be viewed as a variety of D-N explanation.

It *does* follow that we have here a rather special family of explanations (a special family of D-N explanations, as it turns out). There are two ways of explaining the production of the answer '100' by the calculator. One is to appeal to its design and the laws of physics; this is patently a D-N explanation. The other, faster, way, is to take the soundness of its design for granted, and simply do the arithmetical calculation. The latter is an instance of what J.R. Lucas calls *formal* explanation:

> Formal explanations – the successors to Aristotle's
> Formal Causes – are those where we explain a
> proposition – e.g., 'Why is 257 a prime number?' –
> by deducing it from other propositions, and ulti-
> mately from ones that are either analytic or postu-
> lated as axioms.[14]

Lucas has given a satisfactory statement of the differentia of formal explanation, but has failed to settle the question of the genus to which it belongs. It seems reasonable – nay, unavoidable – to include the axioms of logic and mathematics among the laws which can figure in D-N explanations; likewise any principles which we wish to take as being true by definition. If this is done, then it follows at once that Lucas's formal explanations are but one variety of D-N explanation.

(c) A critique of Churchland's L_1

I return to the matter of pocket calculators. *Their* operations provide no grounds for thinking that formal explanation must be distinct from D-N explanation, for this further reason: the very fact that they regularly perform calculations in accordance with the laws of arithmetic is itself a derivative law of physics, deducible from more fundamental physical laws together with details of their engineering design. Likewise, Churchland would say, the fact that humans behave in accordance with the norms of rationality provides no grounds for thinking that R-A explanation must be distinct from D-N explanation, *because* L_1 is a law of nature. At any rate, our use of the R-A schema presupposes that it is. (And in time we may discover more fundamental laws of biology from which L_1 can be deduced.)[15]

Now I am in agreement with Churchland on the subject of pocket calculators, but I nevertheless wish to insist that R-A explanation is not a variety of D-N explanation. It follows that, in consistency, I must deny that L_1 is a law of nature. Deny it I do. I deny, furthermore, that our explanatory practices presuppose L_1. Churchland has shown great ingenuity in formulating the principles of R-A explanation as it is practised, but he has misrepresented the common "folk psychology" in claiming that these practices are rooted in an acceptance of L_1 as a law of nature.

The way to see that L_1 is not something that the inherited common-sense outlook would accept as a law of nature, is to focus on the multiply ambiguous verb 'overrode' in clause (4). What are we to understand by one want's *overriding* another?

Think of John Q. Taxpayer completing his annual income tax return. Let us suppose that in addition to his regular salary, he has received $5,000 in cash income which, by law, is taxable. He has every reason to believe that the government will never find out about this income unless he, on his own initiative, declares it on his return. We have a classic case of conflicting wants. On the one hand, John Q., being a morally scrupulous and law-abiding individual, wants to make an honest and legally proper tax return. On the other hand, he has the normal person's desire to hang onto his hard-earned cash. Whatever he finally *does* – whether he submits a return with or without that extra five thousand entered in the gross income column – we will have an R-A explanation of his behavior. If he declares all his income, his behavior will be explained by his desire to act honestly and obey the law. If he cheats, that will not be hard to explain either. It will simply be a matter of which desire overrode the other.

But what *are* we to mean by "the desire which overrode the other"? The one which in fact determined John Q.'s behavior? If we mean that, then L_1 is trivial and has no explanatory or predictive force. Or are we to mean "the desire which John Q. judged it *better* to gratify"? In that case L_1 is empirically false, and is falsified by every instance of *akrasia* or weakness of will. Notoriously what the weak-willed person does is to act against his own best judgment in order to gratify a desire that conflicts with the one he believes it best to gratify. Should we say, then, that "overriding desire" is to mean the desire which is *felt* most strongly at the time, or the one whose gratification would represent the course of least (psychological) resistance to the agent? In that case, again, L_1 is empirically false. This

252 | Causes, Agents, Explanations, and Free Will

time the falsification comes from people who exhibit *strength* of will. They, notoriously, gratify the desire they think it best to gratify, in spite of the fact that some other, conflicting desire is the one which, at the time, they feel to be stronger and more compelling.

How about a disjunction: we could take "the overriding desire" to mean the desire which *either* is the one most strongly felt *or* is the one which the agent judged it best to gratify. This suggestion will do very nicely for spelling out the R-A schema of explanation as such; it is exactly by taking 'overriding' to have this disjunctive meaning in clause (4) that we can be sure of having an R-A explanation of J.Q.T.'s behavior whether he cheats or pays up. We may then proceed, with the resources of the R-A schema, to distinguish saintly taxpayers, who have no desire other than to be honest and abide by the law; taxpayers of sterling character, whose desire to be honest and law-abiding is stronger than their desire to hang onto their money; strong-willed taxpayers, who pay up in spite of a more strongly felt desire to keep their money for themselves; weak-willed taxpayers, who cheat because they act against their own judgment as to which desire it is best to gratify; utterly depraved taxpayers, who have no desire to abide by the law in the first place; and many other categories besides. But the suggestion that 'overrode' be construed disjunctively is fatal to the claim that L_1 is a law-like truth. If, as one may well imagine, John Q.'s most strongly felt desire is to keep his money, but the desire he thinks it best to indulge is to tell the truth, then L_1 with clause (4) interpreted disjunctively would entail that John Q. would *both* cheat *and* pay up. But in the nature of the case it is logically impossible to do both.

It might be objected that if John Q., despite his acknowledged desire not to part with his money when he can avoid it, nevertheless submits an honest and accurate income tax return, this shows that his desire to be a law-abiding fellow was in fact stronger at the time, although he may well have found it very difficult to do what he did.

But now we face the same problem with the adjective 'stronger' that we have already encountered with the verb 'overrode'. If "stronger desire" means the desire more strongly felt, the statement that his desire to obey the law was stronger is simply false. If "stronger desire" means the desire which in fact determines the agent's behavior, the statement is trivial and lacks any explanatory force.

I contend, then, that the following three propositions all belong to the "Person-Theory of Humans"[16] or the "folk psychology" in terms of which we interpret and explain human action:[17]

(i) Clause (4) is a non-redundant element in R-A explanation of behavior.

(ii) Sometimes people deliberately act against their own best judgment.

(iii) Sometimes people deliberately act in defiance of their most strongly felt desires.

From these propositions it follows that L_1 is not the law-like truth Churchland says we take it to be. Either, therefore, Churchland has misrepresented folk psychology, or folk psychology itself is radically inconsistent.

How, it might be asked, could folk psychology incorporate the R-A schema of explanation – which is, after all, the source of the antecedent of L_1 – and yet have no place for L_1 itself? The answer is that the R-A schema is a pattern for explanation, and no more than that. Explanation is a process that only begins when we have an explanandum on our hands to be explained. A law, on the other hand, has a role to play both in explanation and in prediction. The trouble with L_1, as we saw, is that when its clause (4) is interpreted in the way that best suits the purpose of articulating the R-A schema of explanation, it yields contradictory *predictions*. But a schema of explanation, as such, yields no predictions at all.

Travelers approaching the seashore from inland are apt to smell the ocean long before they are able to see it. In the discovery that L_1 comes to grief over the matter of predictions, while its parent, the R-A schema, does not, we may likewise catch a whiff of the tangy air of libertarianism, which is indeed the conclusion toward which the present argument is conveying us. The libertarian concept of human freedom does involve an element of unpredictability; and as it turns out, it is precisely this element of unpredictability that the R-A schema of explanation can tolerate, but Churchland's L_1 cannot.

Churchland is aware that *akrasia* represents a difficulty for his theory which libertarians will be inclined to exploit. He writes:

> Even if the ordinary man is in some sense cognizant of an *'akrasial'* gap ... in his understanding of how persons function, the mechanics of his ordinary explanatory practices will still be perfectly explicable on the assumption of his implicit use of L_1 if we add a completely unspecific "barring vitiating factors" clause to its antecedent. L_1 would thus be one degree sketchier than first represented, but that is no problem. If *akrasia*, of a sort inimical to L_1, is a part of (better: gap in) the ordinary man's understanding of how persons function, a minor addition to L_1 will include that factor in the story of that understanding.
>
> Footnote: A libertarian will insist that *akrasia* represents not a gap in our understanding of the mental state/behavior function, but rather an *in principle* unfillable gap in that so-called *function*.

Aside from the difficulty of justifying such an insistence, we should note that even if the claim were true, this would not entail the desired indeterminism. It would entail only that the conceptual framework in terms of which we now understand the "working" of humans is, at bottom, inadequate to the phenomena (is an explanatory failure), and should be replaced by some more successful explanatory framework.[18]

This goes to the heart of the matter. I would indeed claim that there is "an in principle unfillable gap" in the so-called mental state/ behavior function. I have indicated that it is not *akrasia* alone, but the whole range of motivational phenomena involving weakness of will *and* strength of will, which together constitutes the evidence for there being such a gap. If anything it is the behavior of strong-willed people that is more mysterious. Why should a person act contrary to his most strongly felt desire? It seems downright absurd.

Folk psychology would have it that the will is something which is in a certain measure functionally independent of both reason and passion. Otherwise the traditional metaphors, according to which the will sides with one or the other of those skirmishing parties, make little sense. I grant that this does not, by itself, entail indeterminism; the thesis of incompatibilism is required as a further premise, and that thesis must be separately defended. I do think that certain propositions of folk psychology, together with incompatibilism, entail indeterminism. Nevertheless, those parts of folk psychology may be in error: that is what the hard determinists have been saying for a long time. So indeterminism, as well as incompatibilism, is a thesis that needs a philosophical defence of its own.

But does the claim that there is an unfillable gap between mental states and behavior entail that folk psychology is an explanatory failure? Only if one takes the logical tightness of D-N explanation as one's standard of success.

We noted in the last chapter that if we have a complete D-N explanation of an event E, then the truth of the explanans S entails that there was no causally possible alternative to E's occurring. Do we employ a similar standard of completeness for R-A explanations of human behavior? The only way to answer that question is to examine our explanatory practices, being careful to avoid having our vision distorted by determinism, the Principle of Sufficient Reason, or some other rationalistic dogma.

I think that an unbiased look at the evidence reveals that we do not employ a standard of success or completeness for R-A explanation that is at all comparable to the standard we find appropriate for D-N explanation. Certainly when I explain John Q. Taxpayer's cheating on his return by saying that he wanted to hang on to his money, that he judged this to be a good means, and that his desire not to part with his money overrode his desire to be a good law-abiding Joe, I do not imply that under the circumstances he was *unable* to do otherwise. So, given the truth of the explanans, an alternative outcome was possible, in the human-agency sense of "possible". This much is entailed by saying that his act was a free act, in the *pre-analytic* sense of "free" – the sense whose extension compatibilists and incompatibilists are agreed on.

Does it then follow that there was a possible alternative, in the *causal* sense of "possible"? The incompatibilist would say yes; the compatibilist (at least one who is a soft determinist) must say no. I submit that the R-A schema of explanation itself is neutral between these two theories. Its use as an integral part of our common-sense conceptual scheme commits us neither to compatibilism nor to incompatibilism.

If Churchland could have shown that our use of R-A explanations rests upon an acceptance of L_1 or some such law-like statement, then he would have shown that we do commit ourselves, by the way we go about explaining human conduct, to a belief in compatibilism. I have argued that Churchland has not shown this. But this merely removes one objection – albeit a most significant objection – to the neutrality of the R-A schema. It does nothing in a positive way to establish its neutrality.

(d) R-A explanation, freedom, and reasons for acting

In the succeeding chapter it will be argued that incompatibilism is true. Since I continue to hold that our common explanatory practices are sound – and here the onus of proof would be on the person who wished to claim that they are not – the argument for incompatibilism may be viewed as being, at the same time, an argument for the proposition that the R-A schema does not presuppose compatibilism.

But neither does it presuppose incompatibilism. This is evident from the fact that in certain cases (cases of unfree voluntary action), it is possible to give an R-A explanation and a D-N explanation of one and the same act. If this is possible in some cases, the principles of R-A explanation cannot of themselves rule out that it be possible in every case.

To say this is not to retract anything that has been said earlier. I have argued that R-A explanation is a distinct type, not a subspecies of D-N explanation. But from this it does not follow that we can never give two explanations of the same bit of behavior – one R-A style and one D-N style. Sometimes, in fact, we can. The examples given previously of actions performed as a result of truly irresistible impulses or desires provide the cases in point.[19]

The use of the R-A schema, therefore, commits us neither to compatibilism nor to incompatibilism. Some acts which we explain by giving the agent's rationale we count as free acts in the minimal sense that the agent was able, in the circumstances, to do otherwise. (Whether this ability to do otherwise is analyzed along compatibilist or incompatibilist lines is another matter.) Some acts are free in the stronger sense that they are not prompted by any kind of compulsion or constraint imposed upon the agent.

A robbery victim who coolly hands over his money, because he calculates that resistance would be too risky, acts freely in the minimal sense. He would have been able to resist, had he so chosen. Obviously, though, he acts under compulsion: if it is the stronger sense of 'free' we are interested in, he is the very paradigm of a person not acting of his own free will. But a robbery victim who handed over his money in a panic might not even be free in the minimal sense; perhaps his terror was so great that he was not able to do otherwise. It is the minimal sense of freedom, rather than the stronger sense, which will be of more significance in the analysis to follow.

The "stronger" sense of freedom I have mentioned is by no means a maximal sense. The maximum of freedom is to act completely on one's own initiative, as God is thought to do when he is credited with activity that is self-causing or *causa sui*.[20] A person who does a favor for another when asked is acting freely in the stronger sense, so long as no coercion is involved. But the person who does a favor *without* being asked comes a step closer to acting freely in the maximal sense.

The central claim I wish to make about the pragmatics of R-A explanation is this. Without committing ourselves to compatibilism, we do sometimes accept R-A explanations of acts which are free in the minimal sense as being complete or sufficient explanations. What I mean by "complete explanation" in this context is the same thing I meant by "complete explanation in the modest sense" in the context of D-N explanation: the question

'What has this explanans got to do with the explanandum?' is no longer in order.

We accept an R-A explanation as being complete precisely when the rationale spelled out in the explanans gives a sufficient reason for the action, decision, or desire described in the explanandum, in a *normative* sense of 'sufficient', and when, furthermore, we are convinced that the explanans gives some or all of the agent's *real* reasons as contrasted with a mere rationalization.

The norms involved here are our minimal norms of rationality, the standards in the light of which the explanandum appears reasonable or appropriate, given the explanans. It is important to realize that nothing stronger than minimal norms of rationality are involved. If such were not the case, we would have little success in explaining the behavior of creatures as "brokenly and imperfectly rational" as ourselves.[21] As it is, we do very well at explaining the acts and choices of the stupid, the weak-willed, the depraved and the insane. By allowing for false beliefs, wicked desires, perverted priorities, and flabbiness of character, the R-A schema covers a multitude of sins.

One may have a complete R-A explanation of an action, and then request an explanation of one of the facts mentioned in the explanans. This is exactly parallel to the situation with regard to D-N and other styles of explanation. The explanations which are trotted out in order to satisfy such a new request may be of the R-A kind, or of any other variety.

Suppose our friend John Q. Taxpayer declares all his income and pays his tax in full, despite having had a golden opportunity to cheat and have an extra thousand dollars or so for himself. An R-A explanation of his behavior will be complete when we have given a rationale in terms of the relevant desires, beliefs, and abilities. Such a complete R-A explanation will serve to classify John Q., in this instance, as a saintly taxpayer, a taxpayer of sterling character, a strong-willed taxpayer, an extraordinarily absent-minded taxpayer, a masochist, or an imbecile. (No doubt there are other possibilities; one cannot claim exhaustiveness for such a list.)

Suppose that one element of the explanation we come up with is that John Q. had a very strong desire, this year, to minimize his income tax payment. Then it would be in order to request an explanation of this fact: "Why was he so anxious to save all he could on his taxes, despite his very adequate income?" The answer to this new question might be an R-A style explanation: "His daughter has been visiting the orthodontist". As Nagel pointed out, a motivated desire may need, and be given, an R-A explanation, just as much as an action.[22] Or the answer might be a D-N explanation, complete or truncated: "He has an anal-retentive personality". Or an S-R (statistical relevance) explanation drawn from psychology or one of the social sciences: "He comes from a family of tightwads". Or one of the informal explanations which explain desires and actions by noting that they are instances of persistent dispositions or character traits: "He's just plain greedy".

Before we leave the subject of R-A explanation, one final point needs to be noted. Some acts are such that we can give complete R-A explanations of them in answer to one question 'Why did H do A rather than X_1 or X_2 or . . . or X_n?' but not in answer to another question 'Why did H do A rather than Y_1 or Y_2 or . . . or Y_m?' Suppose you are out driving at five o'clock on a Sunday morning, and enter an expressway that is devoid of traffic. Having three empty lanes to choose from, you select the middle one. Why? Well, you are on the highway that leads to your intended destination; and you had to select one of the three lanes because it is bad form to drive along straddling a broken white line. But you had no reason for selecting the middle lane rather than the right-hand or the left-hand lane, although you did so deliberately. There may, of course, be subconscious motives or even physiological factors that will account for your choice; but I think it would be an error to suppose, dogmatically, that this must be so in every case. It is possible that there is nothing more to be said.

It was this type of problem which led van Fraassen to the view that an explanans S can only be said to explain an explanandum E relative to some contrast-class X.[23] No such problem arises in the case of D-N explanation, as we have explicated that concept; for in every complete D-N explanation, S rules out all causally possible alternatives to E. For the remaining types of explanation, I prefer to treat 'E and not X_1 or X_2 or ... or X_n' as a different explanandum from 'E and not Y_1 or Y_2 or ... or Y_m'. It then follows, not that there are phenomena for which there is no explanation, but that there may be certain complex facts, each consisting of a phenomenon plus the non-existence of the other members of some contrast-class, for which there is no explanation.

Causation and rational agency

The contrast between a rationalization, which *would* explain an action or a motivated desire *if* it were the *real* reason for the action or desire in question, and the real reason itself, which *does* explain, brings the discussion inevitably from the topic of explanation to that of causation.

Joe Illwill, let us suppose, is one of the most vicious people you know. He entertains his acquaintances by relating fantasies of blood-chilling callousness and violence. When he tells you he has decided to join the Canadian Armed Forces, you have little difficulty in figuring out an R-A explanation for this move: Joe is trying to seek out an occupation in which he can lawfully indulge his murderous instincts. It may cross your mind that his choice is a rather inappropriate one, given the supposed motive. Canadian soldiers have few opportunities to gratify homicidal urges; they are far more apt to find themselves on peacekeeping duty in a country torn by civil strife, being shot at by both sides and not allowed to shoot back. Joe, you surmise, has not really thought this thing through. Imagine your reaction when Joe goes on to explain that his reasons for joining the armed forces are to see the world, and learn a trade, and have a life in which he is sure to keep physically fit. What a bunch of transparent rationalizations! All the more disconcerting, in a way, if Joe himself believes that that is why he chose to join.

The example has been designed to illustrate the point made by Donald Davidson:

> How about the . . . claim that justifying is a kind of explaining, so that the ordinary notion of cause need not be brought in? Here it is necessary to decide what is being included under justification. Perhaps it means only . . . that the agent has certain beliefs and attitudes in the light of which the action is reasonable. But then something essential has certainly been left out, for a person can have a reason for an action, and perform the action, and yet this reason not be the reason why he did it. Central to the relation between a reason and an action it explains is the idea that the agent performed the action *because* he had the reason. Of course, we can include this idea too in justification: but then the notion of justification becomes as dark as the notion of reason until we can account for the force of that 'because'.[24]

One obvious suggestion is that the force of the 'because' is counterfactual: you judge that Joe Illwill would not have decided to join the armed forces if he had not had the urge to kill people; and that since he does have this urge, he would have decided to join the forces even if he had not believed that this was a way to see the world, learn a trade, and keep fit.

This very natural answer, however, is open to the same objection that was urged against the analysis of other kinds of causes in terms of conditionals and law-like generalizations. The basic thing about causes is their *efficacy:* they *bring about* their effects – and this basic fact is independent of what happens in general or what might have happened in a counterfactual situation. Likewise, the real reason for a person's behavior is a cause that actually produces the behavior on this particular occasion.

When people are giving the causes of their own behavior, there is a presumption that introspection gives them a manner of direct access to the factors that are causing them to act as they do. The awareness that *these* factors are motivating my actions and decisions amounts to a direct perception of the efficacy of those causes, just as my awareness that *I did that,* when I deliberately pound my fist on the table, is a direct perception of my own efficacy. But despite its being a direct awareness of what is bringing about our conduct, we find that in this type of case, introspection is notoriously fallible: the example of Joe Illwill was designed to illustrate that very point. When examining or re-examining the causes of our own actions, we have the option of engaging in more careful and sustained introspection, in the hope of arriving at a clear and accurate perception of our motives. But when it comes to working out the causes of other people's behavior, other means must be used to marshal the evidence of experience in support of any hypothesis we might entertain.

The role of the counterfactual conditionals that we so readily produce in expanding on our judgment that *this* was the *real* reason for a person's behavior is similar, but not quite identical, to the role of the causal conditionals backed by laws of nature, to which appeal is made when the concept of nomic causation is being applied. Evidence supporting the acceptance of the counterfactuals is indirect evidence for the hypothesis that these reasons were efficacious in producing the behavior.

Nevertheless, you do not entertain the idea that Joe would have been *unable* to join the armed forces in the absence of an urge to kill; nor that the presence of this urge renders him unable to do otherwise than join. You entertain only hypothetical judgments about the ways in which he would exercise his abilities in different circumstances. What, now, if incompatibilism were true? Then those hypothetical judgments could not be construed as *causal* conditionals, sustained by laws of nature. For the causal conditional $N_c(p \supset q)$ rules out $(p \bullet \sim q)$ as causally impossible. And incompatibilism says that what is causally impossible is impossible (in the agency sense) for any human.

Of course one can have a sufficient reason for one's action, in a normative sense of that term, which is also a *real* reason, in the sense that it was causally efficacious, and yet be able to act otherwise. Nothing could be more central, and more of a commonplace, in the view of human nature that is built into folk psychology. The standard of completeness for R-A explanations is thus seen to be a different type of standard from the one that is applicable to D-N explanations. And *now* if incompatibilism turns out to be true – i.e., my being able to do otherwise entails that it is causally possible for me to do otherwise – it will follow that some acts – viz., acts that are free in the minimal sense – are such that they can be given a complete R-A explanation but not a complete D-N explanation, though it might be possible to give them a complete S-R or D-N-P explanation.

Causation and counterfactual conditionals

We have found that counterfactual conditionals play a significant role in our reasoning when we assign causes to the behavior of rational agents. Some philosophers, however, have attempted to analyze *all* singular causal judgments solely in terms of counterfactual conditionals, and it will be helpful to consider the contribution they have made to the discussion. I begin with the elegant definition offered by Ardon Lyon:

> 'a caused x' = Condition ω & (Condition 1 v Condition 2) Df.

> *Condition ω.* 'a is not a precondition of x (i.e., it is not the case that, if a had not occurred, then it would have been logically improper to say without further explanation either that x occurred or that x did not occur).'

> *Condition 1.* 'In a situation where an event x was preceded by a set of events a, b, c, d, e, . . . etc., if all the events b, c, d, e, . . . etc. other than a had occurred and a had not occurred, then x would not have occurred'.

> *Condition 2.* 'In a situation where an event x was preceded by a set of events, a, b, c, d, e, . . . etc., then there is at least one event b such that, with all other events remaining as before:

> both (i) if neither a nor b had occurred, x would not have occurred,

and (ii) if b had occurred and a not, then x would have occurred,

but also (iii) if a had occurred and b not, then x would have occurred.[25]

For reasons already discussed, I would insist upon two amendments to this definition – one to take care of causes which do not precede their effects, the other to allow for causes which do no more than confer upon their effects a certain probability, greater than zero but less than 1.

Nevertheless, Lyon's proposal has considerable merit. It allows for the fact, noted by J.L. Mackie, that what is most commonly meant by 'a caused x' is that a was necessary and sufficient in the circumstances for x, but that "the sufficiency is less firmly required than the necessity, particularly where the sequence is known to have occurred".[26]

The Cement of the Universe: A Study of Causation CLLP by J.L. Mackie (1980), p. 58. Reproduced by permission of Oxford University Press.

It introduces, in Condition 2, the indispensable complication which is required to cover cases of causal overdetermination, such as the prisoner executed by a firing squad who simultaneously receives two bullets in the heart, either one of which would have been immediately fatal, or the man who walks around wearing both braces and a belt.

Most important, for our purposes, Lyon has here offered us a definition of 'cause' which could be applied to both rational-agency causes and nomological causes. If we let the letters a, b, c, ... stand for the kinds of conditions which can enter into R-A or D-N explanations – i.e., for facts and states of affairs as well as for events – then it seems that the counterfactuals which make up Condition 1 and Condition 2 express exactly what is common to the two types of causes we have distinguished (i.e., rational-agency causes and no-mological causes). The motives and beliefs which cause our actions, in the rational-agency sense, may be rationally and counterfactually necessary for those actions, or sufficient, or both; and some of our actions are overdetermined in the sense that we have two or more reasons for acting, each of which would be sufficient, in the circumstances, to cause us to act so. Analogously, it would seem, with nomological causes and their effects.

The analogy, the common structure, is genuine; yet it is only skin-deep. This becomes evident when we enquire into the truth-conditions of the conditionals associated with rational-agency causation, and contrast them with those of the conditionals associated with nomological causation.

The conditionals which express the relation of rational-agency causes to their effects are ordinary counterfactuals. Hence, if we were to adopt Stalnaker's semantics for counterfactuals, we would read 'If p, then q' as meaning 'In that possible world most similar to the actual world in which p is true, q is also true'.[27] Following the (to me) far more plausible semantics of David Lewis, the ordinary counterfactual 'If p, then q' cannot be interpreted as claiming that either p or $(p \supset q)$ is true in any one particular world, nor yet in all worlds satisfying some restriction that can be laid down once for all. Counterfactuals are, rather, variably strict conditionals. Roughly speaking, the counterfactual 'If p, then q' is non-vacuously true, at a world i, if and only if there is a set W of worlds possessing *some* degree of similarity to i, p holds at one or more of the worlds in W, and $(p \supset q)$ is true in every world in W. But the set W need not be held constant from one utterance of a counterfactual conditional to the next.[28]

That the counterfactuals expressing rational-agency causation are just such variably strict conditionals may be seen from the fact that when we are asked to back them up, or give a warrant for believing them, we do not always appeal to causally necessary laws of nature. Sometimes this would be insufficient, because the set W of possible worlds, similar to the actual world in certain respects and to a certain degree, which we need to discuss in order to spell out the meaning of 'If p, then q', is a proper subset of the set of worlds in which the laws of nature are the same as in the actual world. "If Joe Illwill had not had a desire to kill people, he would not have joined the armed forces": this statement would normally be backed with information about Joe's character; hence it invites us to consider the set of worlds in which the laws of nature are the same as in the actual world, and so likewise is the character of Joe Illwill. (We might possibly call such conditionals "counterfactuals of character".) On the other hand, counterfactuals of this family may expressly envisage worlds in which the laws of nature are different: "If strychnine did not cause death in rats, and this was generally known, rat-catchers would not use it as a poison".

But just in this, it seems to me, we can observe an important difference between these counterfactuals and the ones that express nomological causation. The latter are *typically* supported by an appeal to laws which entail them; it is agreed on all sides that laws play this role in our thinking about what causes what. If this is so, then when we take Lyon's definition, above, as an account of nomological causation, the counterfactuals which figure in Condition 1 and Condition 2 can no longer be viewed as ordinary counterfactuals – *variably* strict conditionals. They are *uniformly* strict conditionals expressing physically necessary connections between their antecedents and their consequents. Each should be flagged with the operator 'N_c', to indicate that here is a conditional which would hold true in every possible world in which the laws of nature were the same as in our world. (I observe in passing that something like Robert Stalnaker's "moderate modal realism" is being assumed here, as it was in Chapter 3.[29])

David Lewis has offered a counterfactual analysis of causation more subtle and complicated than Ardon Lyon's. One important refinement due to Lewis is designed to cope with a special class of causally overdetermined events that Lyon overlooked:

> Suppose that c_1 occurs and causes e; and that c_2 also occurs and does not cause e, but would have caused e if c_1 had been absent. Thus c_2 is a potential alternate cause of e, but is pre-empted by the actual cause c_1. We may say that c_1 and c_2 overdetermine e, but they do so asymmetrically. In virtue of what difference does c_1 but not c_2 cause e?
>
> As far as causal dependence goes, there is no difference: e depends neither on c_1 nor on c_2. So the difference must be that, thanks to c_1, there is no causal chain from c_2 to e; whereas there is a causal chain of two or more steps from c_1 to e.[30]

The notion of a causal chain (alternatively, that of a continuous causal *rope*, otherwise known as a causal sausage) is a notion used in many contexts, and one which seems to be indispensable here.[31] (I earlier used the expression 'causal process', intending this to be neutral as between the chain theory and the sausage theory.)

The conclusion I would wish to draw from this examination of causation and counterfactuals is somewhat different from the conclusion reached by J.L. Mackie, who says of the concept of causation:

> [O]ur concept is in several ways a bit indeterminate: 'cause' can mean slightly different things on different occasions, and about some problematic cases, for example of over-determination, we may

be unsure what to say. But it is still a fairly unitary
concept: we do not have one concept for physical
causation and another for human actions and interactions (as someone might be forced to say who
took our concept of physical causation to be that of
regular succession); we can and do assert similar
counterfactual necessity (and at times sufficiency)
about fields of all different sorts.[32]

The Cement of the Universe: A Study of Causation CLLP by J.L. Mackie (1980),
p. xi. Reproduced by permission of Oxford University Press.

It will be plain that I do not equate nomological causation with mere
regular succession in the actual world. But as we saw, the distinction
between rational-agency causes and nomological causes breaks out
all over again, within a counterfactual analysis of causation, when
we come to consider the manner in which different counterfactuals
are known and warranted. Nevertheless, Mackie is, I think, quite
correct to insist that our concept of causation is a "fairly unitary"
concept. The basic idea of efficacy applies to all sorts of causal connections in the same way; so do the relational concepts of causal
priority and causal ancestry. But the counterfactual conditionals
associated with causation need to be treated differently in the context of rational agency than in the context of nomic causation. This
point serves to create an opening for the defence of libertarianism
that will be attempted in the following chapter.

We began this chapter by noting, with Collingwood, that when
verb 'cause' is used in accordance with the oldest sense that exists
in our language, what is caused is (frequently) "the free and deliberate act of a conscious and responsible agent".[33] When we say
that a solicitor's letter causes a man to pay a debt, we do not imply
that the debtor was unable to do otherwise. In the normal case, it

would be quite within his powers to ignore the letter or even sue the creditor. We do imply that the arrival of the letter was efficacious in producing the debtor's act of paying up, and causally prior to it. We imply, moreover, that the letter's arrival was counterfactually necessary and sufficient (in the circumstances) for the act of making payment. But the conditional judgments involved (If the letter had not been received, he would not have paid; once the letter was received, he would have paid even if other circumstances had been different) are, crucially, counterfactuals expressing the character of the debtor. They are to be understood as variably strict conditionals, not causally necessary conditionals holding true in every possible world in which the laws of nature are as in this world. So if the debtor had chosen to ignore the solicitor's letter, he would, we imply, have been acting out of character. But he would not have done something that, in the circumstances, was causally impossible. This is how we can understand the traditional claim that rational-agency causes "incline without necessitating".

---

1 R.G. Collingwood 1940, p. 290. Although the present account owes a great deal to my reading of Collingwood, my analysis diverges from his when it comes to other senses of 'cause'. I therefore pass over Collingwood's senses II and III.

2 Collingwood 1940, p. 291.

3 See above, ch. 3, pp. 93-95.

4 William Dray 1957, p. 124.

5 J.R. Lucas 1970, p. 42.

6 Paul M. Churchland 1970, pp. 220-221.

7 Churchland 1970, pp. 221-222.

8 Churchland 1970, p. 224.

9 Jeffrey E. Foss 1976.

10 Skinner 1953, ch. vii, esp. pp. 110-116.

11 Churchland 1970, p. 215, n. 7.

12 As Richard Brandt and Jaegwon Kim have insisted. See Brandt and Kim 1963.
13 Tom Nagel 1970, p. 29.
14 Lucas 1970, pp. 41-42.
15 Churchland 1970, pp. 234-236.
16 Churchland 1970, p. 226.
17 The expression "folk psychology" has come to supplant Churchland's term 'person-theory'. Churchland himself regards the two as having the same extension (private conversation).
18 Churchland 1970, p. 224.
19 See above, ch. 3, pp. 93-95.
20 See Collingwood 1938, pp. 88-89.
21 The phrase is due to Brand Blanshard.
22 See above, p. 248.
23 Van Fraassen 1980, pp. 126-130. See above, ch. 5, p. 179.
24 Donald Davidson 1963, p. 691.
25 Lyon 1967, pp. 8, 12, 15 and 16.
26 Mackie 1974, p. 58.
27 Robert C. Stalnaker 1968, Section II, pp. 98-112.
28 For the exact definition, see David Lewis 1973, pp. 13-17.
29 See above, pp. 106-107.
30 David Lewis 1973, p. 567.
31 See above, ch. 3, p. 122.
32 Mackie 1980, p. xi.
33 See above, p. 239.

CHAPTER 7
Free Will

Three objections to libertarianism

The position that has been developed in the preceding chapters on the issues of causality and explanation has implications for the issue of determinism and free will. In particular, it provides the basis for a defence of libertarianism, and the present chapter will be devoted to elaborating a defence of that position.

Libertarianism is the theory that whenever human beings act of their own free will, they exercise a power of choice which is such that in the prevailing conditions it is possible to choose otherwise; thus, one's choosing X *freely* at time t is logically incompatible with there being causally sufficient conditions at t for one's choosing X. I will argue that such a power of choice is also exercised, in many cases, by agents who would not commonly be described as acting of their own free will – e.g., by persons acting under strong, but not irresistible, pressure from others.

The libertarian, as I see it, is obliged to defend this view against three different objections. There is, first, the objection of the determinists. They claim that there are, in point of fact, causally sufficient conditions, obtaining at the same or at an earlier time, for every event that occurs (and also for every state of affairs and every non-event, such as my computer's not bursting into flames). The making of a choice by a human being is an event. Hence, if determinism is true, no such thing as a free choice, as defined by the libertarians, ever occurs. Against this, the libertarian must say that determinism is false: a factual claim.

Secondly, there are the compatibilists (who are apt to be determinists but need not be). Their claim is that it is not self-contradictory to suppose that there are causally sufficient conditions for the making of a free choice, in the sense of 'free' that is needed to give an accurate account of human behavior. Against this, the libertarian will maintain that such a supposition would be self-contradictory: here the claim that is made is a logico-semantical claim.

Lastly, libertarianism must be defended against the charge that the conception of free choice it proposes is incoherent. The objector will argue: either there are causally sufficient conditions for the making of a free choice, or there are not. If there are, then we can readily explain how a person's free choices are determined by his or her desires, beliefs, and character: those precise desires, etc., are causally sufficient conditions for the making of just those choices by anyone. Furthermore, there will be no problem in justifying the standard, and universally accepted, social practice of holding people responsible for the results of their free choices; for it is *their* desires, beliefs and character that were the cause of those choices.

At the same time, we will be able to say categorically that a person could have chosen, and done, otherwise, even with the desires, beliefs, and character he or she had, provided only that this 'could have' of human ability is kept distinct from the 'could have' which denotes causal possibility. Of course it is causally impossible not to choose A in the presence of conditions that are causally sufficient for the choosing of A. But the categorical 'could have' of ability, while it does not entail a categorical 'could have' of causal possibility, *does* entail a causal conditional to the effect that *if* (contrary to fact) the agent's desires or beliefs or character had been other then they in fact were, then he or she would have chosen differently. This is, precisely, the compatibilist account of free choice.[1]

But, the objector continues, what if there are not causally sufficient conditions for the making of a free choice, as you libertarians contend there cannot be? Then the making of a free choice is an event that is not completely determined by prior and simultaneous conditions. It may, of course, be completely determined in certain respects; and even with regard to those respects in which it is not completely determined, there may yet be causally sufficient conditions for its falling within certain limits. But there will be a non-zero range of indeterminacy with respect to at least one of its characteristics: the characteristic's being anywhere within this range will be consistent with all the conditions obtaining at the time and with all the relevant laws of nature. This is what is meant by an event's not being completely determined.[2] In the case of the making of a free choice, it must be indeterminate as between the choice of X and the choice of some alternative incompatible with X.

But to the extent that an event is not causally determined, it must occur by chance; it will be a random happening, occurring without rhyme or reason. Now a random happening, if there were such a thing, would indeed be uncaused; and perhaps there are uncaused events. The compatibilist account of human action does not, after all, entail that determinism must be true. But it would be absurd, and highly unjust to boot, to hold a person morally responsible for uncaused random happenings, even those which were part of her own psychic life. Since they are uncaused, she, the person, cannot have caused them; they simply happen to her. How can these be the things for which, above all else, she is to be held morally responsible?

The libertarian's response to this very telling objection must be to define a concept of freedom which will make it plain that a free choice is a psychic event which is neither completely determined nor *simply* a random happening. Next, it must be shown that this concept provides what is in fact the best characterization of human agency as we encounter it in experience. Then, and only then, will the libertarian be able to grasp the second horn of the dilemma posed by the objector. The first part of this task is an exercise in concept-construction; the second part requires examination of the data of introspection and (more important) the accepted norms of explanation of human actions. John Hick writes:

> It is very difficult to see how such concepts as responsibility and obligation could have any application if human volitions occurred at random instead of flowing from the individual nature of the agent. From the point of view of ethics the cost of equating freedom with volitional randomness would thus be so great as to be prohibitive.
>
> Is there a third concept of freedom such that a free act is neither, on the one hand, the inevitable outworking of a man's character nor, on the other hand, a merely random occurrence? There is such a concept of freedom, and, indeed, it is the one that seems intuitively most adequate to our ordinary experience as moral agents. It is, however, not easily defined. It is roughly the notion of freedom as a limited creativity. This must be thought of as involving an element of unpredictability; for, whilst the action proceeds from the nature of the agent, the nature from which it proceeds is that of "the actual self alive in the moment of decision".[3] Thus,

whilst a free action arises out of the agent's character it does not arise in a fully determined and predictable way. It is largely but not fully prefigured in the previous state of the agent. For the character is itself partially formed and sometimes partially reformed in the very moment of free decision.[4]

SOME CONCLUSIONS REGARDING FREE WILL

(a) Compatibilism refuted

From what has now been said, together with what was said in the preceding chapters, it follows that compatibilism is false. According to compatibilism, it is possible for a human being to act freely, or to make a free choice, while at the same time the action, or the choice, is the result of conditions that obtained at an earlier date, and were causally sufficient for the doing of just that act or the making of just that choice. Acting and choosing freely is held by compatibilists to entail what I have called the minimal sense of freedom: the ability to do otherwise, or to choose otherwise, in the circumstances prevailing at the time.

But the position which has been defended above rules out the very possibility the compatibilists insist upon. On the one side, analyzing causation in terms of agency forges a link between the causal modalities and the modalities of human agency, at the very point where compatibilists need to keep these two families of modal terms strictly separated. On the other side, the inability of any agent existing in time to alter the past, or to do anything in the present that would require the past to have been different, enables us to complete a knock-down argument for incompatibilism without committing any modal fallacies. I will take up these two points in turn.

(i) The 'can' of agency and the 'can' of causal possibility

The link between the modalities of agency and those of causation is expressed by the following two entailments, which are consequences of defining the causal modalities in terms of the 'can' of natural agency. Using 'Ax' for 'x is a natural agent', we have:

$$(7.1)\ N_c p \rightarrow (x)(t)[Ax \rightarrow Na\ (x,t)p]$$

$$(7.2)\ (\exists x)(\exists t)[Ax \bullet M_a(x,t)p] \rightarrow M_c p$$

What (7.1) is saying is that whatever is causally necessary is also necessary in the agency sense for every natural agent. The formula (7.2) is equivalent to it: it says that whatever is possible, in the agency sense, to any natural agent at any time, is also causally possible. Being themselves conceptual truths, (7.1) and (7.2) apply to all *logically possible* natural agents, not just those in the actual world. That these two principles enjoy the status of logically necessary truths may be brought out be re-expressing them as follows:

$$(7.11)\ N_L\{N_c p \supset (x)(t)(Ax \supset N_a(x,t)p)\}$$

$$(7.21)\ N_L\{(\exists x)(\exists t)[Ax \bullet M_a(x,t)p] \supset M_c p\}$$

G.E. Moore was quite right to alert us to the possibility that the word 'could' might be ambiguous,[5] and it is valuable to distinguish the uses of 'could' concerned specifically with physical causality from those concerned with the abilities of persons. But these different uses are intimately connected, and it is bound to lead to trouble if we adopt a theory that obliges us to deny the connection.

Compatibilism, when combined with determinism, implies that a person who acts freely is able to do something (namely, act otherwise) which in the circumstances is causally impossible – an implication which is flatly contrary to common belief. Compatibilists then attempt to defend this counterintuitive position by (1) carefully marking off the 'can' of being able from the causal 'can', and (2) trying, as Moore did, to analyze the 'can' of being able in terms of certain counterfactual conditionals.

Now there is no denying that there is *a* use of 'can' in the language that may be analyzed in this fashion without contradicting common sense. It is precisely the use illustrated by Moore's example of the steamer that *can* steam at twenty knots but is in fact only doing fifteen. It created no conflicts with common belief to claim that the statement 'This steamer can do twenty knots', uttered at a time when the steamer is in fact traveling at fifteen knots, should be analyzed as meaning 'This steamer *would* do twenty knots *if* the captain chose to run at full steam'.

Notice that I have not said that I think this analysis is all right; in fact, I think it is both inaccurate and deceptive. Inaccurate, because there are significant differences between 'can' statements and conditionals. Deceptive, because it creates the impression that we can eliminate modal terms and allusions to unactualized possibilities, whereas in fact we have to bring back one or both of these in order to give an adequate analysis of the non-material conditionals that were supposed to replace them. I said only that the 'iffy' analysis of this particular group of 'can' statements creates no conflicts with common *belief*. And why not? Just because the 'can' statements we are here concerned with are used to ascribe abilities to natural agents that are presumed *not* to have any power of acting or choosing freely. A steamer can do otherwise only in an iffy sense, precisely because it is not acting freely, even in the minimal sense of the word.

What goes for a ship goes equally for a human being who is acting unfreely – e.g., a person in the grip of an impulse that is literally irresistible. Such a person is able to do otherwise only in the iffy sense, *not* in the sense required for even minimal freedom. It is the presence in the language of this use of 'can' and 'able' which has made the compatibilists' argument seem plausible. But the plausibility of the argument vanishes once we perceive the connection between the causal 'can' and the 'can' of being able.

(ii) An alleged modal fallacy

Some philosophers who have been arguing against compatibilism have fallen into a certain modal fallacy – or at any rate have failed to choose their words carefully enough to assure their readers that no fallacy has been committed. Thus, for example, Richard Taylor writes:

> If . . . existing conditions are causally sufficient for my moving my finger, then it follows that it is causally impossible for me not to move it. If, on the other hand, existing conditions are causally sufficient for my holding it still, then it is causally impossible for me to move it.[6]

I believe Taylor was attempting to defend a view not greatly dissimilar to the one I have adopted. But it looks very much as if he is employing an argument of this form:

$$N_c(p \supset q)$$
$$\underline{p}$$
$$\therefore N_c q \text{ (or, equivalently, } \sim M_c \sim q)$$

This of course is a fallacy, whether the modality in question is the causal one or any other. All that ever follows from 'N(p ⊃ q)' and 'p' is 'q', not 'Nq'. But the fallacy is a seductive one, because the premise 'N(p ⊃ q)' is often expressed in English and other natural languages by a sentence of the form 'If p, then necessarily q'. Put another way, when we *say* 'If p, then necessarily q', we often *mean* 'N(p ⊃ q)' rather than 'p ⊃ Nq'.

Richard Taylor was in fact charged with having committed this very fallacy,[7] and his words will indeed bear that interpretation. More significantly, compatibilists have felt justified in suspecting that no incompatibilist will be able to avoid committing the fallacy in one form or another.[8] Our task, then, is to show that incompatibilism is not necessarily the expression of a modal muddle.

One philosopher who at least avoids muddling the different modalities is Roderick Chisholm. His formulation of the thesis of incompatibilism is as follows:

> If we make a choice under conditions such that, given those conditions, it is (causally but not logically) impossible for the choice not to be made, then the choice is one we could not have avoided making.[9]

The 'could not' in the final clause is the 'could not' of agency: Chisholm has grasped the connection between the 'can' of agency and the 'can' of causal possibility without confusing the two. But Chisholm's thesis needs further defence.

I argued earlier that the condition of being able to do X commencing at t_1 exists in some short interval preceding t_1.[10] From this it follows, not only that events in the near or remote past are unalterable by any agent existing in time, but that events and conditions in the immediate present are as well. As has already been argued, no event or state of affairs obtaining at a time earlier than a short interval preceding t_1 is possible to me *in* the short interval preceding t_1, except what *did* occur or obtain prior to t_1. This would include events or conditions obtaining during the short interval preceding t_1 during which I am able to act commencing at t_1.

Suppose now that at time t_0, conditions C obtain, and these conditions are causally sufficient for some human agent A to do X at a later time t_1. Then

$$(7.3) \ N_c[C(t_0) \supset A \text{ does } X(t_1)]$$

All humans are natural agents. So by (7.1) we have

$$(7.31) \ N_a(A,t_1)[C(t_0) \supset A \text{ does } X(t_1)]$$

But by (3.2) we have

$$(7.32) \ N_a(A,t_1)[C(t_0)];$$

and from (7.31) and (7.32) it *does* follow that

$$(7.33) \ N_a(A,t_1)[A \text{ does } X(t_1)].$$

The argument by which (7.33) is inferred from (7.31) and (7.32) has the valid form

$$N[p \supset q]$$
$$\underline{Np}$$
$$\therefore Nq$$

the modality involved being '$N_a(A,t_1)$' – 'It is necessary, in the agency sense, for A, in the short interval preceding t_1'. But the conclusion (7.33) means precisely that at the very time A is able, in the all-in sense, to do X at t_1, A is *not* able to do otherwise. Compatibilism is thus refuted.

(b) The causation of free actions

But having now refuted compatibilism, to the best of my ability, I hasten to add that a free action or a free choice can perfectly well be caused, in three distinct senses of that term.

(1) It can be caused by the desires and beliefs of the agent, in the rational-agency sense of 'cause'. This point is, in substance, quite uncontroversial. Whatever controversy surrounds it is due to confusion over the different senses of 'cause'. As Collingwood noted,[11] nomic causation so dominated philosophical discussions of cause and effect, for a time, that some philosophers ceased to recognize the rational-agency sense of 'cause', despite the fact that it is the oldest in the language.

(2) A free act F may be related to an antecedent condition C that is causally necessary for F, and in this sense caused by C. Many of the examples cited in support of the thesis of compatibilism turn out to be beside the point because they are examples of conditions that are causally *necessary* for a certain action without being caus-ally *sufficient*. A clear instance of this type of *non sequitur* is found in an essay by Antony Flew. Thanks to Flew's crystal-clear writing style, it is abundantly plain that a conclusion embracing causally sufficient conditions has been supported by an illustration – the only illustration Flew employs in this context – which is an example of a causally necessary, but insufficient, condition.

> A paradigm case of acting freely, of being free
> to choose, would be the marriage of two normal
> young people, when there was no question of the

parties 'having to get married', and no social or parental pressure on either of them: a case which happily is scarcely rare. To say that Murdo was free to ask whichever eligible girl of his acquaintance he wanted, and that he chose to ask, was accepted by, and has now married Mairi of his own free will, is not to say that his actions and choices were uncaused or in principle unpredictable: . . . there is no contradiction in saying Murdo chose to marry Mairi of his own free will; and furthermore he would not have chosen to do this if his endocrine glands had not as a matter of fact been in such and such a state, that is, that his glandular condition was one of many causes of his choice. . . .

It might be objected that if Murdo acted because his glands were in such and such a state then he cannot have chosen Mairi because he wanted to be married to her: that the one explanation excludes the other. But this is not so: for the one assigns a cause; gives a, but not presumably the only, precondition the absence of which would have been followed by the absence of Murdo's action. While the other indicates his motive, again perhaps not the only one; and to say that and in what way a piece of behaviour was motivated is not to deny that it was caused. . . .

Now if this sort of argument is sound, then there is no contradiction involved in saying that a particular action or choice was: *both* free, and could have been helped, and so on; *and* predictable, or even foreknown, and explicable in terms of caused causes. . . .

> [I]t really is logically possible for an action to
> be both freely chosen and yet fully determined by
> caused causes.[12]

(3) A free act F may be caused, in the nomic sense, by a set of conditions C to which it is related by a law of the probabilistic kind. Such a law will state that given C there was a certain non-zero probability of the act's being performed. Here we must distinguish two sub-cases.

(a) The law in question may depict the process connecting C and F as a fundamentally random process. This case would be realized, for example, if neuroscientists were to discover the structure of the brain and nervous system to be such that some behavioral outputs are subject to quantum uncertainty. From the point of view of physical theory, there would then be a margin of randomness, and a consequent measure of unpredictability, in human behavior. It must be stressed that a margin of randomness, as such, is not freedom: freedom is the possibility of acting otherwise, and a free act may express the character and personality of the agent through being caused (in the rational-agency sense) by her desires, beliefs and abilities. But the margin of randomness here envisaged in the physiologist's account of human behavior *is* what makes freedom *compatible* with nomic causation of the probabilistic variety. This is connected with the fact that a D-N-P explanation of a piece of behavior is compatible with an R-A explanation that portrays that same behavior as a free action.

(b) Alternatively, the law connecting C to F may depict the process involved as a superficially random process. The laws of operant conditioning, and the familiar statistical laws of the social sciences, would be of this kind. But for reasons already discussed, F could still *be* a free action only if the process linking it with C were, in point of fact, a fundamentally random as well as superficially random process. Should it turn out that underlying the superficially random process there was a causally tight deterministic one, in virtue of which C was causally sufficient for F (perhaps on account of additional background conditions), then F would have been shown to be an unfree action after all. It is as sure as anything that neuroscience can and will increase our knowledge of the limits of human freedom, and uncover causal constraints on people's behavior that, so far, we have not even imagined to be the case.

It must be borne in mind that whatever statistical laws we discover, at the superficial level, linking C to F, will *be* truly lawlike, and truly explanatory, only on condition that there is a nomic connection underlying the superficial statistical correlation. But it matters not at all, for this particular purpose, whether the underlying process is a deterministic or a fundamentally random one. By the same token, the discovery of a seemingly law-like statistical correlation cannot of itself lend any support to the conclusion that we have a deterministic process on our hands.

Some determinists seem to have been misled about this point, one of the most eminent of these being B.F. Skinner. Skinner assumes that no human behavior is free,[13] yet the assumption is entirely gratuitous. It is not needed as a presupposition of the methods which enabled him to discover the laws of operant conditioning. Nor is it supported by their success.

(c) Free will and neurophysiological indeterminism

If the argument of the last section is sound, human freedom is compatible with probabilistic causation, but not with determinism. Earlier, I committed myself to the view that practically all physical processes are fundamentally random processes, since all but a few are instances of *some* laws of an irreducibly probabilistic character.

This I took to be the view of the universe which is best supported by contemporary quantum physics.[14]

But these two points are not sufficient to show that human freedom is a fact. The quantum laws themselves entail that the familiar deterministic laws of classical physics are correct to within a close margin of approximation. Only in rather exceptional conditions does the indeterminacy of interactions at the quantum level have a noticeable effect on the behavior of an ordinary middle-sized physical object, composed – as it always would be – of a huge number of elementary particles. The great majority of observable physical processes are superficially deterministic.

Realizing this, many philosophers drew the conclusion that quantum indeterminacy, supposing that it was a fact, could have no bearing upon the issue of human freedom. The case was eloquently stated by Brand Blanshard.

> [L]et us suppose that the Eddingtonians are right and that what has been called "free will among the electrons" is the fact. Would that imply indeterminism in the realm that most nearly concerns us, the realm of choice? I cannot see that it would. The argument supposed to show that it would is as follows: Psychical processes depend on physical processes. But physical processes are themselves at bottom unpredictable. Hence the psychical processes dependent on them must share this unpredictability. Stated in the abstract, the argument sounds impressive. But what does it actually come to? We are told that, even if there is inconstancy in the behavior of single particles, there is no observable inconstancy in the behavior of masses of them; the particles of a billiard ball are never

able to get together and go on a spree simultaneously. Eddington admitted that they might, just as he admitted that an army of monkeys with a million typewriters might produce all the books in the British Museum, but he admitted also that the chance of a billiard ball's behaving in this way was so astronomically remote that he would not believe it if he saw it.

The question of importance for us, then, is whether, if acts of choice are dependent on physical processes at all, they depend on the behavior of particles singly or on that of masses of particles. To this there can be but one answer. They depend on mass behavior. An act of choice is an extremely complex process. It involves the idea of one or more ends, the association of that idea with more or less numerous other ideas, the presence of desires and repulsions, and the operation of habits and impulses; indeed, in those choices for which freedom is most demanded, the whole personality seems to be at work. The cortical basis for so complex a process must be extremely broad. But if it is, the great mass of cells involved must, by the physicist's admission, act with a high stability, and the correlated psychical processes must show a similar stability. But this is what we mean by action in accordance with causal law. So, even if the physicists are right about the unstable behavior of single particles, there is no reason whatever for translating this theory into a doctrine of indeterminism for human choice.[15]

I once thought that this argument was decisive, but I no longer think so. What changed my mind was a book on the free will problem written by a physicist, Allan Munn.[16] Munn argues that the nervous system of a mammal will, in all likelihood, turn out to be one of those exceptional physical systems in which quantum indeterminacy in the interaction of the minute sub-parts *does* sometimes result in a margin of indeterminacy in the gross behavior of the system as a whole.

That some such systems exist, is established fact. Hence Blanshard's sweeping argument, implying as it does that no such system is possible, must be unsound. Munn uses an example drawn from inorganic nature to make the general point. He describes how one of the world's fairs was opened in a dramatic fashion by pointing a telescope at a region of the sky where the star Arcturus would appear at the precise moment the fair was to be declared open. The light transmitted by the telescope was focused on a photo cell, which generated an electric current that actuated a relay, which in turn closed a large switch, turning on the lights all over the fairground at the precise moment the fair had been scheduled to open. But *if* a star much weaker than Arcturus had been chosen, the light arriving when it appeared in the sky would have amounted to only a few dozen photons per minute. In that case, supposing a sufficiently sensitive device had been installed in place of the photo tube actually used, so that the system as a whole functioned as before, it would still not have been possible to predict the precise instant when the circuit would be closed and all the lights would come on. There would have been a margin of uncertainty, amounting to at least a few seconds, on account of quantum indeterminacy in the reaction of the sensor to the small number of photons arriving each minute from the very feeble light source.

> Here we are dealing with a divergent chain reac-
> tion having its origin in a microscopic event.[17]

Munn turns to the physiology of vision for an example of quantum uncertainty infecting the determination of an item of human
behavior. He calculates that in certain circumstances the retina is
capable of responding to a pulse of light of the order of 2 or 3 photons, thereby transmitting an electrical pulse to the optic nerve. He
invents a fictional example to show how this could produce behavior in a human subject resulting from a cause subject to quantum
uncertainty. A gun-owning householder is awakened on a dark,
moonless night by the sound of an intruder in his house. As luck
would have it, the intruder is a gun-toting burglar. The householder
grabs his gun and emerges from his bedroom onto a balcony over-
looking the living room below. No lights are on in the house, so the
darkness is profound.

> If the average level of light intensity is of the order
> of a few photons (per unit of retinal sensitive area
> and unit response time) it is apparent that whether
> the home-owner sees the burglar and shoots first
> or vice versa is theoretically indeterminate and un-
> predictable. In this case microscopic indetermin-
> ism could make the difference between the death
> of the burglar or the householder.[18]

So far, so good. But it has been taken for granted, in this story,
that both the burglar and the householder have made up their
minds beforehand to shoot as soon as the appropriate target becomes visible. As a result, the example is not one that goes indis-
putably to the heart of the free will problem. For although the act
of shooting would be a free act, in the sense of being the result of

a free choice, it might be maintained that the exercise of free will would have occurred, not at the moment of pulling the trigger, but at some earlier time, i.e., when the resolution to shoot as soon as the burglar (householder) became visible was formed. In that case, the point at which quantum indeterminacy has been brought into the story is not the point at which it is needed for the purpose of demonstrating that it is germane to the matter of free will.

Plainly, what is needed is a paradigmatic instance of the exercise of free will – such as John Q. Taxpayer deciding whether or not to declare all his income – in which it can be shown that the cerebral process which corresponds to the making of the decision, and which triggers the relevant ensuing behavior, is a process whose outcome is subject to quantum uncertainty. Not only that: each of the possible outcomes – e.g., John Q.'s paying his tax in full, or cheating – must have a non-negligible probability of coming to pass. If it developed that there was always an overwhelming probability in favor of one particular outcome, or the probability of an alternative outcome rose to a non-negligible level only after several hours of intense cogitation, then things would look very black indeed for the free will hypothesis. Human freedom – i.e., the familiar capacity which compatibilists and incompatibilists alike are interested in – is a faculty that people are capable of exercising every waking hour, sometimes with only a moment's deliberation. If humans have any such gift of freedom, then, given the above argument for incompatibilism, there must be a *large* number of neural processes in which there is something more than a vanishingly small physical probability of an outcome different from the one that actually occurs. These would be the processes controlling minimally free actions.

Now in most of our free activity we do things that are in character, and would be considered highly probable in the light of our previous background. In such cases, it is to be expected that the neural process governing the overt behavior is such that there is a high physical probability in favor of the actual outcome. But one would expect that in some cases, when a person must choose between two equally enticing courses of action, a corresponding neural process would occur with two possible outcomes, each of which would trigger a distinctive sequence of behavior, and that each of these possible outcomes would have a physical probability of close to 50 per cent.

The existence of free will is thus seen to be an empirical hypothesis, subject to confirmation by discoveries in neuroscience. Equally, neuroscience has an indispensable role to play in establishing the precise extent of human freedom.

As yet we do not know nearly enough about neurophysiology to confirm or to disconfirm the free will hypothesis. But Munn deploys the following argument, making use of some very elementary facts about brain function, to support the speculation that the free will hypothesis is true:

> [I]f . . . electrodes [are] connected to the skin of the head and then connected through a suitable amplifier to a cathode ray oscilloscope, they show that the brain is very active electrically. Analysis of the brain pattern produced shows that there is a basic frequency of about 10 cycles per second with a complex superimposed set of other frequencies. The very large scale circulating currents producing the fundamental frequency require the co-operation of vast numbers of nerves acting in concert, and the power concerned is so large that classical physics would appear to be entirely adequate for their description. In consequence, the human functions corresponding to these must be

entirely determinate. . . . It would seem then that if quantum uncertainty has any part to play it is a small one. This is undoubtedly true, the question being: does it have any role at all? The key lies in the nature of the synaptic mechanism, in the all or none nature of the response. Remember that the size of the transmitted pulse is independent of the stimulating pulse, providing only that the latter is in excess of the threshold. Thus even though the absolute threshold of response is very high in comparison with the energy carried by single ions, the relative threshold must be very much smaller; and consequently when the initial pulses are of the approximate size of the threshold the response can become minutely critical as to their exact size. Small fluctuations up and down about the mean (absolute threshold) value can make the difference between a pulse being transferred or not. For the small number of microscopic entities involved in such fluctuations, Quantum Mechanics with its indeterminism is the only working theory.[19]

He then refers to John Eccles' finding that an impulse discharged by one neurone can, within 20 milliseconds, contribute to the excitation of hundreds of thousands of others.[20]

Munn's own conclusion from these data is a cautious one:

This then is the significance of our discussion in this book. In contrast to nineteenth-century physics and the world picture based upon it which denied the possibility of free-will for man, the new physics reopens the question. When common-sense man, with his introspective belief in free-will, now turns to science for an opinion he receives an entirely new answer. Modern physics, while being unable to prove that he has free-will, at least now concedes the possibility. In general then, a contemporary world picture including both our immediate introspective understanding of what goes on in our mind when we are involved in making decisions, and modern science, is justified in including the concept of 'free-will'.[21]

The relation between free will and an indeterministic scientific picture of the world has been taken up in the twenty-first century by Robert Kane. His discussion occurs in the context of an examination of the issues that brings in both neuroscience and chaos theory. Kane writes:

We must grant . . . that if any libertarian theory of free will is to succeed there must be some genuine indeterminism in nature to make room for it. As the ancient Epicurean philosophers said, the atoms must sometimes "swerve" in undetermined ways if there is to be room in nature for free will. Moreover, it would be no use if the atoms swerved in outer space somewhere far from human affairs. They must swerve where it would matter for human choice and action, for example, in the brain. . . .

Consider a businesswoman who . . . is on her way to an important meeting when she observes an assault taking place in an alley. An inner struggle arises between her conscience on the one hand (to stop and call for help for the assault victim) and

her career ambitions, on the other hand, which
tell her she cannot miss this important business
meeting. ...

Imagine that two crossing recurrent neural
networks are involved, each influencing the other,
and representing the woman's conflicting motiva-
tions. ... The input of one of these neural networks
consists of the woman's reasons for acting morally
and stopping to help the victim; the input of the
other network comprises her ambitious motives
for going on to the meeting. ... In these circumstances, when either of the pathways "wins" (i.e.,
reaches an activation threshold, which amounts to
choice), the woman will be making her choice ...

Kane concludes that in a case of this kind, which at least some neuroscientists regard as being subject to quantum indeterminacy, the
person's choice is one that is willed, and done for reasons, and for
which they are properly held responsible – not at all a random and
inexplicable occurrence.[22]

In the light of these considerations, it seems reasonable to conclude that it is not at all unlikely that quantum indeterminacy of a
sufficient degree is sufficiently prevalent in the functioning of our
brains to allow for the existence of free will. I continue to believe
this after observing how the debate over these issues has unfolded
in the early years of the twenty-first century, informed by remarkable advances in neuroscience and the blossoming of chaos theory.
The debate has not led to a settled consensus. There remain philosophers who contend that free will is compatible with deterministic
causation of the neurological events with which conscious states
are to be identified. There are others who embrace a deterministic
view of the brain and conclude that free will is an illusion. What if,

in the end, neurological research produced overwhelming evidence to the effect that the correct account of the workings of the human brain must be a deterministic one?

Given what has been stated above, I would be unable to adopt soft determinism, since I am committed to incompatibilism on conceptual grounds, not on the basis of empirical evidence. The only option would be to embrace hard determinism.

That would be discomfiting; but it is worth recalling that for many centuries – since the time of the Stoics, to be exact – philosophers nursed a disquieting suspicion that free will might be an illusion, since to a scientific mind it seemed so obvious that determinism must be true. Yet everyone, philosophers included, went on living their lives, and engaging in moral reasoning, in a fashion that presupposed humans do have free will. What *were* they thinking? It seems to me that they were engaging in a sort of Orwellian "doublethink" – simultaneously holding two contradictory beliefs and assenting to both of them.[23] Then in the twentieth century the quantum physicists made the astonishing proposal that at the microscopic level the world is in fact indeterministic – so it was determinism that had been the illusion all along! This, as Allan Munn avers and I agree, reopens the whole question of whether free will is real or illusory. It does not *answer* the question, but it opens up the possibility that free will is real, by the most exacting standard of what would count as real. So then, if one day we were to read, and be obliged to believe, that scientists had come to a consensus that determinism is true after all, how would a reasonable person react? Well, I suppose it would mean that we were obliged to return to the pre-twentieth-century practice of doublethink.

(d) Libertarianism and the "new compatibilism"

We have now completed the defence of libertarianism against the three significant objections discussed at the beginning of this chapter. To the determinists, we have replied that the universe we live in is, in point of fact, an indeterministic one; and we have offered the well-supported speculation that the appropriate type and degree of physical indeterminacy is to be found in the workings of the human nervous system. To the compatibilists, we have offered an analysis of causality and of agency which shows these concepts to be connected in a way that is fatal to their central claim. To those who have alleged that the libertarian conception of freedom is incoherent, we have explained how a free act can be caused – in an old and respectable sense of that term – by the desires and beliefs which constitute the agent's rationale for doing what she did. In such a case, the act is neither causally determined nor *simply* a random occurrence. To think of it as merely a random occurrence is to restrict one's point of view, quite gratuitously, to the probabilistic laws of quantum physics which play a role in its genesis. But to be a chance event – caused, and explicable, in accordance with probabilistic laws – is compatible with being a free act – caused, and explicable, in the sense of those terms which has to do with rational agency. This "new compatibilism" – or, if you will, "soft indeterminism" – appears to be true; and it is a truth which libertarians should be glad to embrace.

It is perhaps useful to remind ourselves of Jerry Fodor's point, cited earlier,[24] that the special sciences have their own taxonomies which do not reduce to the taxonomy of physics, though they apply to the same things. What is true of the special sciences is equally true of the commonsensical "folk psychology" to which the R-A schema of explanation belongs, and in terms of which we understand our own and our neighbors' beliefs, desires and behavior.

Folk psychology and neurophysiology have two different styles of classifying and explaining the *same* trains of events. From one point of view, these are physical events occurring in the brain and nervous system; from another, they are the desires, beliefs and psychological states, conscious and unconscious, which cause and explain behavior. I have said "points of view", but one could equally well speak of two differing conceptual schemes, or two parts of the one, complex conceptual scheme that we in this culture are heirs to. As we have seen, one distinctive feature of the conceptual scheme of folk psychology is that it incorporates a special schema of explanation – the R-A schema – which has no place in the conceptual scheme of physical science. Now it is beyond doubt that folk psychology is constantly altered and enriched by new discoveries in scientific psychology and neurophysiology, and that this process will continue. To cite one obvious example, neuroscience has taught us much, and in future will have much more to teach us, about the limits of human freedom. But it is not to be expected that we will ever find it necessary or helpful to dispense with folk psychology entirely. Such a non-reductive identity theory concerning mental events and neural events fits well with the conclusions I have reached concerning causality, agency and free will.

(e) Postscript

While I believe that the argument I have given succeeds in refuting the important objections to libertarianism, I confess that when all is said and done, I do not find it very satisfying. It is something to have demonstrated that free agency is compatible with probabilistic causation; but we all, I think, hanker after something more exciting than a bare logical compatibility. We desire to arrive at a view of human nature which is coherent in the stronger sense that the different elements mutually support or mutually necessitate one another. The kind of yearning I have in mind would be satisfied by someone who could present a new, daring, fruitful theory about what free will *is*. But I have no such theory. To the question 'What *is* free will?' I can only say that it is what common sense and folk psychology have all along been claiming it to be.

Cartesian dualists would experience no such intellectual desolation. They are able to say, "An exercise of free will is an intervention by the immaterial Self in the material realm". This is an exciting piece of theorizing, all right. If only it were rationally defensible, it would satisfy that craving for insight and coherence which no plodding defence of a logical compatibility can ever hope to assuage. Unfortunately, as I have indicated, I find mind-body dualism untenable; and I can offer no equally exciting version of monism to put in its place.

Perhaps in due course a developed neuroscience will provide us with a physiological criterion for distinguishing instances of free will from the general run of probabilistically caused cortical events; but that is as yet no more than a pious hope. In the present, drastically unfinished state of our knowledge, I see no alternative to the unsatisfying position I have defended in this chapter.

---

1   See, e.g., Bruce Aune 1963; Robert Young 1975, ch. xi; Winston Nesbitt and Stewart Candlish 1978.
2   See C.D. Broad 1952, pp. 208-212; reprinted in Broad 1966, pp. 149-154.
3   Charles Hartshorne 1962, p. 20.
4   John Hick 1977, p. 276.
5   See Moore 1965, pp. 88-92. Quoted above, ch. 3, pp. 128-129.
6   Richard Taylor 1960, p. 87.
7   By Bruce Aune in Aune 1963, p. 408.
8   See Aune 1963; also Stephen N. Thomas 1970, and Nesbitt and Candlish 1978.
9   Roderick W. Chisholm 1961, p. 157.
10 See above, ch. 3, pp. 71-74.

11 See Collingwood 1938, pp. 106-112.
12 Flew 1955, pp. 149-153. The order of the quotations has been altered.
13 See Skinner 1953, p. 111.
14 Above, ch. 5, pp. 214-220.
15 Brand Blanshard 1961, pp. 24-25.
16 Allan M. Munn 1960.
17 Munn 1960, p. 171.
18 Munn 1960, pp. 179, 180, 183.
19 Munn 1960, p. 193.
20 John Carew Eccles 1953, p. 276.
21 Munn 1960, p. 213.
22 Kane 2005, pp. 133-139.
23 See Orwell 2008, p. 223.
24 Ch. 5, p. 184.

BIBLIOGRAPHY

Abro, A. d'

1951   *The Rise of the New Physics: Its mathematical and physical theories.* New York: Dover Publications. Originally published 1939 under the title *The Decline of Mechanism.*

Anderson, Alan Ross, and Nuel D. Belnap Jr.

1975   *Entailment: The logic of relevance and necessity.* Princeton, NJ: Princeton University Press.

Anscombe, G.E.M.

1971   "Causality and Determination". Inaugural Lecture delivered at Cambridge. Cambridge University Press. Reprinted in *Causation and Conditionals,* ed. Ernest Sosa. Oxford: Oxford University Press, 1975.

Aquinas, Saint Thomas

1952   *Truth (Quaestiones Disputatae de Veritate).* Trans. Robert W. Mulligan, S.J. Chicago: Henry Regnery.

Aune, Bruce

1963   "Abilities, Modalities, and Free Will". *Philosophy and Phenomenological Research* 23 (1962-63), 397-413.

Austin, John L.

1956   "Ifs and Cans". *Proceedings of the British Academy.* Reprinted in *Philosophical Papers* (Oxford: Clarendon Press, 1961), pp. 153-180.

Beardsley, Elizabeth L.

    1960   "Determinism and Moral Perspectives". *Philosophy and Phenomenological Research* 21 (1960-61), 1-20.

Berkeley, George

    1901   *A Treatise concerning the Principles of Human Knowledge.* In *The Works of George Berkeley,* ed. Alexander Campbell Fraser. Oxford: Clarendon Press. Originally published 1710.

Blackburn, John

    1968   *A Ring of Roses.* Harmondsworth, Mddx.: Penguin Books. Originally published 1965.

Blanshard, Brand

    1961   "The Case for Determinism". In *Determinism and Freedom in the Age of Modern Science.* Ed. Sidney Hook. New York: Collier Books. Originally published 1958.

Brandt, Richard, and Jaegwon Kim

    1963   "Wants as Explanations of Actions". *Journal of Philosophy* 60, 425-435.

Brier, Bob

    1974   *Precognition and the Philosophy of Science.* New York: Humanities Press.

Broad, Charles Dunbar

    1952   *Ethics and the History of Philosophy.* London: Routledge & Kegan Paul.

    1966   "Determinism, Indeterminism, and Libertarianism". In *Free Will and Determinism.* Ed. Bernard Berofsky. New York: Harper & Row.

Brown, Donald

    1968   *Action.* Toronto: University of Toronto Press.

Carey, Susan

    2009   *The Origin of Concepts.* New York: Oxford University Press.

Carnap, Rudolf

1936   "Testability and Meaning". *Philosophy of Science* 3, 419-471.

1945   "The Two Concepts of Probability", *Philosophy and Phenomenological Research* 5, 513-532.

Cartwright, Nancy

1979   "Causal Laws and Effective Strategies". *Nous* 13, 410-437.

1999   *The Dappled World: A Study of the Boundaries of Science.* Cambridge: Cambridge University Press.

Chisholm, Roderick W.

1961   "Responsibility and Avoidability". In *Determinism and Freedom in the Age of Modern Science.* Ed. Sidney Hook. New York: Collier Books. Originally published 1958.

Churchland, Paul M.

1969   "The Logical Character of Action-Explanations". *Philosophical Review* 79, 214-236.

1995   *The Engine of Reason, the Seat of the Soul.* Cambridge, MA and London: The MIT Press.

2012   *Plato's Camera.* Cambridge, MA and London: The MIT Press.

Collingwood, R.G.

1938   "On the So-Called Idea of Causation". *Proceedings of the Aristotelian Society* 38 (1937-38), 85-112.

1940   *An Essay on Metaphysics.* Oxford: Clarendon Press.

Davidson, Donald

1963   "Actions, Reasons and Causes". *Journal of Philosophy* 60, 685-700.

1967   "Causal Relations". *Journal of Philosophy* 64, 691-703.

Dray, William

1957   *Laws and Explanation in History.* London: Oxford University Press.

Dretske, Fred I.

1977　"Laws of Nature", *Philosophy of Science* 44, 248-268.

Ducasse, Curt John

1926　"On the Nature and the Observability of the Causal Relation". *Journal of Philosophy* 23, 57-68. Reprinted in *Truth, Knowledge and Causation* (London: Routledge & Kegan Paul, 1968), pp. 1-20, and in Sosa 1975, pp. 114-125.

Eccles, John Carew

1953　*The Neurophysiological Basis of Mind*. Oxford: Clarendon Press.

Ehrenfels, Christian Freiherr von

1890　"Über Gestaltqualitäten". *Vierteljahrsschrift für wissenschaftlicher Philosophie* 14, 249-292. English translation in *Foundations of Gestalt Theory*. Ed. Barry Smith. Munich: Philosophia Verlag, 1988. Pp. 82-117.

Ellis, Willis D., ed.

1938　*A Source Book of Gestalt Psychology*. London: Kegan Paul, Trench, Trubner & Co.

Feyerabend, Paul

1975　*Against Method*. London: New Left Books.

Fischer, John Martin, Robert Kane, Derk Pereboom and Manuel Vargas

2007　*Four Views on Free Will*. Malden, MA, Oxford and Carlton, Australia: Blackwell Publishing.

Flew, Antony

1954　"Can an Effect Precede its Cause?" II. *Proceedings of the Aristotelian Society*, suppl. vol. 28, 45-62.

1955　"Divine Omnipotence and Human Freedom". In *New Essays in Philosophical Theology*. Ed. Antony Flew and Alasdair MacIntyre. London: SCM Press. Pp. 144-169.

1961   *Hume's Philosophy of Belief.* London: Routledge & Kegan Paul.

1975   Review of *The Cement of the Universe,* by J.L. Mackie. *Philosophical Books* 16, 1-6.

Fodor, Jerry A.

1975   *The Language of Thought.* New York: Thomas Y. Crowell Co.

Foss, Jeffrey E.

1976   "A Rule of Minimal Rationality: The Logical Link between Beliefs and Values". *Inquiry* 19 (1976), 341-353.

Foster, J.A.

1975   "Testing the Cement: An Examination of Mackie on Causation". *Inquiry* 18, 494-497.

Freeling, Nicholas

1977   *Gadget.* New York: Coward, McCann and Geohegan.

Friedman, Michael

1974   "Explanation and Scientific Understanding". *Journal of Philosophy* 71, 5-19.

Gamow, George

1961   *The Atom and its Nucleus.* Englewood Cliffs, NJ: Prentice-Hall.

Gasking, Douglas

1955   "Causation and Recipes". *Mind,* N.S., 64, 479-487.

Gerwin, Martin E.

1985a   *Causality, Agency, Explanation: A Perspective on Free Will and the Problem of Evil.* Ph.D. dissertation presented to Princeton University. Ann Arbor, MI: University Microfilms International.

1985b   Critical Notice of Bas C. van Fraassen, *The Scientific Image. Canadian Journal of Philosophy* 15, 363-378.

1987   "Causality and Agency: A Refutation of Hume". *Dialogue* 15, 3-17.

1988   "Quanta, Randomness, and Explanation", in *Philosophy and Culture,* Proceedings of the XVIIth World Congress of Philosophy, Montreal, 1983, ed. Venant Vauchy (Montreal: Éditions du Beffroi/Éditions Montmorency), Vol. III, pp. 86-91.

1998   "Natural-Agency Theory as an Alternative to Hume: A Reply to Andrew Ward". *Dialogue* 37, 3-12.

Giere, R.N.

1973   "Objective Single-Case Probabilities and the Foundations of Statistics". In *Logic, Methodology and Philosophy of Science* IV, Proceedings of the Fourth International Congress for Logic, Methodology and Philosophy of Science, Bucharest, 1971. Ed. Patrick Suppes et al. Pp. 467-483. Amsterdam: North-Holland Publishing Co.

Goodman, Nelson

1965   *Fact, Fiction, and Forecast,* 2nd ed. Indianapolis: Bobbs-Merrill.

Grünbaum, Adolf

1963   *Philosophical Problems of Space and Time,* 1st ed. New York: Alfred A. Knopf.

1973   *Philosophical Problems of Space and Time,* 2nd ed. Dordrecht, Holland: D. Reidel Publishing Co.

Hallie, Philip P.

1951   "Maine de Biran and the Empiricist Tradition". *Philosophical Quarterly* 1, 152-164.

1959   *Maine de Biran, Reformer of Empiricism.* Cambridge, MA: Harvard University Press.

Hanson, Norwood Russell

1958   *Patterns of Discovery.* Cambridge: Cambridge University Press.

Hartshorne, Charles

1962   *The Logic of Perfection.* La Salle, IL: Open Court Press.

Hempel, Carl G.

1962 "Deductive-Nomological vs. Statistical Explanation". In *Scientific Explanation, Space and Time,* ed. Herbert Feigl and Grover Maxwell. Minnesota Studies in the Philosophy of Science, Vol. III, pp. 98-169. Minneapolis: University of Minnesota Press.

1965 *Aspects of Scientific Explanation And Other Essays in the Philosophy of Science.* New York: The Free Press.

1966 *Philosophy of Natural Science.* Englewood Cliffs, NJ: Prentice-Hall.

1968 "Maximal Specificity and Lawlikeness in Probabilistic Explanation". *Philosophy of Science 35,* 116-133.

Hempel, Carl G., and Paul Oppenheim

1948 "Studies in the Logic of Explanation". *Philosophy of Science* 15, 135-175. Reprinted in *Readings in the Philosophy of Science,* ed. Herbert Feigl and May Brodbeck (New York: Appleton-Century-Crofts, 1953), pp. 319-352, and in Hempel 1965, pp. 245-290, with a 1964 postscript by Hempel, pp. 291-295.

Hick, John

1977 *Evil and the God of Love,* 2nd ed. London: Macmillan.

Hughes, G.E., and M.J. Creswell

1968 *An Introduction to Modal Logic.* London: Methuen & Co.

Hume, David

1888 *A Treatise of Human Nature.* Ed. L.A. Selby-Bigge. Oxford: Clarendon Press. Rpt. 1960. Originally published 1739.

1902 *Enquiries concerning the Human Understanding and concerning the Principles of Morals.* 2nd edition. Ed. L.A. Selby-Bigge. Oxford: Clarendon Press. Originally published 1777.

1938   *An Abstract of A Treatise of Human Nature.* Reprinted with an Introduction by J.M. Keynes and P. Sraffa. Cambridge: Cambridge University Press. Originally published 1740.

Jeffrey, Richard C.

1970   "Statistical Explanation vs. Statistical Inference". In *Essays in Honor of Carl G. Hempel.* Ed. Nicholas Rescher. Dordrecht, Holland: D. Reidel Publishing Co. Pp. 104-113. Reprinted in Wesley Salmon et al. 1971, pp. 19-28.

Kane, Robert, ed.

2002   *Free Will.* Malden, MA, and Oxford: Blackwell Publishing.

Kane, Robert

2005   *A Contemporary Introduction to Free Will.* New York: Oxford University Press.

Kant, Immanuel

1929   *Critique of Pure Reason.* Trans. Norman Kemp Smith. London: Macmillan & Co. First published 1781, 1787.

Kitcher, Philip

1976   "Explanation, Conjunction and Unification". *Journal of Philosophy* 73, 207-212.

Koffka, Kurt

1935   *Principles of Gestalt Psychology.* New York and London: Lund Humphries.

Köhler, Wolfgang

1947   *Gestalt Psychology: An Introduction to New Concepts in Modern Psychology.* New York and Toronto: Liverlight Publishing Corp.

Kuhn, Thomas S.

1962   *The Structure of Scientific Revolutions.* Chicago: University of Chicago Press.

Lakatos, Imre

1970　"Falsification and the Methodology of Scientific Research Programmes". In *Criticism and the Growth of Knowledge.* Ed. I. Lakatos and A. Musgrove. Cambridge: Cambridge University Press.

Laplace, Pierre Simon, Marquis de

1951　*A Philosophical Essay on Probabilities.* Trans. Frederick Wilson Truscott and Frederick Lincoln Emory. New York: Dover Publications. Originally published 1819.

Laudan, Larry

1977　*Progress and Its Problems: Towards a Theory of Scientific Growth.* Berkeley, CA: University of California Press.

Lewis, Clarence Irving

1929　*Mind and the World Order: Outline of a Theory of Knowledge.* New York: Charles Scribner's Sons.

Lewis, Clarence Irving, and Cooper Harold Langford

1932　*Symbolic Logic.* New York: The Century Co.

Lewis, David

1968　*Counterfactuals.* Cambridge, MA: Harvard University Press.

1973　"Causation". *Journal of Philosophy* 70, 556-567.

Locke, Don

1976　"The 'Can' of Being Able". *Philosophia* 6, 1-20.

Locke, John

1959　*An Essay concerning Human Understanding.* Ed. Alexander Campbell Fraser. New York: Dover Publications. Originally published 1690.

Loux, Michael J., ed.

1979　*The Possible and the Actual: Readings in the Metaphysics of Modality.* Ithaca, NY: Cornell University Press.

Lucas, J.R.

1970　*The Freedom of the Will.* Oxford: Clarendon Press.

Lyon, Ardon
    1967   "Causality". *British Journal for the Philosophy of Science* 18, 1-20.

Mackie, John L.
    1973   *Truth, Probability, and Paradox.* Oxford: Clarendon Press.

    1974   *The Cement of the Universe: A Study of Causation.* Oxford: Clarendon Press.

    1979   "Mind, Brain, and Causation". In *Studies in Metaphysics.* Ed. Peter A. French, Theodore E. Uehling, Jr., and Howard K. Wettstein. Midwest Studies in Philosophy, Vol. IV. Pp. 19-29. Minneapolis: University of Minnesota Press.

    1980   *The Cement of the Universe: A Study of Causation.* Paperback edition with a new Preface, additional notes and additional bibliography. Oxford: Clarendon Press.

Maine de Biran, Pierre
    1942   *Oeuvres choisis.* Ed. Henri Gouhier. Paris: Aubier, Éditions Montaigne.

    1982   *Oeuvres Complètes.* Ed. Pierre Tisserand. Geneva and Paris: Slatkine. Originally published 1920-1949.

McFee, Graham
    2000   *Free Will.* Montreal and Kingston: McGill-Queen's University Press.

Michotte, Albert
    1963   *The Perception of Causality.* Trans. T.R. Miles. London: Methuen & Co.

Mill, John Stuart
    1843   *A System of Logic.* London.

Moore, George Edward
    1965   *Ethics.* London: Oxford University Press. Originally published 1912.

Munn, Allan M.

1960   *Free-will and Determinism*. Toronto: University of Toronto Press.

Nagel, Tom

1970   *The Possibility of Altruism*. Oxford: Clarendon Press.

Nesbitt, Winston, and Stewart Candlish

1978   "Determinism and the Ability to do Otherwise". *Mind*, N.S., 87, 415-420.

Nowell-Smith, P.H.

1960   "Ifs and Cans", Section I. *Theoria* 26, 87-92.

Orwell, George

2008   *1984*. London: Penguin Books. Originally published 1949.

Piaget, Jean

1929   *The Child's Conception of the World*. Trans. Joan and Andrew Tomlinson. London: Routledge & Kegan Paul.

1930   *The Child's Conception of Physical Causality*. Trans. Marjorie Gabain. London: Routledge & Kegan Paul.

1953   *The Origin of Intelligence in the Child*. Trans. Margaret Cook. London: Routledge & Kegan Paul.

1955   *The Child's Construction of Reality*. Trans. Margaret Cook. London: Routledge & Kegan Paul.

Popper, Karl

1935   *Logik der Forschung*. Vienna: Springer.

1957   "The propensity interpretation of the calculus of probability, and the quantum theory". In *Observation and Interpretation: A Symposium of Philosophers and Physicists*, Proceedings of the Ninth Symposium of the Colston Research Society held in the University of Bristol. Ed. S. Körner. Pp. 65-70. London: Butterworth Scientific Publications.

1959　*The Logic of Scientific Discovery.* Translation of Popper 1935, by Popper, with the assistance of Julius Freed and Lan Freed. London: Hutchinson & Co.

1962　*Conjectures and Refutations: The Growth of Scientific Knowledge.* London: Routledge & Kegan Paul.

1974　"Reply to my Critics". In *The Philosophy of Karl Popper.* Ed. P.A. Schilpp. La Salle, IL: Open Court Press.

1983　*Realism and the Aim of Science.* Ed. W.W. Bartley III. London: Hutchinson & Co.

Psillos, Stathis

2002　*Causation and Explanation.* Montreal and Kingston: McGill-Queen's University Press.

Putnam, Hilary

1974　"The Corroboration of Theories". In *The Philosophy of Karl Popper.* Ed. P.A. Schilpp. La Salle, IL: Open Court Press.

Railton, Peter

1978　"A Deductive-Nomological Model of Probabilistic Explanation". *Philosophy of Science* 45, 206-226.

1981　"Probability, Explanation, and Information". *Synthese* 48, 233-256.

Reichenbach, Hans

1944　*Philosophic Foundations of Quantum Mechanics.* Berkeley and Los Angeles: University of California Press.

1947　*Elements of Symbolic Logic.* New York: Macmillan.

1949　*The Theory of Probability.* Berkeley and Los Angeles: University of California Press.

1954　*Nomological Statements and Admissible Operations.* Amsterdam: North-Holland Publishing Co.

1956　*The Direction of Time.* Berkeley and Los Angeles, University of California Press.

1976   *Laws, Modalities, and Counterfactuals.* Berkeley and Los Angeles: University of California Press. A reissue of Reichenbach 1954, with identical pagination, and with a Foreword by Wesley C. Salmon.

Reid, Thomas

1967   *Philosophical Works.* With notes and supplementary dissertations by Sir William Hamilton. Reproduction of the 8th edition (Edinburgh, 1895). Hildesheim: Georg Olms Verlagsbuchhandlung.

1969   *Essays on the Active Powers of the Human Mind.* Introduction by Baruch A. Brody. Cambridge, MA: MIT Press. Originally published 1788.

Rothman, Milton A.

1960   "Things That Go Faster Than Light". *Scientific American* 203, no. 1, 201-223.

Salmon, Wesley

1970   "Statistical Explanation". In *The Nature and Function of Scientific Theories.* Ed. Robert G. Colodny. Pittsburgh: University of Pittsburgh Press. Pp. 173-231. Reprinted in Wesley Salmon et al. 1971, pp. 29-87.

1971   *Statistical Explanation and Statistical Relevance.* With contributions by Richard C. Jeffrey and James G. Greeno. Pittsburgh: University of Pittsburgh Press.

1975a "Determinism and indeterminism in modern science". In *Reason and Responsibility,* 3rd ed. Ed. Joel Feinberg. Encino and Belmont, CA: Dickenson Publishing Co. Pp. 351-367.

1975b "Theoretical explanation". In *Explanation.* Ed. Stephan Körner. New Haven: Yale University Press. Pp. 118-145. Comments by D.H. Mellor and L.J. Cohen, and a reply by Salmon, pp. 146-184.

1977 "An 'At-At' Theory of Causal Influence". *Philosophy of Science* 44, 215-224.

1978 "Why Ask, 'Why?'? – An Inquiry Concerning Scientific Explanation". *Proceedings and Addresses of the American Philosophical Association* 51, 683-705.

1980 "Probabilistic Causality". *Pacific Philosophical Quarterly* 61, 50-74.

1984 *Scientific Explanation and the Causal Structure of the World*. Princeton, NJ: Princeton University Press.

1989 *Four Decades of Scientific Explanation*. Pittsburgh, PA: University of Pittsburgh Press.

Sanford, David H.

1976 "The Direction of Causation and the Direction of Conditionship", *Journal of Philosophy* 73, 193-207.

Sayre, Kenneth M.

1977 "Statistical Models of Causal Relations". *Philosophy of Science* 44, 203-214.

Scheffler, Israel

1963 *The Anatomy of Inquiry*. New York: Alfred A. Knopf.

Scriven, Michael

1957 "The Present Status of Determinism in Physics". *Journal of Philosophy* 54, 727-741.

1959 "Explanation and Prediction in Evolutionary Theory". *Science* 130, no. 3374 (Aug. 28, 1959), 477-482.

Seldes, George, ed.

1960 *The Great Quotations*. New York: Lyle Stuart.

Skinner, B.F.

1953 *Science and Human Behavior*. New York: Macmillan.

Snyder, D. Paul

1971 *Modal Logic and its Applications*. New York: Van Nostrand Reinhold Co.

Sosa, Ernest, ed.

1975   *Causation and Conditionals*. Oxford: Oxford University Press.

Stace, Walter Terence

1960   *The Teachings of the Mystics*. New York: New American Library.

Stalnaker, Robert C.

1968   "A Theory of Conditionals". In *Studies in Logical Theory*, ed. Nicholas Rescher, American Philosophical Quarterly monograph No. 2. Oxford: Basil Blackwell.

1976   "Possible Worlds". *Nous* 10, 65-75.

Stoutland, F.

1968   "Basic Actions and Causality". *Journal of Philosophy* 65, 467-474.

Taylor, A.E.

1955   *Aristotle*. New York: Dover Publications. Originally published 1919.

Taylor, Richard

1960   "I Can". *Philosophical Review* 69, 78-89.

1966   *Action and Purpose*. Englewood Cliffs, NJ: Prentice-Hall.

1974   *Metaphysics*. 2nd ed. Englewood Cliffs, NJ: Prentice-Hall.

Thomas, Lewis

1979   *The Medusa and the Snail: More Notes of a Biology Watcher*. New York: The Viking Press.

Thomas, Stephen N.

1970   "A Modal Muddle". In *Determinism, Free Will, and Moral Responsibility*. Ed. Gerald Dworkin. Englewood Cliffs, NJ: Prentice-Hall. Pp. 141-148.

Thorp, John

1980   *Free Will: A Defence Against Neurophysiological Determinism*. London: Routledge & Kegan Paul.

Toulmin, Stephen

1953 *The Philosophy of Science: An Introduction.* London: Hutchinson's University Library.

van Fraassen, Bas C.

1980 *The Scientific Image.* Oxford: Clarendon Press.

Venn, John

1866 *The Logic of Chance.* London: Macmillan.

von Mises, Richard

1957 *Probability, Statistics, and Truth.* Second revised English edition prepared by Hilda Geiringer. London: George Allen and Unwin; New York: Macmillan.

von Neumann, John

1955 *Mathematical Foundations of Quantum Mechanics.* Trans. Robert T. Beyer. Princeton, NJ: Princeton University Press.

von Wright, Georg Henrik

1971 *Explanation and Understanding.* Ithaca, NY: Cornell University Press.

1973 "On the Logic and Epistemology of the Causal Relation". In *Logic, Methodology and Philosophy of Science* IV, Proceedings of the Fourth International Congress for Logic, Methodology and Philosophy of Science, Bucharest, 1971. Ed. Patrick Suppes et al. Amsterdam: North-Holland Publishing Co. Pp. 293-312. Reprinted in Sosa 1975, pp. 95-113.

Ward, Andrew

1994 "Is Gerwin's Natural-Agency Theory a Viable Alternative to Hume?" *Dialogue* 33, 733-742.

Wertheimer, Max

1912 "Experimentelle Studien über das Sehen von Bewegung". *Zeitschrift für Psychologie,* Part I, Vol. 71, 161-265.

Young, Robert

    1975   *Freedom, Responsibility and God*. London: Macmillan.

Yule, G. Udny, and M.G. Kendall

    1950   *An Introduction to the Theory of Statistics*, 14th ed. London: Charles Griffin & Co.

Encyclopedia Americana. Danbury, CT: Americana Corp, 1980.

Encyclopaedia Britannica. Chicago etc.: Encyclopaedia Britannica, Inc., 1961.

INDEX

S

Salmon, Wesley xiv, 51, 64, 100, 134, 193, 201, 216, 308, 313
screening-off 205, 206, 207
singularist 4
Skinner, B.F. 227, 236, 286, 314
soft determinism 6, 296
soft indeterminism 297
Stalnaker, Robert 106, 268, 315
statistical relevance 165, 201, 202, 203, 205, 206, 208, 211, 260, 313
Stoics 296
superficially deterministic 219, 287
superficially random 91, 214, 215, 219, 220, 226, 227, 228, 229, 230, 232, 285, 286
supernatural agent 98, 104
system TA 85, 88, 134

T

Taylor, A.E. 131, 135, 238, 315
tensed modal logic 79

theory-ladenness of observation 23, 26, 53
Thomas, Lewis 189, 236, 315
Thorp, John 78, 89, 133, 315
Toulmin, Stephen 103, 134, 316

U

unfree 94, 241, 257, 286
unfreely 280

V

van Fraassen, Bas xiv, 179, 209, 316
variably strict conditionals 267, 268, 271
vector completion 55, 56
voluntary action 36, 48, 93, 257
von Mises, Richard 202, 236, 316
von Neumann, John 216, 237, 316
von Wright, Georg Henrik 102, 134, 162, 316

Z

zero probability 144, 152, 153, 154, 285

Printed in the United States
By Bookmasters

Printed in the United States
By Bookmasters